Gerhard Leitner

English Today

Introducing the Varieties of English
around the World

Philipp Reclam jun. Stuttgart

RECLAMS UNIVERSAL-BIBLIOTHEK Nr. 19849
Alle Rechte vorbehalten
Copyright © 2012 Philipp Reclam jun. GmbH & Co. KG, Stuttgart
Gesamtherstellung: Reclam, Ditzingen. Printed in Germany 2012
RECLAM, UNIVERSAL-BIBLIOTHEK und RECLAMS
UNIVERSAL-BIBLIOTHEK sind eingetragene Marken
der Philipp Reclam jun. GmbH & Co. KG, Stuttgart
ISBN 978-3-15-019849-0

www.reclam.de

Table of Contents

1 English today

In 1780 English had fewer than 15 million speakers, most of who lived in England, Ireland, Scotland, the American colonies, and the Caribbean. But John Adams, second President of the United States, 1797–1801, foresaw a world where English would play a major role:

> "English is destined to be in the next and succeeding centuries more generally the language of the world than Latin was in the last or French in the present age. The reason for this is obvious, because the increasing population in America, and their universal connection and correspondence with all nations, aided by the influence of England in the world, whether great or small, force their language into general use." (*from* McCrum *et al*. 1986: 239)

What was difficult to foresee at that time was what the Philippine poet Fermino Abad expressed in these words: "English is now ours, we have colonized it" (*Philippine Daily Inquirer*, 12 Aug 1996). The Indian poet Kamala explains why she writes in Malayalam and in English: "The language I speak becomes mine. Its distortions, its queerness, all mine; mine alone. It is half English, half Indian. Funny perhaps, but it is honest, it is human as I am human." (*see* Leitner 2009) What Adams could not foresee either was the devastating impact English has had on the world's linguistic diversity. Some experts have called English a "killer language", a language that has been suppressing thousands of languages globally.

English has an estimated 350 to 400 million native speakers and between 400 and 600 million second language speakers on all continents today. It is difficult to estimate the number of foreign language users. Vastly different figures are being circulated and especially in Asia. It is probably realistic to think of some 600 to 700 million. The figure may be rising as globalization and modern technologies continue to affect all areas of modern life. In terms of political status, English is the national language in so-called *native*, Anglophone countries (USA, UK, Canada, Australia, New Zealand, Republic of Ireland, Bahamas, etc.), though few of them have declared it their official language. English has (co-)official status in close to thirty countries, most of which used to be colonies (e.g. Ghana, Liberia, India, Western Samoa, Costa Rica). It is the dominant language in many international institutions (UN, IMF, APEC, EU, ASEAN, AU) and outdoes other languages in international media and conferences, in air and maritime traffic, publications, and the web. In Europe, South America, China and all of North Asia, it is an important foreign language. From a sociolinguistic angle, the norms of English no longer emanate from a single source. Even the two most important norm-setting *epicentres*, Britain and North America, together cannot determine the texture of English any longer. English is *pluricentric* in a multi-polar world. National norms appear in countries that have English as a native and a second language. Even foreign language countries seem to be developing norms. China may well be a case in point.

The drifting apart of American English was noticed early on both sides of the Atlantic. It had reached a point that made it possible for a section of the political elite to call for an American language, *Federal English* as it was called in the advent of Independence. It was to reflect the federal structure of the new nation and the will of its people. It was to be a democratic contrast to the feudal English in the United Kingdom. A long way down the path of history, the BBC attempted to steer towards a common spoken form in the 1930s, unsuccessfully. The departures elsewhere in the British Empire went unnoticed for a long time, and their long-term impact of fostering disintegration was underestimated. They were eventually commented upon in the 1920s, when the secretary of the BBC Pronunciation Committee, Lloyd James, said in 1928: "In our study of the growth of the Empire we forget that this territorial expansion of our language sowed the seeds of disintegration" (Leitner 1989: 12).

The English conceded defeat in the 1950s: English had escaped their control; they no longer 'owned' it. Its many manifestations created confusion as there were no longer just two forms, a British and an American one. There was Australian English, Indian or South African English. Accepting the multitude of varieties, the word English, a singular noun, acquired a plural form, *Englishes*. Englishes differ from one another and show considerable internal variation. They can show influences from local languages, extreme simplification as in the pidgins of the bazaars of the 18th and 19th centuries in Malacca or be like the established creoles in the Caribbean. The educated varieties at the top are closer to the international and global variety of English.

A level higher is the culturally free-floating international and global English that is devoid, so many experts believe, of connotations of Britishness or Americanness. It is globally understandable if it avoids local associations. The *Reith Lecture* of the Burmese pro-democracy leader, Aung San Suu Kyi, is a case in point:

1.1 "When I agreed, with great trepidation, to take on the Reith Lectures, it was based on the simple desire to discover what we are. By 'we', I mean the National League for Democracy, the NLD, as well as other groups and individuals who are engaged in the campaign for democracy in Burma. We have been engaged in the struggle for democracy for more than 20 years, so, you might think, we should know what we are. Well yes, we *do* know what we are, but only up to a certain point. It is easy enough to say that we are members of a particular party like the NLD or organisation, but beyond that things start to get a bit fuzzy." (http://www.bbc.co.uk/programmes/b0126d70; http://downloads.bbc.co.uk/rmhttp/radio4/transcripts/2011_reith2.pdf, transcript)

Her speech is in Standard English. There are traces of an accent: one can detect some /r/ sounds after a vowel and a few other signs, which could occur in the English of Burmese and other South-East Asians. Her English is the opposite of what is meant by *Englishes*, which would show local loyalties to Burmese, British, American, Australian, Indian, or Singaporean English. It is on the layer above.

Pluricentricity creates conflicting challenges to the education systems. What is 'right', what 'wrong'? Can one accept "The young student *that* you met" or "*Who* did he look at?", let alone "He looked *at who*" for 'whom' or, as above, "most of *who* for "whom". Should one accept all stable varieties or choose the one or ones that secure the greatest communicative mileage? Will the conflict between active competence and passive awareness of variation widen? Will it be necessary to expose learners to 'localizations' or *Englishes* to achieve the goals of competence and of intercultural competence? What will be the role of native-speaker countries? Such questions are relevant at a time when globalization creates and requires contact across the world and when English no longer guarantees equal access.

English exerts power – linguistically, socially, and politically. It divides the population of many nations into those that know and have access to English and those that do not. Its implantation into traditional habitats of languages has created very localized, 'low' forms such as *Hinglish* in India, *Singlish* in Singapore, or *Chinglish* in China. They are treated with suspicion in these countries as they are unable to cope with science and technology, in international trade and relations, according to experts and politicians. While an international variety is felt to be required, localization is a reality and the question of how much of it can be tolerated must be dealt with. Even countries with an Anglophone past invest in the teaching of international English, often at the expense of local languages. Investment costs are logically larger in foreign language countries. As countries invest in English, their resources may be exhausted and make them reluctant or unable to invest into other, desirable languages.

English exerts power by streamlining a nation's cultural and financial resources and stretching those of individuals. It exerts power over the structure of languages with which it is directly or indirectly in contact. The debates about Anglicisms in German, Malaysia and other languages are well known. A study of the Hindi press has revealed that more than seven percent of its words were English. The BBC News Asia-Pacific reported (21 Dec 2010) that "China bans English words in media" such as *OL* for 'office lady'. In Malaysia a word like *debut* 'debate' caused concern. A reader complained that there are Malay words like *bahas* or *perbahasan*. In multilingual societies one can find heavily mixed texts so that it is not clear if they are in the one or the other language. This allows speakers a new dimension in their ways of speaking as they can switch between different languages. The following examples show what is called code-switching, which ends up mixing the grammars of two languages. In 1.2 the newspaper uses extensive borrowing, the writer of 1.3 mixes Bahasa Malay with English and the speaker of 1.4 switches between English and Hindi:

1.2 "[Headline] Devotion to the word. Sikh women reciting a *bani* [prayer] from *aw gutka* [small book of verses] at the *gurdwara* [the Gateway to the Guru (for Sikhs)] in Kuching yesterday." (*New Straits Times*, 15 Apr 2010)

1.3 "Maka, sebagai kumpulan 'scholar' dan *intelekual*, yang mempunyai pertimbangan dan *rationaliti*, maka 'scholar' dan para ilmuan UBD terutama sekali tenaga tempatan tidak akan terus terpengaruh dengan apa yang dipaparkan dalam *Internet*.

As a group of scholars and intellectuals who have a sense of balance and rationality, scholars and academics of UBD, especially local staff, will not be directly influenced by what is available on the Internet." (*Pelita Brunei* [Brunei], 16 July 1997, on speech by Minister of Education)

1.4 *Controversy* mein   bhi *hit-flop*   kaa   khel
    Controversy in   too hit-flop   PART-GEN   play
    "The play of hit-flop in controversy, too."
    (http://criticalstew.org/?p=716)

Example 1.4 looks difficult. I might rephrase it as "Controversies indeed about Hit-flop play". The word order is like in Hindi: Complement+*bhi*-[]-Adv-[*be*]-Subject. *Mein* is a preposition or, better, post-position, as it follows the noun; *bhi* 'too' is an adverb that highlights the significance of the preceding complement. I translate it as 'indeed'. We will find similar phenomena elsewhere, but this example foreshadows the deep embedding of English in novel multilingual contexts.

This study embeds English into its historical, political

and educational contexts worldwide and explores what it is like today. Leitner (2009) covered some of these topics from a geo-political and historical angle. The chapters below, in contrast, are more focused on what English is like as a language and have many more illustrations to make concrete what had to remain abstract there. The book serves the needs of general interested readers, of those in the teaching and learning business. No book like this one can do without some technical language, but an attempt is made to keep the demands low and technical terms are often illustrated in the following chapters and explained in the glossary.

Signs and Abbreviations

c.	*century*
ch.	*chapter*
ed./eds.	*editor/editors*
e.g.	*exempli gratia* (for example)
esp.	*especially*
et al.	*et alii* (and others)
ibid.	*ibidem* (in the same place)
i.e.	*id est* (that is)
p.	*page*
'	marks a stressed syllable
´	marks rising intonation
`	marks falling intonation
*	marks a linguistically incorrect form
Ø	marks a lexical gap

2 Speaking about English

Language has many functions. It is used to convey information, to engage in a debate, to express happiness or sadness, pride or inferiority, friendship or animosity. It is used to signal personal and national identities, or to unite, as the Australian writer David Malouf said:

> "The language is what holds us together. You know when people are always looking round for what defines our Australian identity, or defines us as a community ... it seems to me to reside ... in the fact that we share that language with one another and have changed that language to fit us, but fit us socially rather than fit the land. ..." (*from* Leitner 2004a: 340)

At the level of society and politics language can unify groups or be divisive, as I have said earlier. It gives power to those that are competent in it (or in a standard variety) and marginalizes those that are not. Minority language groups suffer especially from the rejection of their language and language varieties. They speak of the "loss" of identities in another language. Identities are transported by characteristics in pronunciation, lexis, grammar, and the (pragmatic) ways of speaking and writing. This expression of gratitude by an Egyptian writer, for instance, rings unfamiliar: "In the meantime, I truly appreciate for your recommendation." As language appears in different guises according to users and functions different expressions can be used.

We need a 'language' to speak about language in its multifarious forms, its psychological, social or political functions. Linguistics and *Anglistics* are most closely associated with English and so I will turn to them to provide the very basic vocabulary we need. I should add for readers' benefit that the rest of this chapter can well be read after the chapters that follow or be browsed when concepts come up that appear difficult. To facilitate reading the concepts have been put in bold; for further details see the glossary.

Explaining the inexplicable

Most people find it difficult to talk about language. A Malaysian taxi driver once said to me: "Malaysian English has no grammar" – a crude statement. I learnt to understand. But it is useful to be able to say more, explain. This section will elaborate on a number of important concepts. I will begin with those that may be familiar and continue with those that deal with the structure of language.

To begin with, we need to have a way of talking about manifestations or **varieties** or *Spielformen* of English. That is not easy. Most often they are named after their geo-political location. One speaks of Australian and New Zealand English, of Malawi and South African English, or of Singaporean and Malaysian English, though the pairs of countries mentioned are neighbours and often share a common colonial past. Have they become different from one another? The technical terms used bear a great similarity to dialects and in the past Australian English and others were indeed seen as **dialects** of English. This view is no longer current. Sometimes widely disparate varieties are clustered under a single common name. **Southern Hemisphere English** is a case in point; it includes Australian, New Zealand and South African English because they share a number of features and a com-

mon colonial history. **Northern** (types of) **English** is another term that comprises the English of the north of
England, of Scotland and Ireland for a similar reason.
The opposite of Northern English is **Southern English**.
Both types have had a formative input into American
English. To avoid the problem of having to list the names
of individual forms of English the neutral **variety** (or often *variety of ...*) has come into use. One can then just refer to 'varieties of English' or to 'Englishes'.

Some concepts like **pluricentric** and **epi-centre**, **native**,
second, and **foreign language** were used above. There are
two points that need to be added on the last three. The
first is that they apply to the individual and the nation. A
native language is learnt at home, but need not be one's
most frequently used personal language for life. In native
English countries like Great Britain, the USA or Australia English seldom needs political support. It is the **native
language** of the vast majority and dominates in the public
domain or education. It is the almost sole language there.
In such a situation native is equivalent with **national** language. An **official** language means that English is the one
or one of several languages that is sanctioned in legis-
lation, parliament, or mainstream education. There are
situations where support is felt to be needed in light of
migrations and/or close-knit migrant settlements. The
USA's 'official language debate' of the past two decades
is a case in point. Conservative politicians wanted to declare English the official language in light of massive im-
migrations and close-knit settlements. Liberal politicians
and most linguists opposed that move as unnecessary. Migrants would integrate naturally. The issue is far from settled. Along similar lines some foreign language countries
are trying to impose defensive policies to safeguard the
native language in light of the strength of English.

English as a **second language** is often mentioned in constitutions to define its status vis-à-vis other national languages. Its use may go back to a colonial past. Today it is typically learnt in educational contexts and is used in, say, higher education, higher courts, business and trade, and the sciences in these countries. Its status may vary considerable between countries. In Singapore it is extensively used, while in poverty-stricken and war-ridden East Africa it will have a peripheral role today. As a **foreign language** English is largely confined to education and has limited functions inside a country. Its functions may be increasing in typical international contexts such as conferences, export businesses, diplomacy, higher education, and tourism. As mentioned above, that increase is of concern and some nations, as I just said, develop policies to monitor its use, ensure the use of their native language(s) and multilingualism. *Native*, *second* and *foreign* language are, in other words, overlapping concepts that describe the functions of English in society and for the individual and have a political dimension.

The second point mentioned above is that these three concepts may have implications on the **texture** of English, i.e., its pronunciation, grammar, vocabulary and rules of speaking and writing. A foreign language speaker of English will normally be aware of mistakes, such as when a German pronounces *think* as 'sink'. One will always look for guidance and correction. A native speaker will not do that as they are said to have an almost innate *Sprachgefühl*, a natural sense of correctness. A second language speaker will be similar to the foreign language speaker in showing the effect of one's native language but different in that this effect may be seen as a genuine part of local English. The impact of, or **inference** from, other languages creates different varieties of English. English in India will differ from English in South-East Asia because the languages of India, for instance, have a very complex system of consonants and combinations while those of South-East Asia do not. English in the context of Nigeria or China might show traces of tone – a melody on a word that is essential to express its meaning. As English is mainly learnt in school there is a counter-effect, the learning context that leads to similarities across the world. These developments are not alien to English as a native language as it is transplanted to new geo-political and language situations. English in America or in Ireland was necessarily brought into new kinds of contact. There was a novel situation between, say, English dialects that were vastly separated 'at home'. And there were the local languages such as American Indian or Gaelic. A Cockney speaks English differently from a Scot; you could not know what was edible in North America unless you had some factual and linguistic guidance. These developments have gained a political dimension. A Pakistani minister of education once told the author that "what a quarter of the users of English say – he meant Asians and Africans – cannot be wrong". A clear sign of rejecting the natives' domination!

As we look at English worldwide, we will see that the concepts of 'native', 'second' and even 'foreign' English play a crucial role. They can be used to categorize English in the world (*see* next section) and will reveal important linguistic differences. Readers may be familiar with the observation that foreigners often comprehend each other better than when they speak to a native speaker! "Bad" English has its occasional advantages. We will find that it is the area of English as a second and foreign language, say in India and China, that presents the greatest challenges to the teaching and learning of English in Europe.

As for categorizing variants inside these varieties, one needs terms like **regional**, **social**, or **ethnic** (**varieties**) to make more precise what is meant. One might speak of "regional varieties of British English", etc. Compounds ending in *-lect* perform a similar role. One speaks of **dialect** (= regional variety), **sociolect** (= social variety of, say, the upper middle class), of **ethnolect** (of Asian migrants in England), or **genderlect** (the varieties used by men and women). Regions are often referred to metaphorically by *London English* or *Belfast English*, though it is arguable if there is a (single) 'London English' that is distinct from its neighbours in the south-east of England.

Another dimension of variation refers to the situations in which English or any other language is used. It may be used to have a chat with friends, to give a power-point presentation, to read a manual of the new I-phone or read a novel or poem. The language of chemistry differs from that of literature. There is also the dimension of who speaks to whom: a friend to a friend, an apprentice to the superior or boss, a stranger to another stranger. There are, as one can expect, several dimensions there. One is a scale of formality that ranges from **formal** to **informal usage** and to **slang**. A particularly important scale is that from **standard** to **non-standard**. A third one relates to stable areas of use in domains such as business statistics, sports reports, political commentaries. The language they use is referred to by the term **register**. Registers differ in the employment of lexical and grammatical systems. A chemist article differs from a live horse-race call. A chemist's language is unemotional and objective, that of a horse-race caller full of 'colour' and tension. Often less neutral concepts like **jargon** are used for registers. All languages change permanently. The distinction between contemporary or **synchronic** and historical or **dia-**

chronic linguistics is easy to understand. What is more difficult (when one understands more about the development of a language) is to set up broad, overarching periods such as *Old English*, *Middle English* and *early Modern English* or *contemporary English*. A crucial issue is what the criteria are that delimit one period from the next. Are they socio-political (such as the beginning of the Middle English period is marked by the Norman Invasion) or are they based on linguistic developments? **Contact** springs to mind as the growth of varieties of English is often seen as related to contact of English with other languages or between varieties of English that find themselves in a new mixing constellation, as was the case in Australia? Or, finally, are periods related to purely internal rules of the language? These are questions that will come up again and again in the remainder of the book.

That takes us to the next question. How do we describe the **internal hierarchy** of English? If a variety of English has a standard variety such as British English, one can set up a vertical dimension that ranges from the formal end of the standard to the colloquial, informal layer and to the non-standard, sometimes even sub-standard. But if there is none or not a fully established standard, things become fuzzy. I will turn to this in the next section. But as I have already mentioned the concept of *Englishes*, I might add that that term has been used widely to refer to such situations. The standard/non-standard dimension is, as I have just said, related to the formality of a situation. If there is no standard (as in many second language nations like Ethiopia) one tends to refer to **educated English** and the amount of exposure speakers have.

The process of **standardization**, the growth of a standard variety, is equally difficult to describe. Do all layers of a language such as pronunciation, grammar, etc., have to 'standardize' at the same rate? Can some lag behind? What are the functions of a standard variety? Do all varieties of English have a standard? There is no simple, perhaps no answer at all, and readers will find that the problems with this concept are dealt with throughout this book.

Having clarified some linguistic concepts, I will turn to **methodological** questions. Varieties differ from one another. How do we find out and know that they differ? There will be many examples in subsequent chapters, but a few examples may be helpful here. One finds *wee* as an adjective in *wee hours* 'early morning' or as an adverb in *wee bit* 'a little bit' in Malaysian and Indian English. One finds sentences like 2.3 where the verb is missing, and in 2.4 an emotion verb is used with the progressive aspect in Malaysian or Indian English.

2.1 "… gathered with their telescopes at Universiti Sains Malaysia's … Padang Kawad in the *wee hours* to witness." (*The Star*, 24 May 2011)
2.2 "… may help make rating agencies a *wee bit* more relevant." (*The Star*, 23 Apr 2011)
2.3 She texted me that she Ø *not liking* him so much anymore.
2.4 I'm lovin' it (McDonald's slogan)

In Anglo-American English *wee* counts as a Scotticism. The progressive would produce a shift in the meaning in 2.4 and signal a deliberate action (as if making an effort to enjoy). In the McDonald's slogan it is accompanied by a picture of a man enjoying a burger; that illustrates the so-called instantaneous present (moment), That semantic shift would go unnoticed in Indian English as the progressive is the typical form with such verbs. To explore the

nature of varieties of English, past research has often re-
lied on subjective collections and deep syntactic or semantic analysis. More objective, systematic reading programmes were used, for instance, in the compilation of
dictionaries like the *Oxford English Dictionary* or *Webster's Third International Dictionary*. Grammar writing,
too, benefitted from extensive empirical data. Today, data
collection and analysis have made a large step forward.
They now rest on large computerized collections or **corpora** of what has been printed, hand-written or spoken at
particular periods of time. Further progress has been
made as corpora are required to be representative – of
the language as such or of sub-varieties. Analyses are
speeded up and gain depth by automatic grammatical
analysis. The *Oxford English Dictionary* and *Webster's*
like all modern dictionaries are corpus-based today. Spoken English is increasingly taken into account, which was
barely possible in the past – either because of the lack of
recording techniques or the costs of transcription. There
are corpora of many hundreds of millions of spoken and
written-printed data of British and American English.
There are smaller ones for the English in India, Nigeria,
Jamaica, etc. There can be explorative, small corpora of,
for instance, the speech of British adolescents, of press
commentaries or sports registers. Corpora are the most
sophisticated technique to acquire first-hand knowledge.
Intuition and selective sampling are still necessary to
identify lead questions. Even the cultural embeddedness
can be advanced by corpus analysis as one investigates
the contexts in which some expression occurs. *A fair go*
'equality of chances' is such a cultural icon in Australia
whose understanding will benefit in this way.

To return to the question of how we know that some
variety is different from another or how it has developed

away from its former parent, it is best to adopt a **contrastive** but **non-judgemental** angle. Such a perspective opens the eyes to new features and reveals the individuality of varieties, but also their connectedness with one another. Today, that is taken for granted. But for a long time the angle was a British one, loaded with negative **attitudes** or **prejudice** against anything that was perceived as non-British. American English was the first to suffer under this prejudice. Scottish and Irish English suffered too, as I will show in Chapter Four. Australian English was considered no more than London's working class dialect 'Cockney'. As late as the 1940s, when Australia saw itself confronted directly with American English, a journalist linguist, Sidney Baker, stood up and declared that Australian English should be described from 'within', not from the purview of Oxford. Prejudice was even worse for the English in trade colonial settings and worst of all for the pidgins that arose in maritime trading contexts, on the farms in the Caribbean and similar environments. So a neutral and contrastive angle that may, but need not emanate from corpus studies is the best way to see and interpret new features in new "Englishes".

Descriptions of varieties of English from without, by comparing them with another, will not lead to a genuine picture. They ignore the background, the cultural or other meanings attached to some expression. Yet, that practice cannot be done away with. There may not be enough information about some varieties. And in general a comparison simplifies the presentation. Linguists like Lionel Wee are right to say that an external perspective is "purely intended to facilitate the description of CollSgpE [= colloquial]; it is conceptually a separate issue from the more controversial one of whether CollSpgE can in fact be analyzed as an autonomous linguistic system." (2008:

266) The reference variety is a tool, a meta-language, he says.

When one asks whether some variety constitutes a **linguistic system** of its own, one has to have some knowledge of the concepts of linguistics. They may seem to pose a great hurdle, but they need not really. I will keep the technical survey short and explain more as we go along understanding varieties of English. Instead of using technical jargon, I will replace it by examples or use them to clarify it.

To begin with, the terms **accent** and **dialect** must be distinguished. We hear when someone has a ring of American, British or Scottish English in the way he pronounces words like *fair*. We hear the tone of voice of African Americans. **Accent** refers to the pronunciation, i.e., the sound system, rhythm and intonation. The word **dialect** refers to the grammar, the vocabulary, styles and ways of speaking. When someone uses *wee* for 'small', the speaker may be a Scot, when we hear "I'm loving chocolate" we may have to do with someone from India. *Dialect* here means something different from regional dialect, used above.

Describing accents is a matter of **phonetics** and **phonology**. We speak of **vowels** and **consonants** as sounds and phonemes are units in the system of an accent. Exchanging two sounds in *minimal pairs* like in *tie, lie* and *sigh*, or in *lie, lay,* and *low,* we can identify sounds that create different meanings. If that happens they are called **phonemes** and are inserted between slashes, as in /aɪ, əʊ, l, t, s/. When we look at the three plosive sounds [p, t, t] (note the angled brackets) in *potato* we see that [tʰ] in "-ta-" is aspirated, as a puff of air escapes as the mouth opens. There is a much weaker puff of air in "po-", and none in "-to". Such variants of phonemes are called **allophones**.

All phonemes have allophones, and these will be significant differentiators between accents. When we speak of the pronunciation of a word we typically think of it as spoken in isolation. That is called the **citation style**. Varieties differ in citation style, but more so when words are pronounced as members or constituents of a sentence or a whole utterance. We then speak of **connected speech**. Words carry **stress** as some **syllable** (a sequence of sounds or phonemes) stands out more than others. In '*bigger* the syllable *big-* is stressed and marked with a stress symbol. In *be'coming* it is *-com-* etc. The time (in milliseconds) it takes from one stressed syllable to the next defines the *rhythm* of a language. **Rhythm** is particularly important in English as there can be considerable differences between varieties. Native English is often said to be **stress-timed**, while Singaporean English (or Italian for that matter) would be **syllable-timed**. What this means is that the length of time it takes from one stressed syllable to the next does not depend much on the number of unstressed syllables in between, while each syllable takes about the same amount of time in syllable-timed languages. The italicized passage in "*He won't be* coming" would take as much time as, say, "*Joe* said" where both words are stressed. In connected speech, such as in conversations, many things can happen. Words may lose stress or be articulated in ways not seen in citation style. For instance, /n/ is *alveolar*, i.e. normally articulated in the same place as the /t/, that is behind the teeth, while *th-* (/θ/) in *thin* is *dental*, i.e. articulated at the teeth. In a word like *ten<u>th</u>* /n/ moves front or is *assimilated* to /θ/. Languages have fairly strict rules as to which phonemes can combine or ·*cluster* with one another (– **phonotactics**). As for combinations, English disallows /ps-, kn-/ at the beginning of word like *psychology* and *knight*. At the beginning of a syllable

English permits three consonants and four at the end.
The word *stress* /stres/ shows the 'maximal syllable onset'
with three consonants, *twelfths* /twelfθs/ the 'maximal syllable coda' with four. Varieties can differ in all areas.
What makes differences especially interesting is their cumulative effect on comprehension.

Many features we are going to find in the 'accents' of
English worldwide have a somewhat uncertain status, a
status between being part of an underlying system (of an
accent) or being the typical usage in speech (as variants
of an ill-defined accent). To capture that uncertainty, I
will use the term **pronunciation** in most of the following
chapters and frequently raise the issue of whether they
are (already) part of the system of some national accent
like Singapore's or variants that are typical of some segment of speakers. The term pronunciation is able to be
vague enough to describe these unstable patterns.

As mentioned earlier, dialect refers to anything other
than pronunciation. That 'anything other' is words (= **lexis**), the forms of words in sentences (= **inflection, morphology**), **syntax**, **semantics**, and **pragmatics**. **Word-formation** deals with the formal relationship between words
as between *daily* and *day* or *shoplifter* 'someone who
steals (*lifts from*) in shops' with *shop* and *lift*. If a pattern
becomes the source of other words like *carlifter* 'someone
who steals cars' or *childlifter* 'kidnapper', we speak of a
productive pattern. To illustrate the grammar associated
with words (= **lexico-grammar**), English has a clear-cut
distinction between countable nouns such as *letter* and
collective nouns like *staff*. To refer to an individual, one
must say "a member of staff". In many second language
varieties such nouns have been converted to countable
ones. One can speak of *a staff* 'member of' or *an alphabet*
'one letter'. Often the grammar of verbs is simplified. In

native English one needs *to fill in/out a form* but in many Asian varieties one finds "Lots of tedious *forms to fill*".

Dialect includes **syntax**, which deals with the ordering of words in sentences. It covers the grammatical systems that operate within sentences such as time reference (= **tense**), the voice of a sentence (active or passive), the types of sentences such as questions, statements or commands, etc. The German sentence "Die Wurst isst die Frau" could mean that the sausage eats the woman, which is unlikely, and that the woman eats the sausage. That meaning cannot be expressed in English by "The sausage eats the woman", as the English **word order** is S-V-O. There is a range of constructions that allow modifications of the order of words (or, technically, constituents). The passive, "The sausage was eaten by the woman", does maintain the S-V order, but the (logical) subject now appears as an adverbial. There are radical alternatives. The existential *there*-construction in "There is a book that John took" serves to introduce a new topic. The two types of split or **cleft sentence** (the essential elements are italicized), i.e., "*What* the woman ate *was* the sausage" or "*It was* the sausage *that* the woman ate" highlight a topic. We will see differences in syntax.

Dialect also covers the area of how people do things with utterances (= **pragmatics**). How does one ask a question, make a request or offer something politely? Questions, for instance, require 'inversion' in native English as in "Did you do that?" or "What did you do?" In South-East Asian English, the inversion of the verb and the subject is replaced by a rising speech melody (= **pitch** or **intonation**).

I need to add a few words on style. **Style** is a cover term for a variety of things that are really quite distinct. The following texts illustrate some areas that come under style:

2.5 [Headline] *Storm* will finally *stir things up*.
   (a) It's nearly December, so the *Seattle Storm* women's basketball team is probably the last thing on your mind …
   (b) *Stirring up a Storm* fan base has been as hard as predicting the weather.
   (c) *Theories* abound on why. But the main problems are … the timing of the Storm's season. It runs from May to August, when *the crack of the bat drowns out the squeak of the sneak* in almost every city …
   (d) So during this off-season, I bring you *tidings of great joy*: The Storm just won the first-round pick in the WNBA draft.

2.6 "This is the language *by which* Mr. Blair deceives us" (*The Independent*, 8 May 2003).

The passage in 2.5 conveys the message that it is hard to write about the women's basketball team *Seattle Storm* as they play during the off-season. The team's name itself is used metaphorically in the headline and again in (b). There are metaphoric expressions such as *the crack of the bat*, *drown out*, and *the squeak of the sneak* in (c) that allude to the shift of interest from basketball, a winter game, to baseball, a summer game, and 'explain' the difficulty of writing about the *Seattle Storm*. The report brings *the tidings of good joy* in (d) that they won the first round in a competition. Metaphors produce colour and can be seen as semantic-pragmatic readings of sentences that deviate from what the sentences express literally. The metaphors in 2.5 can be understood in the context of the symbolism surrounding the two national games. Many linguists would refer to this as expressions of culture – an important theme in varieties of English.

   Choices in syntax can refer to situations like sentences (a) in 2.5. They can create meaning as in the headline.

The headline in 2.6 referred to the performance of former Prime Minister Tony Blair, who was seen as lying while he pretended to be honest. This contrast between self-image and perception is expressed metaphorically by the hyper-correct construction "*by which*" instead of the common "*which* Mr. Blair … *by*". Hyper-correction is frequent with people who are uncertain and are trying to avert risks. Here it has a strategic purpose.

Politically correct language is expressed through the lexis, morphology and syntax of English. The 1960s saw a protest against 'man-made' language that aimed to redress the situation by, for instance, enforcing the replacement of masculine words with neutral ones. A verb like *to man* was to be replaced by *to staff* or *to operate*. Non-biassed language was extended to linguistic bias against race, disabilities, life-styles. This movement, ridiculed as 'politically correct', was a world-wide success. But there are 'pockets of resistance', as in this quotation from a Malaysian newspaper:

2.7 "… there are not enough *nurses to man* operations at full capacity" (*Malay Mail*, 14 June 2011).

We have come a long way in providing background to the description of varieties of English and some common themes. (I will say more on internal variation below.) I must return to national varieties like Malaysian English and discuss how we can integrate a considerable level of variation into a common framework or model.

Models of English

What do we mean by 'English' today, when there is so much variation? Can we still be certain that the norms of usage derive from Standard British English or, if you like, from a mixture of British and American English? Clearly 'no': English is **multi-polar**, **pluricentric**, and **global**. English is both **localizing** and **globalizing** (*see* Leitner 2009). Localizing means that it develops varieties that we identify with nations (for the purposes of this book) such as the United States, Great Britain, Australia or India. At the same time there are overarching pressures such as from the politically correct language.

When we hear on an Australian evening news broadcast something like "The PM has met with his British counterpart this morning", when a Malaysian says "Can have or not", when a Nigerian writes "Tat's te biggest problem" or when a German says "I sink sat is rong", are we talking about errors or regular properties of the English in the region concerned? We seem certain that the Australian is right and that the German's pronunciation is wrong. But the Australian broadcast contradicts 'our' rules! What about the Malaysian and the Nigerian? Linguists avoid talking about errors in such cases and classify them as 'features' or 'variants'. They need to assess their signifance inside the grammatical system of English. The present perfect with a past time adverb above relates to the system of tense – in a marginal manner. The Malaysian expression goes deeper as so much is omitted – the subject and object. We do not know the intention and whether it is a polite request or question. The German 'sink' reduces the phoneme inventory of English – like it is done in many varieties. Occurrences require analysis. They also require to ask the question if they are regular overall, in some style of speech or writing or in some section of those that speak English? Even if they are regular, what do Anglophones in the countries concerned think of them? Are they considered to be the right way of using English? Or are they used but still considered wrong? Are they acceptable in the school system? These are crucial questions when we want to integrate them into some 'model' of English that enables us to understand what English is today. Occurrence, analysis, allocation to some style or segment of speakers, and attitudes are crucial questions that need to be resolved. Depending on the answers we can speak of gradual variants of English or new regular systems.

I will use the terms **localization** and **globalization** so as to capture the 'departures' from some native mode and the local or global origin. Localizing differences emerge naturally and are indeed the reason for distinguishing varieties in the first place. They result from the **adaptation of English** to new environments such as a new topography, a new fauna, flora, people, social practices, material culture, fashion, or contact with other languages (or, not to forget, the input varieties). When speakers of different varieties mix in circumstances such as the settlement of America or Australia, adaptations reduce the amount of variation that the settlers carry with them. Pronunciations accommodate to reduce variation. Words are retained while they disappear at home; they shift in meaning; and new words are created or introduced from other languages. Grammatical variation is levelled out. In the case of native varieties, the linguistic base, say, varieties of British English, continues to dominate the developments. In the case of non-native contexts, the contact with local languages and the role of inference increases. We will see that all types of English, i.e. native or second language, undergo similar developments until they reach a new system. But in the case of second language varieties the role of language contact and of language acquisition are more visible.

Such changes are connected with social factors or with pressures exerted by the linguistic system. Hindi has postpositions after a noun as in 1.4, Indian English does not and will not. Often both factors collaborate, so to speak, to create a new national variety. As these differences emerge, they collectively turn the language into a different *de facto* **variety** and begin to signal new linguistic identities. These new varieties may become legitimate forms of, say Australia, India or Malaysia, if they find acceptance amongst the relevant elite. If not, they continue to be mere characteristics of language use. Yet, do they challenge the unity of English as a (single, cohesive) language? Their impact has given rise to two schools of thought emerged.

Braj Kachru is known to have seen radical departures from what was considered the core of English. In a radical move in the 1970s he argued that English was no longer a unified system of linguistic expressions and was no longer tied to a single speech community. It existed in the form of interlocking **Englishes**, which, though loosely related to a common system, differed in respect of linguistic texture, showed different effects of contact, and developed local norms. Such norms or shared practices were accepted by a growing number of speakers, who acquired them in their daily lives. *Englishes* were owned by local **speech fellowships**, a concept that would later be replaced by **language communities**. Kachru's model is best known in the form of three concentric circles (*see* Fig. 2.1).

The Inner Circle contains the traditional native varieties, the Outer Circle second language varieties (most of

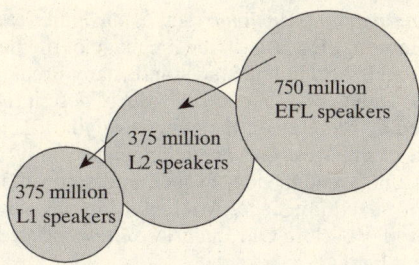

Figure 2.1: Kachru's Three-Circle Model

them in former colonies); the Expanding Circle is for English as a foreign language. The allocation of some variety to any one circle is based on the likelihood of developing norms of 'good' usage or standard varieties. Inner Circle varieties are most likely to do so, though not all have and some like the English on the Falklands Island will never do. Outer Circle varieties may develop norms, which are quite visible in India, Singapore or Hong Kong. Varieties in the Expanding Circle were assumed to never develop norms of their own, though the growth of English in China may well lead to such varieties in the future. Englishes need to be described in reference materials. The Three-Circle model has been recast into one with overlapping circles to depict the dynamics of English that is mainly associated with the Outer and Expanding Circles (Graddol 1997: 10).

Unlike the Australian *Macquarie*, most dictionaries have, however, remained rather conservative. The *New Oxford Dictionary of English* (1998), e.g., describes English as "the language of England, now widely used in many varieties throughout the world". The *Webster's*

Third International Dictionary takes an American angle when it says that English is "the language of the people of England and the United States and many areas now or formerly under British control". Such descriptions are supported by remarks on the genetic origin of English as a branch of the West Germanic language family, and the impact from Scandinavian, French and Latin that made English a mixed language. A straight line is drawn from English today back to Old English to show the strength of its descent line.

That is the background to what is called the **core-periphery approach**. It assumes that English worldwide is based on a single but flexibe system. Standard English has global validity and, as it embraces a lot from British and American English, it is inherently variable. To give a few examples, spelling differences such as in *honour* and *honor*, the pronunciation of *dance* with /ɑː/ or /æ/ or even /a/ would be acceptable. Both *fall* and *spring* or the simple past in "Did he come yet" for British "Has he come yet" would be acceptable. So would *that* as a conjunct introducing the subject in a relative clause as in "That's the professor *that* we met". The replacement of dental fricatives in *this* and *thumb* by [d, t] would be on the margin. There is also, I should add, a core non-standard English, which contains *ain't*, *-in-* for *-ing*, double negation and a few other properties that will be illustrated in Chapter Three. Trudgill/Hannah (2008) have suggested a quite stringent typology of native varieties of English (*see* Fig. 2.2).

A few explanations may be useful. The well-known pronunciation of *path* /paːθ/ occurs in one form or another in the Republic of Ireland, England and Wales, South Africa, Australia and New Zealand. The pronunciation /pæθ/ combines Scotland, Northern Ireland, Canada and the USA. Feature 2 shows that England, Wales, South

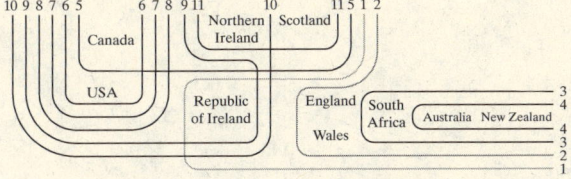

1. /ɑː/ rather than /æ/ in *path* etc.
2. absence of non-prevocalic /r/
3. close vowels for /æ/ and /ɛ/, monophthongization of /ai/ and /ɑu/
4. front [aː] for /ɑː/ in *part* etc.
5. absence of contrast of /ɒ/ and /ɔː/ as in *cot* and *caught*
6. /æ/ rather than /ɑː/ in *can't* etc.
7. absence of contrast of /ɒ/ and /ɑː/ as in *bother* and *father*
8. consistent voicing of intervocalic /t/
9. unrounded [ɑ] in *pot*
10. syllabic /r/ in *bird*
11. absence of contrast of /ʊ/ and /uː/ as in *pull* und *pool*

Figure 2.2: Family relations in English

Africa, Australia and New Zealand omit the /r/ after vowels. They are non-rhotic, while all others, including Ireland, are rhotic. Scotland and Northern Ireland share features (11, 5), as well as non-rhoticity (2) and /æ/ (1), but are separated by not having a syllabic /r/ in *bird* (10). It is easy to see a basic division between what are called *Northern English* and *Southern English*. The latter merges England, the former on Scotland, Northern Ireland and the USA (*see* Fig. 2.2).

Trudgill/Hannah's model adds substance to the core-periphery concept and identifies areas of patterned varia-

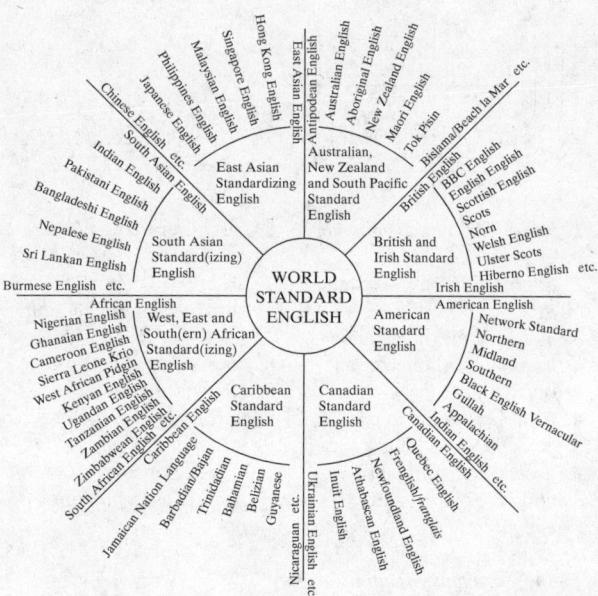

Figure 2.3: McArthur's circle of World English

tion in phonology. It is compatible with the observation that English had become quite diverse by the 1920s when people could hear English on the radio. But it marginalizes second language varieties altogether and does not apply in the same way to other levels of language structure. There is a variant of the core/periphery approach that is owed to McArthur (1998a). It is not confined to phonology. It takes Standard English as a starting point and puts it into the centre of three overlapping circles. Other varieties are the more remote circles the greater they differ from the Standard (*see* Fig. 2.3).

McArthur, thus, represents the relationship between varieties in terms of the linguistic differences between them. **Standard English** may look like a Swiss cake with 'holes' pointing to variable areas that have not been made explicit. John Algeo's (2006) work on American and British English helps understand what McArthur has in mind. Variable areas in grammar, he says, rarely refer to large grammatical systems such as tense or aspect or nominal class systems. Generally, they are small patterns in the grammar of words (= **lexico-grammar**) and in the way they are used together (= **collocation**). Americans tend "to protest a decision", while in Britain one would "to protest *against* a decision". British English has no definite article in "he plays Ø piano" while American English and Northern English such as in Scotland and Ireland have "he plays *the* piano". The present perfect in Standard British English is obligatory with adverbs of recent time like *yet*: "*Has* John *come* home *yet*?" In American English the simple past is (normally) used. Findings like these have been replicated in many corpus linguistic studies and have supported the concentric circles. That model too has been taken up willingly in the educational sector.

These models are persuasive and have their strengths in organizing a more than complex area of variation. But there are problems. Kachru's circles lack dynamism: never any variety has been moved from the centre outwards or from the periphery inwards. There is also a problem with 'norm', which is seen as an all-embracing concept; a variety does or does not develop a norm. It took nearly two centuries for general American English to emerge as a standard variety and it took many decades for Australian

English to do so. The development of norms does not necessarily make a variety the accepted target of teaching. Despite such observations, the simplicity of the model has made it a good organizing principle for many text books. The core-periphery model is quite unable to incorporate the growing evidence of regular, rule-guided variation.

As a dynamic element was seen missing, some experts were motivated to look for alternative ways. Leitner (2004a/b) and Edgar Schneider (2007) have developed alternatives that are **dynamic**, inclusive, and apply to native and second language varieties alike. Leitner's model is detailed with regard to English in Australia, while Schneider's uses examples from around the world. Schneider argues that there are five stages that all varieties of English can go through as they move away from some parent and reach their own system: (i) foundation, (ii) **exo-normative** stabilization, (iii) nativization, (iv) **endo-normative** stabilization, and (v) differentiation. The details are well-described in, e. g., Schneider (2011) and Leitner (2009). A few remarks will clarify the background.

The **foundation** phase is crucial. A variety is based on the dialects of the first settlers or learners and is influenced by the nature of settlement and the nature of contact with local peoples. Australian English, for instance, shows heavy influences from the south-east of England. American English has relics of Elizabethan English. In economic and exploitation colonies such as in Africa the situation is different. Even though English is mainly transmitted through education, its daily use outside school reflects the local languages of its speakers. Attitudes on what is good English remain tied to the country of origin for a long time and accentuate exo-normative stabilization, Schneider argues. What he means is that those countries go on seeing the English of Britain (or

America, as the case may be) as the proper form to emulate. This is true even today of Singapore, where the target of education still is British English.

Novel features develop naturally in areas where English has been transplanted to. The outcome of this phase is called "*de facto* variety". But as new features accumulate, there is bound to build up a conflict about whether they should be accepted as proper 'local' English. That conflict is resolved by moving on to stabilization, which is often referred to as nativization, stage (iii). Australia did that around the time it became independent in 1901 and the United States around 1776. Both countries then moved on to stage (iv), endo-normative stabilization. They adopted positive attitudes to local English. Second language countries are willing or forced to entertain that conflict for a long time and remain 'stuck', so to speak, at a stage before endo-normativity. Few countries have moved on to endo-normative stabilization, stage (iv). The final stage, differentiation, is reached, Schneider says, when internal variation patterns stabilize. Thus, there may be clear regional and social dialects and registers that mark communities and increase the expressive capacity of the wider variety.

Schneider's model has another characteristic. As English was transported to, and implanted into, social contexts with native peoples such as the Aboriginal Australians, the Maori New Zealanders or the First Nations in North America, English developed two varieties, i.e., the one of the **settler strand**, the majority, and the one of the **native strand**. In countries like India or Malaysia where there were few Anglophone settlers, English is now spoken by a vast majority of non-native speakers. The descendant of the original transplanted varieties has become the language of the minority of expatriates, if it has persisted. Terms like Anglo-Indian (of the expatriates) and Indo-Anglian (of the Indians) show the currency of the linguistic effects of the coexistence of the two strands. Schneider argues that the two strands, i.e., that of the settlers and that of ethnic communities, will ultimately find a common purpose when the varieties move on to stage (iv) and develop norms of their own. That may happen. In many Islamic countries the content and language of Western culture will be replaced by those that fit into the local culture. Thus, scenes that involve alcoholic drinks will disappear from teaching materials. In contrast, conflicting views on how to represent interactions between boys and girls may develop and accentuate, as English is inevitably the language that represents modernity. Schneider fails to see that societies are built on conflict, resolution, and renewed or persistent conflict. He presents English based on a social consensus model.

A variety like British or American English is, one might say, 'self-controlled'. Britons and Americans do not look across the Atlantic to ask what is right or what is standard or non-standard. There is a consensus that there is no single dimension such as between Standard English and anything 'below'. There are regional dialects, there are sociolects in different social strata and differences between age groups, genders and ethnicities. These internal variations are taken for granted and become problematic only in educational contexts. There is another dimension of variation, that between speech and writing, that is close to that between formality or informality.

These dimensions of variation intersect and there is no easy way to model them, though they are often simplified as a two-dimensional triangle. The model below intersects social class and geographical variation. Standard English would cover an area that reaches down to somewhat below the upper middle class (*see* Fig. 2.4).

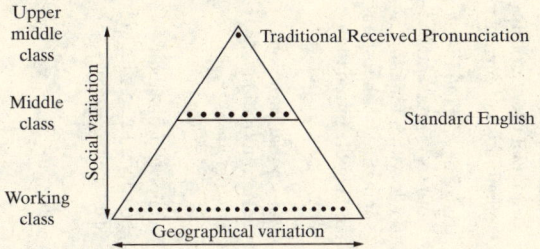

Figure 2.4: One model for the depiction of internal variation

While the model generally holds for Great Britain, it may not capture other varieties. But it has been replicated for varieties of English worldwide. This is often done on the assumption that there is a cline or a scale that is quite similar to the social class scale in Britain. It does not assume segregation of the social classes but an implicational scale. The bottom variety that is a typical outcome of language contact is called **basilect**. A level higher is a wide spectrum of **mesolect**, and above it is the **acrolect** (Collins/Mees 2008: 3). The differences are normally defined in terms of the distance from the assumed Standard English of Britain and the proximity to the structures and cultural affiliations to the local languages habitats. Even very educated speakers may use the basilect, at least to some extent, to signal common descent. A common representation is this, which is based on Azirah/Tan (2012) (*see* Fig. 2.5).

To sum up, my position in this book is that English

1. is still one language system
2. has a distinct set of national varieties with internal stratification, called *epi-centres*

	Acrolect: Standard MalE, formal use, international intelligibility	Mesolect: dialectal MalE, informal use, national intelligibility	Basilect: patois MalE, colloquial use, patois intelligibility and currency
Phonology	Slight variation tolerated so long as it is internationally intelligible	More variation is tolerated, including prosodic features especially stress and intonation	Extreme variation – both segmental and prosodic with intonation so stigmatized – almost unintelligible internationally
Syntax	Rules of international standard fully observed	Some deviation is acceptable although it is not as stigmatized as broken English	Substantial variation/ deviation (national intelligibility)
Lexis	Variation acceptable especially for words not substitutable in an international context (to give a more localized context)	Lexicalization quite prevalent even for words having international English substitutes	Major lexicalization heavily infused with local language items

Figure 2.5: Internal variation in non-native Englishes

3. has an overarching International English or Standard variety
4. has tensions between national varieties, internal varieties and international English that lead to mixed outputs

Despite these clarifications it will not be easy to present the manifestations of English from a single perspective. Often it is not clear whether what we see is a signal of a new system that goes way beyond little differences like saying "sink" for 'think' or "The PM has met with his British counterpart this morning". It is often not clear what their implications are. Too often, observations are couched in different ways, as standard, education, (upper) mesolect, etc., terms that are interpreted differently. I will choose a perspective of the educated speakers and writers in formal contexts. Whether big or small, those differences occur often enough in particular countries or regions and are often part of literature. They are a challenge to the teaching and learning of English. And when we understand them, we will have a better access to the cultures of the countries concerned. The coverage will not be comprehensive. Africa and East Asia will get considerably less space than the rest of the world.

3 From the English Heritage to the Core

Many people around the world treasure British English. They aim to imitate it – some may say 'ape' it or speak 'flash'. England is the birthplace of English. English started out there as a member of the West Germanic branch of Indo-Aryan languages and is related to German, Dutch and Frisian. It is the outcome of the transplantation of West Germanic dialects to Britain. Norwegian, Swedish

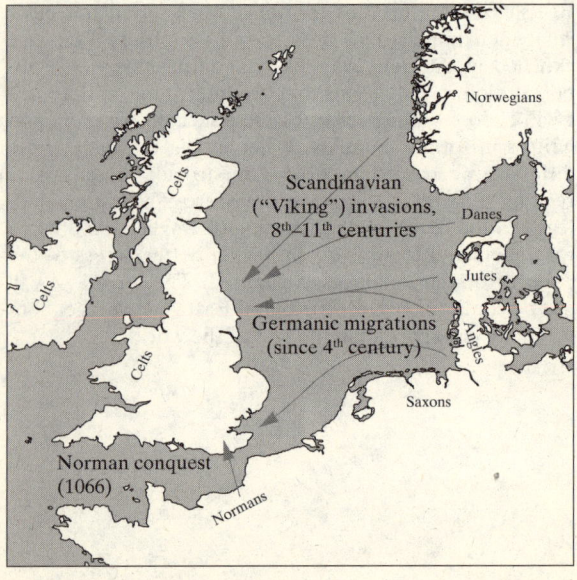

Map 3.1: The roots of English

and Danish are members of the North Germanic family, which occupied an adjacent region on the continent and later mixed with English in Britain. The main steps of the development to 1500 are summed up by McCrum *et al.* in these terms (*see* Map 3.1):

"The making of English is the story of three invasions and a cultural revolution. In the simplest terms, the language was brought to Britain by Germanic tribes, the Angles, Saxons and Jutes, influenced by Latin and Greek when St Augustine and his followers converted England to Christianity, subtly enriched by the Danes, and finally transformed by the French-speaking Normans." (1986: 51)

After 1,000 years English began its travels to the remote corners of the British Isles, to the New World and Asia – passing along the coasts of Africa. That is a topic for later, but that had repercussions that helped the rise of Standard English and the prestige of the precursors of the *Received* Pronunciation. The timeline below therefore includes the main dates of the expansion of English during the colonial period so that these repercussions become visible.

Timeline 1: England

407	End of Roman period in Britain
449	West Germanic tribes, i.e., Angles, Saxons, Jutes, and Frisians, begin to invade Britain and settle up to Edinburgh
500	**Old English Period**
563	Spread of Christianity by Irish missionaries in north England; foundation of the monastery of Lindisfarne

597	On Pope Gregory's initiative St. Augustine begins to Christianize the south of England
793	Start of Viking pillages, destruction of Lindisfarne
9th c.	Viking settlements in north England, expanding southward
867	England ceded Strathclyde and Lothian to Scotland
878	Truce with Vikings; establishment of *Danelaw* boundary
1016	Canute becomes the first Danish king of England
1066	Battle of Hastings and beginning of Norman supremacy
1100	**Middle English Period**
1476	Caxton introduces printing in London
1154	Power shifts to House of Angevin and Plantagenet in France
1170	Supremacy over Wales and Ireland (1170); over Scotland (1175)
1500	**Early modern English Period**
1536	Unification of England and Wales
1600	Foundation of East India Company; first trading post in India
1603	Union of Scottish and English crowns (United Kingdom)
1607	First settlement in America: Jamestown (later Virginia)
1607	*Authorized Bible* foll. by *Common Book of Prayer*, etc.
1630	Foundation of Bermuda
1642–51	English Civil War
1707	Act of Union with Scotland (Kingdom of Great Britain)
1756	Seven Years' War: Territorial expansion in Africa, Asia
1783	Recognition of Independence of United States

1788	Foundation of Australian colonies
1801	Unification with Ireland (United Kingdom and Ireland)
1806	First settlements in Cape colony (more in 1820)
1819	Singapore; later part of Straits Settlements
1857	India becomes Crown Colony
19th c.	(late 19th c.) Scramble for Africa
1918	English and French official languages of League of Nations, International Labour Office
1922	Republic of Ireland (hence United Kingdom and Northern Ireland); Britain is given mandate over Palestine
1947	Decolonization (beginning with India)
1973	Great Britain joins European Community
1998	Devolution of Scotland and Wales; Ireland (2002)

The story of English

The Roman Empire began to withdraw from Britain from around 409, leaving behind the Britons, who were threatened by the Celtic Picts. The West Germanic Angles, Saxons, Jutes and Frisians soon filled the vacuum and settled an area from Kent and Somerset to Edinburgh. Seven kingdoms, the Heptarchy, emerged, but only Mercia, Northumbria, Kent and Wessex gained enough power to have an impact on the newly forming "language". The invaders, says Crystal (2004: 19), "did not bring with them three 'pure' varieties – Anglian, Saxon, and Jutish – but a wide range of spoken varieties, displaying different kinds of mutual influences." Kent, the main entry point, "must have been an especially mixed sociolinguistic area", he adds (2004: 21). It would be wrong to think that a homogeneous language could emerge in the absence of a pre-national government or cultural centres. There was no sign of, and no need for, an overarching form of Old English. What the founding generations did achieve was a base, Anglo-Saxon.

The beginning of a world language

Two invasions and Christianization made Old English a mixed language or a hybrid. Ongoing nativization helped transform the basis into a core that all epi-centres of English have inherited.

Christianity, the cultural revolution, began in Kent around 600 and in the north around 630 by Irish missionaries who brought the Celtic tradition. Church centres were founded in Lindisfarne in the north and Canterbury in the south-east. The Church introduced Latin as the language of religious matters and of historical writing. Latin was also the carrier of Greek and Hebrew words. Old English was enriched by these three languages (*see* Map 3.2).

The Vikings or, as they were also called, the Danes (or Norwegians), were responsible for the second invasion in the 8th century. They began with raids but settled in the north-east and pushed south a few decades later. Appealing to a sense of Englishness, King Alfred of Wessex was able to enforce a boundary at the end of the 9th century that gave him control over London and the Thames Estuary, leaving the Danes the Danelaw, a large area in the east and north of England. From a sociolinguistic angle it is worth noting that the word *englisc* was now used for the first time to refer to the people and the language in the south and south-west. The socio-political and linguistic importance of Wessex promoted an Old English stand-

Map 3.2: Viking settlement areas

ard in writing that was to survive into the 12th century.
That can be seen as the beginning of the endo-normative
development. A note on Scotland may be useful here.
The end of warfare between the Angles and the Celtic
tribes in the 10th century led the Anglian dialect in Scotland to a break from the common Anglian in the north-
east of England. Anglian became a flourishing national
language, *Scots*, and a regional dialect south.

The Vikings introduced new sound patterns and a
North Germanic vocabulary. Many loan words passed into the common vocabulary – quite unlike the uptake of
most Latin words. A few examples will illustrate this (the
first word is Old Norse, the second in brackets Old Eng-
lish): *to call* (*ceallian, kalla*), *fellow* (*feolaga, felagi*), *wrong*
(*wrang, vrang*), *knife* (*cnif, knifr*), and *take* (*tacan, taka*).
A number of lexical doublets developed such as (the first
is Old Norse) *dike* and *ditch*, *sick* and *ill*, *skirt* and *shirt*,
skin and *hide*, and *skill* and *craft*. Where both words have
survived, they often underwent semantic differentiation
such as *skirt* and *shirt* or *skill* and *craft*. Sometimes one of
the words was lost; *kirk* has survived in Scottish English,
in England it was lost. The Vikings introduced the personal and possessive pronouns *they*, *them* and *their* and the
3rd person singular *are* of *to be*. *Both* and *same* are of Scandinavian descent, as are *till* and *from*. The Vikings initiated or, at least, sped up the decline of the inflectional systems of English, which was part of the cause of English
becoming a fixed word order language.

The Battle of Hastings (1066) marks the beginning of
the third invasion, i.e., that of the Normans. It happened
because Denmark and Normandy could not agree on a
successor of King Edward the Confessor, who died with
no heir. At the end of the battle Duke William II of Normandy became King William I. Norman and French rule

were to last nearly four centuries. French and Latin became the *high* or prestigious languages in the public domain where they assumed complementary roles in politics, administration, and the Church. Latin was the language of learning, where it dominated up to and beyond
the early Modern English period. French was the national, public language, as well as the native language of the
French aristocracy. In this *triglossic* situation English was
demoted to the rank of the *low* language, that of the common people. The West Saxon proto-standard in writing
continued to act as a form of writing for some time but
stalled eventually. English was reduced to a cluster of
regional dialects. As time went by, there emerged a level
of bilingualism among the Norman elite and the urban
English. A shift to English occurred when the descendants of the French faced the loss of their possessions in
France in the late 13th century and decided to remain in
England.

A peak marks the beginning of a decline, and so it did
in England around 1400. The children of the French had
become bilingual for some time and French was the foreign tongue for many. The Hundred Years' War (1337–
1453), the pestilence and other unforeseeable catastro-
phes further reduced the status of French so that English
acquired a high status in the public domain. At that time
it was no longer a direct descendant of Old English as
contact had turned it into a hybrid. It had absorbed thousands of French and Latin words and incorporated grammatical constructions from both. We can refer to them as
de facto differences from Old English or as nativization,
in Schneider's terms. A move to endo-normativity is
more than obvious. As standardization began, English acquired a formative centre, the famous triangle of London,
Cambridge, and Oxford. As a result Standard English be-

gan to be identified with the south and south-east. Its spread to the nation at large reduced the status of the descendants of the Anglian dialect, i.e., Northumbrian, in the north further.

By 1600 English had the properties needed for a developed language. (Dr.) Samuel Johnson, writer and lexicographer, reflected upon the achievements in the 18th century with these words:

"But as every language has a time of rudeness antecedent to perfection, as well as of false refinement and declension, I have been cautious lest my zeal for antiquity might drive me into times too remote, and croud my book with words now no longer understood. I have fixed *Sidney's* work for the boundary, beyond which I make few excursions. From the authours which rose in the time of *Elizabeth*, a speech might be formed adequate to all the purposes of use and elegance. If the language of theology were extracted from *Hooker* and the translation of the Bible; the terms of natural knowledge from *Bacon*; the phrases of policy, war, and navigation from *Raleigh*; the dialect of poetry and fiction from *Spenser* and *Sidney*; and the diction of common life from *Shakespeare*, few ideas would be lost to mankind, for want of *English* words, in which they might be expressed." (Preface to *Dictionary of the English Language* 1755 [note the spelling of *crowd* and *authors*, G.L.]; http://ethnicity. rutgers.edu/~jlynch/Texts/preface.html)

By the 18th century English was rich enough to express almost any thought, and Elizabethans were proud that it "hath it equally with any other tongue in the world", if articulated properly. At this point it may be good to stop for moment and illustrate the developments from Old to Modern English.

The core of English: a Germanic-Roman hybrid

The English that was felt to be rich enough to take it up
with any other (European) language had been a different
one from the English of the King of Westminster Alfred.
It grew out of the mixing of Old English with Latin and
French (above all) and settled in the 16th century that
would be referred to as "core". A standard dialect and,
somewhat later, a prestige accent were beginning to
emerge that was based on that core and became the angle
from which all older histories described English. New
varieties of English inherited that core as part of their
formative input. The developments after transplantation
will concern us in later chapters. I will now illustrate what
the core was as it developed away from Old English.

The following excerpts from Luke 2,1 tell the story of
the birth of Jesus. The first two excerpts represent the
West Saxon dialect of Old English (3.1) and Wyclif's translation in Middle English (3.2) from somewhat before 1420.
The early modern English text (3.3) is from William Tyndale and example 3.4 from the *New English Bible* (1970).

3.1 Sōþlīče on þām daȝum wæs ȝeworden ȝebod fram þām
cāsere Augusto, þæt eall ymbehwyrft wǣre tōmearcod.
þēos tōmearcodnes wæs ǣrest ȝeworden fram þām dēman
Syriȝe Cirīno. And ealle hiȝ ēodon and syndriȝe fērdon on
hyra čeastre. Đā fērde Iōsēp fram Galilēa of þǣre čeastre
Nāzareth on Iūdēisče čeastre Dāuīdes, sēo is ȝenemned
Bethleem, for þām þe hē wæs of Dāuīdes hūse … (West
Saxon, *MS. Corpus Christi College Cambridge 140*).

3.2 And it was don in þo daies, a maundement wente out fro
þe emperour (August), þat al þe world schulde be discryued. Þis firste discryuyng was maad of Cyryn, justice of
Sirie; and alle men wenten to make professioun, ech into

his owne citee. And Ioseph wente vp fro Galilee fro þe citee Nazareth into Judee into a citee of David, þat is clepid Bethleem, for þat he was of þe hous ... (Wyclif-Purvey, *MS.: BM., Old Library 1 century 8* [probably before 1420]).

3.3 And it chaunced in thoose dayes that ther went oute a commaundment from Auguste the Emperour, that all the woorlde shuld be taxed. And this taxynge was the fyrst and executed when Syrenius was leftenaunt in Syria. And every man went vnto his awne citie to be taxed. And Ioseph also ascended from Galile, oute of a cite called Nazareth, into Iurie: vnto the cite of David which is called Bethleem, because he was of the house ... (Willam Tyndale, 1534).

3.4 In those days a decree was issued by the Emperor Augustus for a registration to be made throughout the Roman world. This was the first registration of this kind; it took place when Quirinius was governor of Syria. For this purpose everyone made his way to his own town; and so Joseph went up to Judaea from the town of Nazareth in Galilee, to register at the city of David, called Bethlehem, because he was of the house of David by descent ... (*New English Bible*, 1970).

Like German, Old English had a free word order with adverbials (*Sōþliče on þām daʒum*) preceeding the verb (*wæs ʒeworden*), the subject (*ʒebod fram þām cāsere Augusto*) and the complement clause. The Middle English version (3.2) is much the same as the Old English one, but its word order is now Subject-Verb-Object. The Early Modern English version (3.3) is like 3.2. We see the existential *there*-construction "*there*+V", which is a 'modern' pattern. It marks information as 'new' or 'old' in Modern English in 3.4.

Turning to inflection, Old English has case in, e. g., *(on)* *þām daჳum, (fram) þām cāsere*. The past participles *ჳeworden* and *ჳenemned* are marked with the prefix *ჳe-* and the *-en/-ed* suffix. That was largely lost by Middle English. What we still see is that simple past endings had not lost the vowel, as in *discryued*. There is a subjunctive in Old English *ware*, which is rendered with the 'putative' *should* in Middle and Early modern English. In Modern English it is replaced by a non-finite passive construction with a (modal) meaning of obligation.

A look at lexis is revealing. For one, the vocabulary of English grew by thousands of words and had acquired, one might say, an inherent preference of borrowing. What was a small vocabulary before the French invasion has become the largest one of all languages. This is not necessarily an asset as no individual could know more than a very small portion. But it gives English an un-matched expressive power and permits multiple layers of differentiation.

An interesting question is what was responsible for that growth of the vocabulary. There are deliberate word crea-tions and derivations; there is language contact with loans, hybrids, loan translations, and semantic processes. Dictionaries like the *Oxford English Dictionary Online* contain information on the etymology and on dates of the first appearance of a word but are too complex for the purposes at hand. Studies of smaller dictionaries like the *Advanced Learner's Dictionary*, the *Concise Oxford Dic-tionary*, and the *General Service List* (of frequent words) (1953) have shown that the Germanic word stock was re-duced to between 26 per cent in the *Oxford* and 37 per cent in the *Advanced Learner's*. Around 28 per cent of the words were Latin, 30 per cent came from the other Ro-mance languages. The results in the *Service List* were different as it was specifically meant to contain frequent and useful words for American schools. It is revealing that 51 per cent was of Germanic and 38 per cent of Romance origin, as that confirms the consensus that Germanic words tend to be found in colloquial and common English. Romance words are, on balance, still educated and formal. The percentages for words from continental languages are minimal. The internal composition of donors of loan words keeps shifting. A recent study of 100,000 loan words found Latin declining (6 per cent), while Spanish, Chinese, Arabic or Hindi have provided few per cents but a comparatively larger number of recent loans (this is the interpretation of Algeo/Pyles 2005: 292).

A third aspect is the impact that Romance and Greek words have had on the socio-educational reality of society. A class of words emerged that was unknown on the continent, the *hard words*. Borrowing led to such a large number of new words within a very short period of time that it became a fashion of the cultural elite to borrow or create ever more new words. As many of them were not understood, they were felt to be *hard words* or, to use a contemporary term, *inkhorn terms*. Glossaries appeared for the uninitiated. One might say that English lexicography goes back to this transformation process of English during the 15th century. Hard words became a source of humour as the uninitiated but aspiring middle class often used them wrongly. Over time a debate was inescapable on whether English should not return to a *plain English* style.

There were other consequences that had an impact on the texture of English and on the role that English 'in its new clothes' played in society (Leisi/Mair 2008; ch. 9). Borrowing often left a large number of doublets and triplets and led to an over-abundance of words for much the same object or phenomenon they referred to. That called for semantic differentiation. There were lexical sets like *edifice* and *building*; *manly*, *masculine*, *male*, and *virile*; *womanly*, *womanish*, *female*, and *feminine* that could not co-exist. For decades *pig* and *pork*, *cow* and *mutton* referred to both the meat and the animal until differentiation restricted the one to the animal and the other to the meat.

Loss was another option to resolve the situation. It is interesting to note that it was often the Germanic words that were lost. The Germanic transparency between derivatives was replaced by opaqueness, as the link between related words disappeared; semantically related words became disassociated. To take a few examples, German *Dreifuß* is related to both 'drei' and 'Fuß'. English *tripod* is no longer associated with *three* and *foot*; there are no words *tri* and *pod*. *Appendix* does not connote like German *Blinddarm*; *son* and *filial*, *smell* and *olfactory*, *word* and *verbal* are not *consociated*, a term Leisi/Mair suggest. Borrowing obscured or 'darkened' the relationship between words and constrained the word-formation potential of the Germanic word stock. While the influence of Latin and Greek was not confined to English, that impact was nowhere as serious as in English.

There were a few advantages. Borrowing created words that could replace others that had acquired negative connotations. German *Vielweiberei* is a case in point. *Weib* became a derogatory word. *Polygamy* was neutral, but educated, to refer to such practices. Allegorisms of Antiquity could be better maintained in English, while they could not in German. The words *justice* and *fame* represent both the well-known concepts and the antique figures. They are translated as *Fama* and *Justitia* in German, as the common words *Ruhm* and *Recht* cannot be used to refer to the figures. *Galaxy* ('Milchstraße') is a metaphor for decorated officers (*the whole galaxy*), which is impossible to translate into German. German has remained plain and had to resort to later borrowing. German now has *Polygamie*, *Galaxien* and *galaktisch* – like English.

There are some other developments that go back to that period and have become significant properties of the core of English. English creates new words by adding a particle to a word. One can *get* a present, but may not *get on* or *along* with someone else. One may *take* something but *take up* an idea, *take in* migrants, *take on* a task or *take to* a stranger. A formal field of lexemes is thus built around *take*, whose semantic cohesion may become quite loose. One should add the nominal verb compounds such as *have* or *take a look*. These resources are more typical of the colloquial, informal and spoken language, according to Leisi/Mair (2008).

I will close with a remark on the social consequences of Latin and Greek. As hard words remained a property of the educated and aspiring members of society, Standard English has become socially divisive and, what is more, created a climate of opinion that denigrated anything that was not standard. When English 'went global' or, more modestly, 'colonial', its mixed character and the attitudes about the social role of Standard English and dialects were part of the package transplanted at different periods of time.

The standard dialect and the prestige accent

An account of the further development of English makes it necessary to distinguish the accent from the dialect. Standard English continued its path into what it is today

and became fully accepted in society. An equally accepted accent did not emerge. What did happen was that the
accent of the Court acquired more and more prestige and
enforced itself as a general and divisive model. Its prestige remained confined to England, but its impact em-
braced the whole world.

Standard English

"What is Standard English?" ask Randolph Quirk and
Gabriele Stein in *English in Use*. To answer the question,
they recount an episode from Molière's *Le bourgeois gen-
tilhomme* in which Monsieur Jourdain is assured that he
speaks prose when he asks in bewilderment: "What!
When I say 'Nicole fetch me my slippers' … that's prose?"
Quirk and Stein explain:

> "Something of the sort can be said about Standard English.
> There is nothing esoteric, obscure, or special about it: who-
> ever or wherever we are in the English-speaking world, we
> have been familiar with it all our lives … Virtually all the
> English we respond to on television and radio is Standard
> English." (1990: 112)

Standard varieties like Standard English do not draw attention to themselves, while other varieties do as they are
used to create effects like humour, belonging, or ridicule.
Standard varieties typically start out in writing; they are
widely intelligible across a nation and used in public communication. They are linked to a nation's past, its literature; they are creative and flexible. They exert power and
empower some segments of society more than others, as
we have seen in connection with the 'hard words'. Their

power may be quite subtle, disguising as the 'normal', 'expected'. When a newspaper quotes the demands of striking hospital staff in Standard English or cites Australian Aboriginal voices in Standard Australian English it could be seen as a kind of internal 'colonization' as their speech is denied them. That theme would take us into the area of the politics of mass media language, which I will not go into.

It took time for the standard variety to gain the kind of power Standard English has today. Authors of the late 15th century still used their native dialects. John Gower and Chaucer, for instance, wrote in London English at the beginning of the 17th century. It took more time still for the prestige accent to be the 'natural' choice, as I will show in the next section.

The term *standardization* describes the steps that a variety undergoes as it becomes a standard. There are four processes, says Haugen:

> "The four aspects of language development that we have now isolated as crucial features in taking the step from 'dialect' to 'language', from 'vernacular' to 'standard' are as follows: (a) selection of a norm, (b) codification of form, (c) elaboration of function, and (d) acceptance by the community." (1972: 110)

Once a base has been selected, *codification* deals with choices in the form of language. There is a lot of variation within and between the dialects or sociolects prior to codification. Should one print *egges* or *eyren* for 'egg(s)', wondered William Caxton, who introduced printing into England 1478. He settled on the 'southern' *egges*. The objective will be "maximal variation in function, minimal variation in form" (Haugen 1972: 107). West Saxon was a base, but the political power behind it did not last long enough for it to fully standardize. The base of modern Standard English was found elsewhere, Sidney Greenbaum says:

> "… in the fifteenth century a national standard was emerging that was based on the dialect of London, the judicial and political capital of the country, and also its commercial, social, and intellectual centre. … The London dialect of the educated drew on the provincial dialects to form a supra-regional dialect. Then as now, the country needed a standard dialect that was not only generally intelligible but also, because of its neutrality, did not distract through its regional peculiarities from efficient communication …" (Greenbaum 1988: 3f).

McCrum *et al.* argue that the triangle of Oxford, Cambridge and London "shared the same kind of English, which may be said to have become the basis for Standard English in the twentieth century" (1986: 79). It was power, trade and learning that excluded competitors such as from Northern English. The variety was codified and expanded stepwise from domain to domain, as Manfred Görlach (*adapted from* Leitner 2009) has shown (*see* Fig. 3.1).

Standard English began in the formal domain of bureaucracy where it competed with, and replaced Latin and French. It was under pressure to develop appropriate expressions in lexis and grammar. No wonder it was only in the 18th century that its use increased in speech. No surprise that speech and writing differed so much. Contracted forms such as *it's*, *she'll* or *the car's seats* were frequent in speech, and could not be used in writing. The spoken dialect permitted a higher level of style shifts,

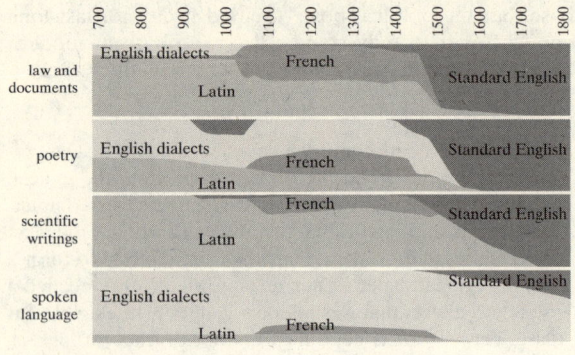

Figure 3.1: The shift to English

while writing demanded a greater level of consistency. Speech and writing have gone different paths for centuries, supported by a class system that was the continuation and transformation of feudalism in the 19th century. The media felt the gap to be too large in the 1970s and shifted the ground.

Standard English dates back to the 16th century, with precursors being identifiable as early as the 14th century. Though a spoken standard has never developed, the accent that acquired prestige, the feudal accent at Court, was suggested for emulation in polite society in the 17th century. It spread nation-wide (but not in Scotland, nor in Ireland), became the accent of the upper classes and during the 19th century that of the public schools and universities. It was not taught but acquired, one might say, by exposure or osmosis in these environments. It was not deliberately codified either. Indeed, many experts saw it as a cluster of idiolects, the accents of a range of individuals,

ACCENT	DIALECT	
formal standard, RP etc.	formal	standard dimension
less formal, colloquial	informal/colloquial	
informal, influenced by middle and lower class speech, regional accents		non-standard dimension
	slang	sub-standard dimension

Figure 3.2: The varieties of English in terms of accent and dialect

whose speech became part of a broad band. The English phonetician Daniel Jones at University College described it as the "accent I meet around me". Yet, he aimed to provide a learnable description in his *Outline of English Phonetics* (1918). It has become a difficult accent that will be described in more detail below. Given the demands made of the standard variety, it is not invariant:

> "A complete language has its formal and informal styles, its regional accents, and its class or occupational jargons, which do not destroy its unity so long as they are clearly diversified in function and show a reasonable degree of solidarity with one another." (Haugen 1972:108)

The dimensions of style variation and the correlation between speech and writing can best be shown in this way (*see* Leitner 2004a: 239; *see* Fig. 3.2).

Some systems of modern Standard British English

Codification is not a pre-planned long-term programme. It seems guided by some long-term consensus of significant segments of the elite. The direction codification takes need not be straightforward, quasi-linear; it may go sideways or return. It is often part of much more general processes that affect all or many dialects. Its crucial 'objective' is to secure the greatest expressive power with the smallest amount of variation. That does not lead to a mono-stylistic variety but to structured variation that leaves enough space for flexibility and creativity. I will survey some of the properties of Standard English and add on to what I said in Chapter Two. I will begin with spelling.

Spelling is chaotic, and yet it is one of the most codified systems of English. It can be a source of linguistic humour:

3.5 I take it you already know
     Of tough and bough and cough and dough?
     Others may stumble, but not you
     On hiccough, thorough, slough and through?
     Well done! And now you wish, perhaps,
     To learn of less familiar traps?
     Beware of heard, a dreadful word
     That looks like beard and sounds like bird.
     (excerpt from "ENGLISH" by anonymous T.S.W.; http://
     www.wordhord.com/humor/english-pronunciation-poems)

Ignoring American English for a moment, there is little variation. Indian English has *upto* 'up to' in standard spelling. One finds *alot* and similar words in Malaysian and Singaporean English. One often finds approximations to pronunciation (= phonetic spelling) as in *wid* 'with' and *goin* 'going'. Some 'phonetic' variations that Noah Webster proposed for American English did not catch on. The deletion of "gh" in *nite* and *rite* were not picked up. Electronic English has more deviations from standard conventions. One finds phonetic spellings, symbols and clips that can well be unintelligible to the uninitiated:

3.6 *Wat*, *wut* and *wot* 'what'; *onli* and *oni* 'only'; *juz* 'just'; *fren* or *fwen* 'friend'.
3.7 while waiting for Anne @ Sarapung
3.8 *c* 'see', *y* 'you', *r* 'are' and *y* 'why'

There are a few variable areas in spelling that may even signal change. Compounds tended to be spelt as separate words up to the late 20th century such as *word formation*, *train station* or *school children*. Today, one can find *train-station*, *wordformation*, *schoolchildren* or *policymaker*. American norms can merge with British conventions so that there appear inconsistencies. Spelling is also a source or medium to express ambiguity, as in a press photo caption about cancer children in Malaysia who have lost their hair: "Hair-oic effort".

To turn to grammar, the paucity of inflectional morphology has already been mentioned. Articles and adjectives lack inflexion, nouns have lost all contrasts, retaining only number and the possessive case, which has an analytic variant as in "the roof *of* the car" for "the car*'s* roof". The genitive can mark a whole noun phrase:

3.9 "Pregnant snatch-theft *victim's* death. Man held." (*The New Straits Times*, 20 May 2009)
3.10 "Media Prima Group Editor (News and Current Affairs) of NTV7, TV8, TV9 and Radio Networks Datuk Manja *Ismail's* youngest son" (*The Star*, 23 March 2010).

Modern English only distinguishes the singular and the plural as the Old English dual has been lost. There are lexical remnants such as *both*, *either* and *neither*. The regular plural form is *-s* in spelling; its pronunciation is predictable. There are irregular remnants such as *umlaut* in *goose/geese*, *-en* in *ox/oxen* and *child/children*, and zero in *sheep/sheep*. *Children* is a lone case as it acquired two plural forms during its history. It was *čildru* in Old English but then moved into the 'weak' noun class and acquired *-en* that we know in *oxen*. In non-standard English and Irish English *children* can be *childru*. Elsewhere it can be *childrens*. There is variation between plural and singular in cases like *medium/media*. The latter is both singular and plural with reference to, e.g., *broadcast media*, the singular refers to 'medium of transmission' etc. *Data* is both singular and plural.

Verbs have no inflectional contrasts for mood such as the subjunctive. *Were* is a remnant, which tends to be replaced by *should* in British or the 'bare' or zero infinitive in American English (e.g. "I suggest he (should) resign from office"). What remains is a 3rd person singular in the present tense (*he goes* vs. *I/you/they/you go*), a simple present and past tense (*I like / I liked*), and the progressive, which is marked by *-ing* (in combination with a form of *be*). A striking aspect is a small number of 'strong', but frequent, irregular verbs. Some have three forms (*go, went, gone*), some two (*buy, bought*), some but one (*put*). Adverbs with initial stress and two syllables have the *-ly* suffix (e.g. *beautifully*). Others are formed analytically (e.g. *in the most friendly fashion* as **friendlily* cannot be formed). Non-standard, dialectal varieties and speech can have unmarked adverbs (e.g. *right*). There is a large amount of variation within and between dialects and in varieties worldwide.

We mentioned expressions like "John, have you had a look at this paper" for 'have you looked at' it. *Take a seat* for 'sit down', *take a shower* 'to shower', *give a smile* 'to smile' and *have a chat* 'to chat' earlier. They are instances of nominal-verbal complexes that are rare in German. There are prepositional verbs like *run up* (a hill), phrasal verbs like *run up* (a bill) or (a plane) *takes off*, and there are phrasal-prepositional verbs like *come up with* (a good idea). These constructions have frequently been mentioned as typical, productive features of English. They make up for the weakening of the word-formation capacity of English that was alluded to earlier. The communicative effect is colloquial, in general. There is variation with regard to the choice of, e.g. *take*, *have*, as both can sometimes be used. Nominalization creates 'particle nouns', which are often marked by the shift of the stress to the verb as in *to take 'off* and *'take-off*.

Pronouns have more inflectional characteristics. Personal and possessive pronouns have a nominative, possessive, and objective case (e.g. *I*, *my/mine*, *me*) and natural gender (in the 3rd person singular). *Wh*-pronouns such as *who* and *which* have (natural) gender (human/non-human, e.g. in *who* and *which*), and genitive and objective case (*whose*, *whom*). The objective is replaced by *who* in most contexts but is most secure after a preposition. But even this dogma is faltering, as this example shows:

3.11 You've got to know *who to* ... – *Who* not to listen to
(from a song by Grant Amy)

A widely discussed gap is the lack of a second person plural form, which is available in German (*du, ihr*) or French (*tu, vous*). Many varieties have lost it, but some have re-created it. American English has *you/you all* or *y'all, you guys* or Irish English has *you/youse*, which is a calque on Gaelic *tu, sibh*. Closely related is the use of the first name as the universal address form. It is said to express social intimacy and proximity in contrast to the social distance in German and other languages. Call centre staff universally give their first name, "I'm / my name is Mary". But the impression of informality is not necessarily true. The first name can easily be followed by "Sir" or a formal title such as "Professor". The use of first names is not as old as one might believe either. In the 1970s and 1980s the last name with 'Mr', 'Mrs' or 'Miss' was still common to express a sense of equality. *The Independent* of 20 July 2001 carried a story on a BBC call-in programme and wrote this: "Marghanita Laski [one of the most prominent broadcasters at the time] was a sharp, clever woman, and when one of her fellow panellists tried to argue with her, saying 'Look, the thing is, Marghanita …', she immediately cut across him with: 'Miss Laski, if you *don't mind* …'" Today, the paper says, "we are forced into intimacy." Most varieties accept the intimacy with first names, but some struggle with formality and respect in titles.

Turning to syntax, there is a trade-off with inflectional morphology. English is essentially a Subject-Verb-Object language, while other Germanic languages have variation. German has two standard orders, i.e. 'verb-second' and 'verb-final' (= SOV) in main and dependent clauses respectively. 'Verb-second' means that any order (SVO, OVS, AVS/O, etc.) is correct for as long as the verb comes second. There is less flexibility in English, but it is not entirely absent, as these examples show: "The young student I like for his sense of humour" (OSV); "Down he came" (ASV); "Here comes the train" (AVS). SOV is impossible, except in verse. Mention must be made of cleft ("It is his sense of humour I like"), pseudo-cleft ("What I like is his sense of humour"), and existential constructions ("There is an interesting programme on TV"). These constructions are related to the information structure in discourse. Interrogatives manifest subject-auxiliary inversion, which is regular in polar questions ("Can he do that? Wasn't that a great show!"). Though a side issue, questions can (now) be expressed with a high rising intonation contour that is superimposed on a declarative construction ("So, you are having an affair?"). That construction permits the inference that the proposition contained is assumed to be true. Many second language varieties in Asia extend this pattern to ordinary polar questions ("He came home late?") without that inference. Different patterns have been reported from Australian, New Zealand, Irish English, some northern dialects, and American English: they have a high rising tone with declarative word order to express meanings of empathy, friendliness, etc., without the intention of asking a question as in "My name is John." Tag questions are appended to a declarative sentence and make very subtle implications on expected answers. So-called polar tags like in the examples below expect confirmation. They are called polar because they are negative if the main clause is positive and the other way round. Non-polar or constant tags imply a conclusion of the speaker and hence expect confirmation by the addressee.

3.12 You've seen that film, haven't you?
3.13 You haven't seen that film, have you?
3.14 You've seen that film, have you?
3.15 You haven't seen that film, haven't you?

There are many more variations if intonation is included, but the complexity of this core system has been reduced in many varieties of English. Some varieties have simpler forms, at least in colloquial speech such as the particle *eh*, witness "You've done that, eh?"

Turning to grammatical relations, English contrasts with many other languages in ruling out sentences with no subject such as German *mich friert* 'I am cold'. Such sentences occur in spoken registers like sports casting if the subject is retrievable. Many Asian varieties can delete a lot more syntactic functions as long as they are recoverable.

One of the most important generalizations about English grammar is the 'loose fit' between form and function. Syntactic categories can express a variety of meanings. The subject is a case in point, as these examples show:

3.16 John can certainly act wonderfully well (agent)
3.17 Money buys you everything, really (instrument)
3.18 Berlin can be a rather cold city in winter (location)
3.19 The headmaster is Dr. Jones (theme)

It refers to the agent in 3.16 who does something, an instrument in 3.17, whereby something is achieved, a location in 3.18, and a theme, a technical word, in 3.19. Sentence 3.17 can only be "Mit Geld kann man wirklich alles kaufen" in German. Transitive sentences need an object (3.20). When they are used in the passive, it can disappear as in 3.21. Some verbs like *break* permit an intransitive version that has a meaning like the passive (3.22):

3.20 John broke the glass
3.21 The glass was broken
3.22 The glass broke

There is a construction where the verb is used in the active voice but seems to express a passive meaning in that some kind of propensity is attributed to the subject; that 'passive'-type of meaning comes out clearly if manner adverbs occur and if the verb is used in the present tense:

3.23 The window pane breaks easily
3.24 Potter's latest book sells extremely well

To turn to tense, aspect, and modality, the future is expressed analytically by *will* ("There *will* be rain in the afternoon"). In more traditional and older varieties of English *shall* was almost prescribed for the first person singular and plural as in "I shall / we shall carry on". That usage is almost impossible today. There are other ways, e.g. "the chair *is going to* dip over, be careful", "the Foreign Secretary *is about to* go to Kuwait", "I'*m* com*ing*, don't worry" or "we *leave* for London tomorrow". They all express subtle shades of future time reference, often merged with modal meanings. A sentence like "I will come and see you later, John" is both a promise and a prediction. Modals can express three types of meaning, i.e., deontic meaning ("I must be gone" = 'I am obliged to'), epistemic meaning ("He can't be there, the light's not on" = 'from what I know'), and what has been described as 'ability' meaning ("I could swim when I was a small child" = 'I was able to'). These meanings interact with negation and question formation in ways that cannot be gone into here ("You mustn't [= deontic] be too strict with the boy" versus "He *mustn't / cannot [= epistemic] be at home yet"), but which suggest that there will be a lot of variation. In Scottish and Australian English that sentence is grammatical.

Apart from the 'instantaneous present' in, e.g., sports commentaries ("Michael Ballack kicks the goal"), the simple present has to be compared with the progressive

to refer to present time (*"Billy goes to school (now)" for
'Billy *is* go*ing* to school (now)'). On its own, it expresses
habitualness, etc. The simple past refers to a definite past
time, even if it is unexpressed ("Billy *went* to school"),
while the present perfect expresses indefinite past time
and notions like current relevance ("I know New York, I
have been there" [= indefinite past]; "Shakespeare has
written important plays" [= current relevance]). A sentence like *"Shakespeare has lived in Stratford" is un-
grammatical and requires the simple past; there is no con-
ceivable current relevance. Here, too, there is great deal
of variation. American English, for instance, has a so-
called colloquial simple past, the perfect is more formal
(in contrast to, say, German and French, where the opposite would apply). There are constraints on the combination of the perfect with adverbs, such as *yet*, *already*.
Once again, varieties differ a great deal. Standard British
English, for instance, disallows *"Did John come in yet",
American, Australian, and non-standard British English
do not. The present perfect, with its *have* and *-ed* construction, was part of a major change in English. There
were two patterns, one with *be* and *-ed* for intransitive
verbs and the *have* and *-ed* construction for transitive
verbs. This excerpt from Virginia Woolf's essay "Street
Haunting: A London Adventure" shows the former.

3.25 "But we *are come* to the Strand now, and as we hesitate
on the curb, a little rod about the length of one's finger
begins to lay its bar across the velocity and abundance
of life." (Woolfe 1945, *The Death of the Moth and Other
Essays*)

The progressive aspect, i.e., a form of *to be* with an *-ing*
inflection of the verb, is a fairly old system, but its use has

been increasing since the 18ᵗʰ century. This is true in general, but more interesting is that, e. g., the 'interpretative' progressive has grown considerably more. Here is an example:

3.26 What I *was meaning* to say was …

To close with the separation of a relative pronoun from a preposition that 'belongs' to, this example illustrates what is meant:

3.27 The language *by which* Mr Blair deceives us … But because Mr Blair is always drawn to stating what should be the case, that there was no disquiet, he spoke as if he had checked with every relevant official – which of course he hadn't.

The example was mentioned earlier, but it may be good to introduce the technical term that a preposition is left 'stranded' at the end of a sentence. That is common usage today but was rejected by prescriptive grammarians for centuries. In this passage the hyper-correct use points to a conflict between the ideal and the real.

An interesting example of contemporary usage problems is the choice between *less* and *fewer*. The BBC reported on the 31ˢᵗ of August 2008 that the food store Tesco was "to change the wording of signs on its fast-track checkouts to avoid any linguistic dispute" from "10 items or less" to "Up to 10 items". The advice had been given by the *Plain English Campaign* movement because *less* is for quantities, such as 'less sugar', and *fewer* for things counted such as 'fewer items'. "Up to 10 items" dodges the issue and is easy to comprehend. The dispute over the correct use of *less* and *fewer* with countable things is old, as Burridge (2004: 89f) shows. There was a parallel development from Old to early modern English. *More* was used with quantities as in 'more water' and *mo* with countable entities as in 'take mo/mae baths'. That difference was lost and *more* was used for both quantities and plural nouns, which impacted on *fewer* and *less* and weakened *fewer*. Chain reactions are a typical way to streamline a system. During the Age of Authority the distinction was enforced again and *fewer* became the 'correct' form with countable items.

To close with a remark on lexis and word-formation, some patterns have become very frequent in the past decades only. A case in point is clipping and blending:

3.28 "*Staycationing* may be an inelegant description, but it was music to the ears of Britain's beleaguered tourism industry ..." (*The Independent*, 12 June 2011)

Having returned to the more colloquial end of Standard English it may be good to close this section with a few excerpts that show its flexibility, its ability to cope with style shifting and to create meanings far beyond the words used. The first is from an article in *The Times* (29 Sep 2010) about policies to be pursued by the, then new, British government. It was headlined by "Cowabunga! Here comes compensation for the cuts":

3.29 "There's a *cow* on the line," [there is an accompanying picture of a cow, G.L.] the conductor said ... Five *beefy* stewards strode up the train ... to reopen the buffet ... We have all become so *cowed* [the word now takes a whole new meaning] that we stay strapped into our dreary lives. ... There can be *no sacred cows* on the coalition's line.

The opinion article (3.29) opens with the story of the un-expected, lengthy stoppage of a train because a dead cow was lying across the rails. It uses that entrée to turn to the proposed, and unwelcome, financial cuts by the con-servative government. The writer suggests de-bureaucra-tization might be a solution. Having begun with a real 'cow', she ends with the metaphor of 'sacred cows' and draws a parallel between the train line and the govern-ment's line. In this multi-layered article the word *cow* has a significant literal and metaphoric meaning. The word 'cow' is motivated by the picture and the word *cowabun-ga*. In fact, *cowabunga* has nothing to do with cows at all. It means something like "Wow!" It is a popular trade name. It is a young word created by one TV serial writer in the USA in the 1940s and has had a history that in-volves the surfers in Hawaii! It does not contain the word *cow* at all, except the sounds. The writer used a humoris-tic clip when she cuts off the three letters "c-o-w" to cre-ate the word 'cow'. Creativity is a trademark of good writing.

   The next two passages show how Standard English can incorporate aggressive and non-standard expressions, once again to create colour in what is being reported:

3.30 "That lucky, *privileged bastard* . Roughly speaking, *I hate* the bankers, *toffs*, *Eton schoolboys* … *I hate* who-ever was complicit in, or responsible for, our downfall …" (*The Independent on Sunday*, 6 Dec 2009)

3.31 "For Arsenal took the lead with a *galumphing header* from Sol Campbell in the 37th minute, a classic, old-Ar-senal *set-piece goal*, and then set about defending it. They *damn near pulled it off*, too. For about 40 minutes they clung on …" (*The Times*, 18 May 2006)

This somewhat long section has dealt with the properties of modern Standard English in lexis, word-formation, inflection, and syntax and style. It looked beyond British English in a number of places to reveal patterns of variation worldwide but also what can be seen as a part of the core of English that will figure large in the background to the chapters to follow.

Non-standard English

"How many killas you got on your mother fuckin pay roll nigga?", from the American rapper Snoop Dogg's "Ain't nutin personal" illustrates the mixing of linguistic choices in lyrics to increase the effect. A few features such as the orthographic display of pronunciation in *killa*, *nigga* and *fuckin'* and the vulgar style suffice to foreground ethnicity and class. A conservative British politician punctuated the shift from one topic to the next with: "You ain't seen nothin' yet." David Crystal used that fixed phrase in a talk on the Australian Broadcasting Corporation to emphasize the role of Indian English. It also occurred in the title of a BBC programme on American and British English. An Australian prostitute countered the provocative question of a journalist about her preferences with "I *ain't* saying I'm *no* golddigga but I *ain't messin'* with *no* road sweeper" (*The Sun* [Australia], 28 Jan 2009). Could there be more colour in classless speech? Non-standard English transcends class and, as we will see, ethnicity. When the *New Straits Times* of Malaysia headed an editorial with "It ain't so bad" (22 Sep 2009) to explain the cautious hopes for an economic recovery, it introduced the non-standard *ain't*, or perhaps the fixed phrase *it ain't so bad* into Malaysian English and succumbed to the ubiquitous prestige of non-standard American and British English.

On one interpretation, non-standard English includes anything that is not standard. Regional varieties were seen as non-standard and well established varieties such as Northern English were degraded. That shift in attitude was noticeable in the 18th century, which Crystal called "a century of contradictions". He found it remarkable "that writers, scholars, and senior figures in the establishment of the 1760s should have been prepared to follow the dictates of a small number of self-appointed pundits, such as Johnson [the lexicographer], Lowth [the grammarian], and Sheridan [the elocutionist]" (2004: 413; angled brackets added). One might add John Walker, author of a pronouncing dictionary, and Lindley Murray, a grammarian. Denigration was soon extended to colonial varieties. Usage guides like, for instance, *The King's English* (1906) by the Fowler brothers at the beginning of the 20th century or Henry Fowler's *Modern English Usage* (1926) can be seen to make it perfectly clear what was standard and what was not, though they did not include such crude prejudice. Henry Wyld's *The Historical Study of the Mother Tongue* (1907) and his *History of Modern Colloquial English* (1920) reflected the intellectual power of Standard English in framing accounts of the history of English. Crystal's *The Stories of English* (2004) and some other recent books redress the imbalance.

There emerged a consensus on a list of features that count as non-standard (Kerswill 2007; Crystal 2004):

(a) multiple negation
(b) *ain't*
(c) *never* as a past tense marker
(d) *-s* 3rd p. sg. present concord

(e) relative pronoun *what*
(f) adverbs without *-ly*
(g) *them* as article and demonstrative
(h) unmarked plural in quantifier phrases
(i) irregular verb forms
(j) subtractive word-formation

As most items were illustrated earlier, I need not expand further. The examples below show *never* to signal past tense, adverbs without *-ly*, the non-use of the plural in unmarked quantifier phrases and irregular verbs:

3.32 I *never* threw it	*see* c)
3.33 The boy played *brilliant*	*see* f)
3.34 *Six pound* of potatoes, please	*see* h)
3.35 See, *seen*, seen	*see* i)

Graddol *et al.* (2006: 208f) add a selection of irregular verbs like *break, broke, broke* and *go, went, went* to the list, which come from Tyneside and Irish English. There are derivational features such as clipping and complex word-formation patterns that count as non-standard. Good examples are words like *bro* 'brother', *bod* 'body', *Maz* 'Mary', *Tone* for 'Tony', *mag* or *cig*. Clipping combines with *-ie* or *-o* and occurs in *compo* 'compensation', *journo* or *bikie*. Subtractive derivation is perhaps one of the dominant processes today that have a touch of the non-standard. To close with a very effective example from *The Times Online*:

3.36 "They look like *smurfs* in their bright blue uniforms …
       but they *ain't* very *'appy* like those *smurfs* on the *telly*!"
       (22 May 2006)

The prestige accent: Received Pronunciation

Even today the BBC is cited as the most likely source to hear the best of English pronunciation: *BBC English*. Whether this is still true remains to be seen, but *BBC English* has become a trade-mark with a commercial branch (Leitner 1989). The World Service has one site with a series of talks and learning materials (http://www.bbc.co.uk/worldservice/learningenglish/grammar/pron/).
The presenter Alex says, 'good' English today is broader, not purely native-like and allows articulations in a number of accents around the world. She presents her own one, which she calls Standard British English, which is far from the pronunciation of the stereotypes of the banker or army officer talking 'down' with a 'stiff upper lip'. Their accent sounded 'normal' at the time. It was perceived as arrogant and outdated in the 1970s, when one thought that the underlying class structure of society had given way to one based on merit in the 1960. It has not, as an article argued that appeared just before the general elections in 2010. The writer described the behaviour of the country's elite cynically as "buffing their accents into something resembling normal speech" and expressed his class hate or hatred.

3.37 "The people I am prejudiced about … are still sticking their noses in the trough, while *PR-buffing their accents into something resembling normal speech* in order to fool us again that they have our best interests at heart rather than their own." (*The Independent*, 6 Dec 2009)

Received Pronunciation was a divisive accent that never reached the wide acceptability of Standard English. For some like the author of the excerpt above it still is divisive. Received Pronunciation was, and for some is, loaded with power as anyone who could not use it, was ineligible for some types of professions. George Bernard Shaw's *Pygmalion* and the musical *My Fair Lady* portrait the effects of the wrong accent. Eliza, a street flower girl wants to work in a flower shop but speaks Cockney and not Received Pronunciation. She turns to Professor Higgins, a character modelled on Daniel Jones, who succeeds in making her pass as a lady, not without showing a considerable amount of facile class prejudice. Eliza succeeds in fiction. Others have not in real life. The BBC's pronunciation advisor in the 1930s recounted a story of a business man travelling on a train in the north of England and sitting in a compartment with some office girls. But, he says, he could not have employed any of them for their accent. Accent was divisive and, while this might have become a political issue, it was treated as an educational disadvantage that could be remedied by speech education. *The Times* article quoted above (3.29) shows how strong this association can be.

As mentioned in connection with Standard English the antecedents of Received Pronunciation evolved at the Court in London spread amongst those associated with the Court countrywide. It was subsequently propagated as a polite accent. A feudal accent, it was passed on from generation to generation without the need to teach it. It was acquired. The Industrial Revolution and the growth of the Empire from the early 19th century required a large number of 'educated' people for a wide range of professions in Britain and the colonies that could not be met by members of the aristocracy and the upper classes. Their accent reflected the right background, the right education, but it was necessary that the accent was learnable and teachable.

It was transformed from a feudal and upper class accent to one of the upwardly mobile, upper middle class bourgeoisie. It retained its association with education and employability. It was seen as not giving away one's region of origin, it was a national accent. The children of this segment of society learnt it during their educational career in the famous Public Schools and especially in the triangle of London, Cambridge and Oxford. Immersion was so successful that Daniel Jones, the most prominent phonetician of the 20th century, called it *Public School Pronunciation*. He was careful not to refer to it as a standard of pronunciation:

> "I do not consider it possible at the present time to regard any special type [of pronunciation, G.L.] as 'Standard' or intrinsically 'better' than other times. Nevertheless, the type described in this book is certainly a useful one. It is based on my own (Southern) speech, and is, as far as I can ascertain, that generally used by those who have been educated at 'preparatory' boarding schools and the 'Public Schools'." (1918: 12)

It had other names such as Oxford or the King's English. When broadcasting started on a national scale, the question of accent was put on the agenda. What kind of speech should be put to a nation-wide audience? There were numerous criteria such as mere functional adequacy, i.e., intelligibility. There were wider objectives such as the BBC's Charter that stipulated education, information, and entertainment in that order. That called for a neutral but 'high' accent. Broad societal and political considerations, such as the fear of arousing the masses, the fear of Communism, the needs of the colonial expatriates that wanted to link up with the Centre and the image that

Britain wanted to send to the 'colonized' elites called for an accent that projected authority. And the BBC itself wanted to be seen as objective and credible. That called for an accent that did not arouse attention to itself. This heterogeneous spectrum of objectives made Received Pronunciation the only choice. It was known nation-wide, was neutral, did not arouse emotions, and carried authority. What was deliberately overlooked was that it projected social class divisions, was authoritarian, and was, despite everything else it had in its favour, a southern accent. The North, Scotland and Ireland resented it. It was resented even more, as the need for nation-wide comprehension was interpreted as requiring homogeneity. Even the slightest sign of variation was ruled out (Leitner 1989; *also* 2004a).

That was the accent used in the major editorial domains such as news reading, children's programmes, serious music announcements, etc. Light entertainment and farming programmes were different and the competition with Radio Luxembourg and other outside stations made a less authoritarian accent a necessity. The BBC formed a pronunciation committee to ensure homogeneity of pronunciation and to decide on what was called doubtful words or, in other words, where educated speakers could use different pronunciations. *England* is an example as it could be pronounced as /ɪŋglənd/ or as /ɪŋlənd/. The BBC favoured the first form. Better technologies soon permitted outside broadcasting. When the war broke out, ordinary citizens were brought to the microphone. The social climate of the 1960s turned away from a strict hierarchical society and favoured egalitarianism, women's rights, etc. The status of Received Pronunciation eroded and found competitors in the so-called "Estuary English" in the south-east of England in the 1970s. Independent developments in other parts of the country created regional standards. The BBC responded by shifting from the formality of the past to a more colloquial style that was immediately denounced as 'demotic' by a conservative section of the public. Today the position of Received Pronunciation is weak. Many experts refer to modifications or further developments and replace the term by *Standard (Southern) British English*, *general English* or *Non-Regional English*. The new accent is assumed not to be confined to the upper middle classes and more open socially and regionally. The BBC's English programmes admit, in theory, pronunciations from around the world, if educated.

Turning to its characteristics, Received Pronunciation (and South-Eastern accents) has an exceptionally complex system. (I will not go into great details as it is well described in practically every learner's dictionary.) Consonants are a fairly straightforward set. Compared with most other languages, the dental fricatives in *thin* and *this* pose a problem and are, indeed, the most variable pair in accents worldwide. At the level of connected speech dental fricatives make neighbouring consonants shift or assimilate to their place of articulation. A word like *width*, for instance, has a dental [d̪].

Vowels are more complicated. Even though I will confine myself to some basic points, I need to give enough detail to understand the patterns of variation in other varieties of English worldwide. Every desktop dictionary for foreign learners will contain an adequate section on English vowels. There are 20 vowels which pattern according to:

(i)   place of articulation (front, mid and back and high to low),

(ii)   vowel length: /ɪ, e, æ, (ə), ʌ, ɒ, ʊ/ and /iː, uː, ɑː, ɜː, ɔː/
(iii) syllable type (checked, CVC, free, CV): /ɪ, e, æ, (ə), ʌ, ɒ, ʊ/
(iv)   (in-)stability of vowel target:
    (a) centring diphthongs: /ɪə, ʊə/, but also /eə, ɔə/
    (b) rising diphthongs: /eɪ, aɪ, ɔɪ/ and /əʊ, aʊ/

All short vowels, except schwa /ə/, occur only in checked syllables like in *neck*, *back*, or *put*. Unlike in German there are hardly any pairs of long and short. The vowels in *feet* and *fit*, and *moot* and *put* are also distinguished in quality. The vowel in *fit* /ɪ/ is somewhat lower and more central than in *feet*. Given there are few front and back monophthongs, there is, what experts refer to, considerable phonetic space. Vowels can be articulated in a higher or lower position without risking overlap. Varieties have made consistent choices such that Received Pronunciation has quite open vowels, while they are closer in Scottish and Australian English. The beginning (or onset) and end (or offset) of long vowels and rising diphthongs are phonetically somewhat unstable. The vowel in *feed* can begin with a lower position or end in one, which would lead to pronunciations like /əi/ or /iə/. Such shifts in onset or offset are marked in contemporary pronunciations and, if they are quite pronounced then they are more typical of, say, Cockney or Australian English. They are then considered, by speakers of Received Pronunciation, as outside their phonetic space.

The centring diphthongs that end in schwa in *hear*, *hair*, *lure*, and *lore* are of interest as they are generally due to the loss of /r/ after a vowel. The loss of the /r/ in such words is, naturally, connected with other processes that we will not go into here. The following modified table from Wells (1982: 215) shows some of the intermediary stages. For those readers that want to have a better grasp of this illustration, let me add that 'breaking' means that a vowel is 'broken up' or divided into two segments or two syllables, which is what happens to the vowel in *feed*. 'Laxing' means that a vowel is somewhat lowered or articulated in a lower position. Syllabicity loss means that a segment, the /ə/ below, no longer counts as a syllable of its own but is attached to the preceding vowel. They become the centring diphthongs. What is not shown is that the /r/ was lost.

	beer	*idea*	*chair*	*more*	*sure*
Input	biːr	-diːə	tʃeːr	moːr	ʃuːr
Pre-R Breaking	biːər	-diːə	tʃeːər	moːər	ʃuːər
Syllabicity Loss	–	-diːə	–	–	–

Figure 3.3: Stages towards non-rhoticity

The processes shown above occurred in the late 17th century, the loss of /r/ in the 18th century. As a consequence, American English is largely rhotic, while English in England and its colonies became non-rhotic. Unlike rhotic accents, Received Pronunciation and other southern accents have developed the so-called *r*-insertion in, say, *war and peace* or the *idea of it* ("linking r").

Closely related to centring diphthongs is the fact that words like *poor* (with /ʊə/) and *pore* /ɔə/ merge so that *poor* sounds like *pore*. They can merge with *paw* /ɔː/. Some differences between Southern English and Received Pronunciation on the one hand and Northern English, Scottish and Irish English on the other are due to the Great Vowel Shift. Northern English has retained the older /ʊ/ in words like *luck*, *stud*, *putt*, or *pub*, while southern types have shifted to /ʌ/.

I said earlier the vowel system is complex in Received Pronunciation. In contact situations, many accents in trade colonies like Nigeria or India have simplified this complexity by, for instance, deleting the length distinction and by shifting the phonetic quality of some vowels so that they merge with others.

Stress in English words like *seek* or *do* is simple as there is no choice but the one syllable. When there is choice, the stress pattern is difficult to predict. (The stress sign ['] is before the stressed syllable.) Why is a word like *'diplomat* stressed like it is, while we say *dip'lomacy* or *diplo'matic*? Why *'Madison Street* but *Madison 'Avenue*? Stress is puzzling and connected with the kind of final syllable (of the root). It is connected with the origin (or etymology) of a word and its history in English. Latin suffixes like *-atic* or *-acy-* and French ones like *-ee* in *diplo'matic*, *Japa'nese* or *employ'ee* influence the stress placement. Germanic ones like *-ness* or *-hood* in *kindness* or *parenthood* do not. Stress is too complex an area to be gone into in this book (*see* Eckert/Barry 2002), and a few examples will suffice to show differences between the two related languages English and German.

'student, 'metal	Stu'dent, Me'tall
'gourmet, 'cafe	Gour'met, Ca'fe
'calender, 'cylinder	Ka'lender, Zy'linder

Though Received Pronunciation has been at the top of an accent triangle that mirrors the correlation between social status and regional background, it has always been influenced by the accents 'below', especially by those in London. The replacement of mainly alveolar stops by glottal stops or their glottalization is a much discussed issue. Glottal stops occur frequently in London's traditional working class accent, Cockney, and have spread into Received Pronunciation. It is a strong marker of social class, but John Wells says this:

> "The increased use of glottal stops within RP may reasonably be attributed to influence from Cockney and other working-class urban speech. What started as a vulgarism is becoming respectable." (1994: 201)

Received Pronunciation is, one might say, being influenced by its surrounding accents, its habitat, that acts as a resource. Many other features remain outside. Another case is the replacement of /θ, ð/ by labio-dental /f, v/; *thin* sounds like /fɪn/ (= *th*-fronting). As the prestige accent is losing some of its class associations, it incorporated even a few regional features such as a front [a] for /ɑː/ in *dance*. A related process is the vocalization of /l/ after a vowel that turns into a back vowel /ɔ/. Thus, *school* sounds like [skuːɔ]. A regional variant that is not accepted is the vowel /ʊ/ in the north of England in *luck*; *luck* is to be pronounced with /ʌ/. The /h/ in *hair* is never lost as it is in many regional and other social accents. The class association has been loosened up, so to speak. Especially, since many speakers today are not keen to associate with it. As attitudes have shifted away from class associations competitors have emerged. *Estuary English* was mentioned earlier. It is an accent in the Thames Estuary that developed with the shift of industries like banking, the press, etc., there. It has been spreading around London and is used to a certain extent away from London. Another development is the growth of 'supra-localized' educated accents in the proximity of large cities like Birmingham, Leeds or Newcastle. Accents like these mark social and regional alternatives and foster a less London-centred ac-

cent spectrum. Received Pronunciation is on the retreat,
one might say. The consequences have been discussed for
some time and John Wells, one of the experts, foresees a
future in which

> "some new non-localizable but more democratic standard
> may have arisen from the ashes of RP: if so, it seems likely
> to be based on popular London English." (Wells 1982: 118)

The Handbook of the International Phonetic Association
(1999) and McMahon (2002) have suggested the term
"(Standard) Southern British English" accent. They still
point to the dominance of southern England but no longer to London alone. David Crystal says this:

> "There is certainly plenty of anecdotal evidence that many
> people these days wish to avoid the 'establishment' conno-
> tations of Received Pronunciation, and try to speak in a
> way which they perceive to be more down to earth …
> What seems to be happening … is the gradual replacement
> of one kind of standard by another – a process which was
> characterized by several newspaper commentators in 1993
> as the linguistic cornerstone of a future classless British so-
> ciety." (Crystal 1995: 327)

Norms of what is good, acceptable or inexcusable keep
changing.

Changing English

All languages change, they always do. What strikes most
is the 'little changes' such as when you hear *'ouse* on the
BBC or "people *protesting* a government decision". The

one is non-standard, the other American. There are three dimensions of change. For one, there are the changes in the texture of the accent or dialect of which we have seen many. Secondly, the relationship of varieties to one another may shift. We have seen the loss of prestige or Received Pronunciation and the rise of competitors. Finally, new varieties may spring up such as Estuary English or ethnic ones like British Black English.

Change in the standard and the prestige accent

We have seen that words like *dance* are often heard as [da(ː)ns] today, as Northern English makes inroads. One can find *John's* in formal writing, which used to be 'John is'. Swear words are no longer sanctioned but have come to be used in press writing. Some Anglicists have tried to group the accumulation of 'small' features like these into a broad, overarching schema. Mair (2006) and Svartvik/Leech (2006) have grouped them under these headings:

1. The approximation of speech and writing (esp. public writing)
2. The informalization of speech, esp. in the public domain
3. The Americanization of English

The difference between speech and writing was wide, given the origin of Standard English in bureaucracy and its continued use in formal writing. It was wide as the social class structure required a considerable social distance between the speakers. A good example is Tom Hooper's film *The King's Speech* (2010). Of course, the Australian speech therapist treated the King but that would not rule out a trace of an Australian accent today. It did in a totally hieratic social class society. In other contexts the rules of Standard English have given way to common usage. Prepositions can now be left stranded at the end of a sentence (*see* 2.6). Some companies like Tesco have changed their shop notices to make them more comprehensible. The express cashiers' former announcement *less than 10 items* has been rephrased as 'no more than 10 items'. *Less* was 'wrong' as it is used with mass nouns like *sugar*, while for count nouns it should have been "fewer than 10 items". The broadsheet papers have for long adopted a more colloquial style. Commercial broadcasters had shifted to a spoken speech style that was closer to that of their audiences in the 1960s. The BBC adopted a slightly more colloquial style somewhat later.

Colloquial speech narrows the gap between writing and speech. Contractions or *clitics*, such as the negative adverb *not*, the 3rd person singular *-s*, the reduction of *will* to *-ll*, colloquial lexical items such as *cop*, even slang and obscene words like *shit, tits* can make it into the press and broadcasting. There are features of the younger generation such as the quotative *like* that introduces direct speech in narrations: "I'm *like*, 'Can I please speak to Antonio?'" (*see* Meyerhoff 2006: 238). It also occurs in sentences like "You just have to *like* go there."

Americanization, too, is a big issue as American English has been the most dominant variety of English for some time. Its effect can be found on all levels of language organization (*see* Chapter Six).

New ethnic varieties

Great Britain is one of the most multicultural countries in Europe and cities like London are host to several hundred languages. Mark Gibson (2007: 259) explains that "The British Isles has experienced ongoing and sustained immigration throughout its recorded history." The Romans, the West Germanic tribes, the Normans, Vikings aside, he mentions Flemish weavers in the 16th century, Huguenots in the 17th, Arabs, and Europeans in the 19th century. Asians and Africans came in small numbers as a result of the slave trade and colonialism as the East India Company employed South Asian and Chinese seamen from the early 17th century onwards. Some were left stranded in England and formed communities. The slave trade brought Africans who found employment in upper class households. There was a second wave of immigration that resulted from the decolonization of former colonies in the 1950s. It accounts for large numbers of Asians, Africans, and Caribbeans. A third, smaller wave were the Hong Kong Chinese who came around the handover of Hong Kong to China in 1997. A fourth wave brought Eastern Europeans after the entry of their countries into the European Union in 2004. These migrations led to younger but stable communities in the larger cities. They brought about demographic shifts in former working class areas such as the East End, the home of the Cockney. It is home today to South Asians, Jamaicans and other immigrant communities.

British Black English

The story of Africans and Caribbeans goes back a long way. The first Caribbeans arrived at the beginning of the 16th century, when slaves were brought to London and other seaports. Queen Elizabeth I had black servants and they figure in Shakespeare's plays and in Italian operas. Elizabeth I issued a proclamation in 1601 that "the great number of Negroes and blackamoores" should leave Britain. By the early 19th century Black Londoners were part of local working class communities. During the anti-slavery movement at the end of the 18th century Africans and Caribbeans began to be transported to Freetown, now the capital of Sierra Leone. Not much seems to be known about the fate of their English. A new wave of Caribbean immigration started in 1948 when there was a shortage of labour. By 1958 some 125,000 Caribbeans had settled in Britain. Most were in their 20s and skilled workers – but the jobs offered were unskilled and well below their capacities. In the mid-1960s London Transport, for instance, recruited staff in Jamaica and Trinidad, British hotels did in Barbados. The 2001 Census has nearly 600,000 Black Caribbeans and 500,000 Black Africans.

What is important socio-linguistically is that the English of Jamaican and Black Africans is subsumed under the label *British Black English*, which has become a marker of identity, a distinct and pronounced Black and British identity that sets itself off of the Caribbean descent. Others call it a '*post-native* variety', as it is not acquired as a first language but often after the 'critical period'. An expert, Mark Sebba, adds that the shift to British Black English is frequently no more than a style shift. "Creole", he says (1997: 281), "is a *performance*. This is different from the notion of Creole as a distinct language …, which would be more appropriate to the Caribbean."

British Asian English

South Asians have had a long-standing presence in Great Britain, as mentioned above. They came from the late 17th century with the East India Company as *lascars* or militiamen on ships. Hundreds were stranded in London, leading to a growing community. A small group were educated Indians who came under separate circumstances. By the middle of the 19th century more than 40,000 seamen, scholars, officials, businessmen and others had settled. But the community that matters most today is due to the post-war migrations from 1948. The 2001 UK Census shows that there are about 2.3 million British Asians (3.9% of the population). More than one million are of Indian origin (2.7% of the population).

There is a variety of South Asian ethnolects which can vary in relation to descent and settlement. One can note semantic shifts in English words such as *bliss* 'cold weather', *vex* 'being annoyed', *sick* or *ill* 'good', *garms* 'clothes', *fronter* 'someone posturing' or *bredren* 'someone you know, friend'. A reversal of meaning is in *sick*, a semantic extension in *vex* or *fronter*. The examples below show the interaction with local non-standard English:

3.38 look ye *dis ain't no* Asian slang it's Black British slang, don't get it twisted

3.39 "They are *kinda* correct in wat they Ø saying, but sometimes they Ø not *being* accurate. I think being bilingual is a *gud* thing, yep *de* best of both worlds and apparently being exposed to a second language at a young age makes it easier to pick up a new language later in life. The 3rd *geezer* looks like a toad by the way – aren't I right??" (http://www.bbc.co.uk/berkshire/content/ articles/2005/08/19/voices_asian_english_feature.shtml; a blog of the BBC World Service)

One can see double negation in 3.38, the Cockney word *geezer* for 'man' in 3.39, but also the South Asian replacement of *th* in *this* (*see* 3.38). There is the extension of the progressive into static relations in 3.39. None of these features is used consistently and both passages are full of features of common English.

Ethnic features are spreading beyond the confines of ethnicity, especially when white British form a minority or where ethnicities mix in youth gangs. Research has revealed distinct friendship groups that can be grouped in three categories: Anglos with predominantly Anglo friends, Anglos with more than 80% non-Anglo friends and non-Anglos amongst themselves (Cheshire *et al.* n.d., p. 10). In such circumstances ethnic accents spread beyond a single ethnic origin. *The Guardian* believes that "a combination of Indian and Jamaican dialects have created a new multicultural London English among young people. 'We have got young people from many different ethnic backgrounds and have found that it is this blend that is responsible for the change. It is a move away from the traditional cockney speech, which was previously used by working-class Londoners,' she said." (*The Guardian*, 12 Apr 2006) Cheshire *et al.* maintain "it's the nature of a speaker's friendship group that is a key factor in the diffusion of linguistic innovations, and … this interacts with ethnicity." Elsewhere they say that "non-Anglo speakers have the largest proportion of the innovative features" and that "all speakers draw on a range of linguistic forms that cannot necessarily, or at least can no longer, be attributed to specific ethnic groups." *The Independent* carries an article on "From the mouth of teens" that begins with the following dialogue between two teenagers (http://www.independent.co.uk/news/uk/this-britain/ from-the-mouths-of-teens-422688.html):

"Safe, man," said one. "*Dis* my *yard*. It's, *laahhhk*, *nang*, *innit*?
> *safe* 'hi'; *my yard* 'my home'; *nang* 'good'; *innit* 'an invariant tag question'

What *endz* Ø you from? You're looking *buff* in *them* low *batties*."
> *endz* 'neighbourhood'; Ø lack of *be*; *buff* 'attractive', *low batties* 'trousers that hang low on your waist'

"*Check the creps*," said the other. "My *bluds* say the *skets* round here are *nuff deep*."
> *creps* 'trainers', *bluds* 'mates', *skets* 'sort of slutty girls', *nuff* 'very', *deep* 'harsh; out of order'

"Wasteman," responded the first, with alacrity. "You *just begging* now."
> *wasteman* 'you say to someone when you're fed up with', *begging* 'chatting rubbish'

There are signs of '*th*-hardening' in *dis*, the lowering and lengthening of the diphthongs in *laaahk* 'like', which is typical of British Black English, of *innit* 'isn't it'. The deletion of *be* shows the mixture with local non-standard English. The lexical differences are quite radical such as the noun *wasteman* to refer to a person doing nothing. It is unclear if *nuff* comes from 'enough' and has undergone a semantic upgrading. Such ways of speaking do mix traditional forms with innovations but must count as very different varieties.

We have seen in this chapter the development of English from its beginnings in the 5th century down to the current time. To structure the story, I focused on Standard English and the prestige accent, Received Pronunciation. I illustrated the style shifts and the loss of class associations, as well as the shift towards a more popular way of speaking. Non-standard English and ethnicity rounded off the picture, while regional dialects were interspersed in various places.

4 The Celtic Regions: Scotland and Ireland

The bagpipe and the kilt can be heard and seen in the remotest corners of the Australian bush, the Himalayas, or cities like Singapore. Their ubiquity rests on the Scottish involvement all over the world. We saw that *wee hours* was used in Malaysia and India in Chapter Two. Here is another example:

4.1 "It was alleged that Tiz had contacted Jejai in the *wee hours* and that she was a party girl." (*New Straits Times*, 14 May 2011)

This "Scotticism" made it to Asia, Australia and America as Scots came to make a living as settlers or do a job as administrators, officers, sailors, teachers or missionaries. The Irish and Welsh too have left linguistic traces around the world. They all speak Celtic varieties, which are also common in Manx and Cornwall. If this is the outward impact of Celtic speakers of English, one must not overlook the fact that their English resulted from the acts of suppression from around the late 12th century, as Dick Leith explains:

> "I take Ireland and Scotland as case studies, arguing that many aspects of the growth of English usage in these formerly Celtic-speaking areas can be seen as an early colonisation process which in some ways provided a model for later English colonisation overseas." (in Graddol *et al.* 2006: 185)

It is doubtful if Scotland is a matter of colonization. The Germanic tribes were invited by the Britons and went as far as the Firth of Forth. Ireland and Wales may be clearer cases of colonization. Leith is not alone in likening the internal expansion of England to colonization. Yet, its equation with the spread of English and the role of Christianization is unconvincing. Ireland was Christian before the invasion of the Normans. Should he refer to the suppression of Highland Scotland and Ireland during the 17th century, then conversion was a different case from Christianization. For us Celtic English will be cases of the expansion of English inside the British Isles.

This chapter will explore the historic situation and give enough space to the linguistic impact.

English in Scotland

Some Scottish newspapers divide the "Latest News" into "Scotland" and "UK/International": England is a foreign country in this respect. Ever since the national regions of Northern Ireland and Scotland got more political independence, which is known by the name of devolution, language policy was an area they had to deal with. They were always caught in a dilemma about the primacy of support. Should funding go solely to Gaelic or be divided between Gaelic and Scots?

English is part of England, it is the language of the Sassenachs, the Saxons, many Scots maintain. What is the status of Scots and Standard Scottish English? If one includes Gaelic, the question is whether the nation is bi- or trilingual. Another question is about linguistic relationships. Are the two varieties of English closely related as if they were poles on a scale, as some experts believe? Or are they distinct, as others do? The answer bears upon sociolinguistic issues about national identity and, of course, government funding. Paul Johnston concludes that Scotland is "one of the most interesting multi-varietal situations in Western Europe" and shows that "the attribution of 'language-hood' is as much of a socio-political judgement as a linguistic one" (2007: 105). The timeline below has some crucial background.

Timeline 2: Scotland

525–633	Angles settle south-eastern Scotland
563	Beginning of Christianization (from Ireland)
800	Beginning of Viking invasions
1057–93	Murder of Macbeth, Malcolm III; beginning influence of English through marriage with English Princess Margaret
1066	Acceptance of refugees from England, later of Norman families
1306	Robert (de Bruce), King of Scotland, recognized as Scottish king by 1328
1376–1603	"Golden Age" of Scottish literature
1390	Parliamentary records written in Inglis, later called Scots
1580	Church of Scotland reprinted the English Geneva Bible
1603	Union of Crowns; James VI becomes James I of the United Kingdom
1611	*Authorized Version* of the Bible; no translation into Scots
1707	Union of Parliaments
1715	(First) Jacobite uprising against the Hanoverian dynasty
1745	(second) Jacobite uprising defeated; followed by Anglicization
late 19th c.	Scots revival during Scottish Renaissance
1999	First modern Scottish Parliament

The story of English in Scotland

As English in Scotland comes in two guises, there are two
stories to tell. The story of Scots is similar to that of English south of the border. The Christianization by Irish
monks from around 563 was the Cultural Revolution
McCrum *et al.* spoke of. True, there were the Viking invasions and that of the Normans. English in Scotland was
enriched by Danish, Latin and French. There were differences from England. There was no fixed border with
England until 1328. Yet, *Inglis*, as it was called, developed
away from the English in the south and expressed a national identity. *Scots*, as it was called later, expanded to
the north-eastern Lowlands around the 14th century and
was then a truly national language. It was used at the
Court, in bureaucracy, literature, and the public domain –
in the Lowlands. It almost became a distinct language,
and was seen as such in continental Europe. But the
strength of Gaelic in the Highlands hampered its further
expansion and made Scotland a bilingual nation. The
proximity with England and its greater economic, political and cultural standing made it difficult to maintain a
distinct cultural and, importantly, linguistic identity. The
introduction of printing and the prestige of writing in
England limited the use and prestige of Scots. The Union
of Crowns and the shift of the Court to London in 1603
amounted to the partial loss of national Scottish domains.
The Union of Parliaments in 1707 completed that loss.
Scots was reduced to the language of low functions in the
country and the family, while English rose to the language of the state, the church, and culture. But domination had its price. The invading language had to adapt
and became Standard Scottish English.

Since we are interested in English as a pluricentric language, we may refer to Scots as the first epi-centre, long before the United States of America made English its national language and that of its identity. At the time of America's formative stage Scots began to decline. At the time of America's independence it had ceased to lead an active life. It recovered during the Romantic period in the literary domain under the name of Lallans. Robert Burns' poem "To a Mouse" (*see below*), for instance, uses the revived Scots but also shows that English intruded into the language of Scottish poetry. The first stanza is in Scots, the second in English (the English translation is in the right column).

4.2 "To a Mouse"

Wee, sleekit, cow'rin' tim'rous beastie,	Tiny, sleek, cowering, fearful mouse,
O, what a panic's in thy breastie!	O, what a panic is in your breast!
Thou need na start awa sae hasty	You need not start away so hasty,
Wi' bickering brattle!	With pattering noises!
I'm truly sorry man's dominion,	I'm truly sorry that my world,
Has broken Nature's social union,	Has broken into your world,
An' justifies that ill opinion …	And justifies your ill opinion of men …

The status and texture of Lallans was always controversial as many 'true' Scots felt it to be artificial. Scots also survived in a modernized form in the urban environments of Glasgow and as a small-town and rural language in the north-east. It is associated with the working-class in Glasgow and a traditional middle class north-east. With such opposing social associations it is hard to see it rise to the integrative, national language of Scotland it once was. Johnston's (2007: 106f) description of this complex situation is worth quoting:

> "While the bulk of sociolinguistic studies have been done in the urbanised Central Belt [the region between and including Edinburgh and Glasgow] ..., where Scots is the most tied to social class and middle-class members tend to primarily use it 'in quotation marks' ..., there are still large regions within Scotland, notably Caithness and the north-east, including at least one major city, Aberdeen, where people of high social prestige speak Scots on a daily basis ... Even in the rural around the periphery of the Central Belt, upwardly mobile middle-class members are not pressured to give up Scots ..."

Such speakers may feel they code-switch between Scots and a variety of Standard Scottish English. As they do switch, their Scots may bear signs of the approximation to Standard Scottish English. Johnston is uncertain as to the best way to explain the situation. Following a Scottish linguistic tradition, he argues that variation could be represented as if it constituted a cline from a broad Scots to a highly educated Standard Scottish English. Other experts have argued that the scale constituted the total repertoire of language that speakers have available as a resource to choose from. But Johnston also says that Scots has numerous grammatical and other features that are constitutive of a language. Does he imply after all that there are two distinct English languages that people code-switch between and that Scotland is really trilingual? He provides further depth in this passage:

"As a general trend, all types of SSE [= Standard Scottish English], including mainstream varieties, seem to have become more Scottish-accented since World War II, and the near-RP ('Panloaf') [a derogatory term, G.L.] and elocuted, hyper-RP-like types (the so-called 'Morningside/Kelvinside accent' ...) are approaching extinction as their last speakers die off ... SSE also forms the basis of Highland and Hebridean English ..." (2007: 109).

It seems that Scots reached the final stage of endo-normativity and differentiation in the early 17th century; it had norms, regional and social varieties. It lost its linguistic independence, as the English from south of the border was introduced in the public domains and, somewhat later, into the Highlands. In the Scots areas the two mixed, in others English started as an implanted and enforced quasi-colonial language. The "television stations in Aberdeen will broadcast a version of the international standard with a Scottish accent", say McCrum *et al.* (1986: 127). Endo-normativity is far off today because of the unresolved controversy about the two varieties of English.

Features of English in Scotland

This survey assumes that variation is located on a cline. Some expressions are Scots and may sound a bit archaic, rural or from the Aberdeen region. Others don't have much of a trace of their Scottish character but betray it by their pronunciation. The following examples show what this means. I begin with the most famous of Scottish ballad "Auld Lang Syne" by Robert Burns (1788) – the year when the First Fleet sailed to Australia:

4.3 Should auld acquaintance be forgot
    And never brought to mind?
    ...

    We twa hae rin aboot the braes [have run about the
        slopes],
    and pu'd the gowans fine [picked the daisies]
    But we've wander'd mony a weary fit, [many a weary
        foot/step]
    sin auld lang syne. [since a long time ago]

    [wi twǫː heː rɪn ə.but ðə breːz
    ən puːd ðə gʌu.ənz fəin
    bʌt wiːv wɑn.əɾt mʌ.ne ə wiːɾɪ fɪt
    sɪn ǫːl laŋ səin]

The next example is from a Scottish TV serial. It features two Canadian Scots, who return after a long time
and who can't fail to realize that their Scots has become
weaker.

4.4 "We'll aye come back and see ye" (= "We'll always come
    back and see you") (http://www.youtube.com/watch?v=
    gX_8knnjbbo)
    GREG HEMPHILL (actor): Well, first of all we've *gotta* head
        into the city center, gotta *chook* in there, get the keys
        from my poor auntie's *hoose*. And then get down to se-
        rious business again, a few rounds of golf while we're
        here, y'know?
    SECOND MAN: Ah, Glasgow ... hey! It's twenty-seven years
        since we left Glasgow. Twenty-seven years! I'm proud
        of one thing: We've both still got *wur* [our] accents.
    GREG HEMPHILL (actor): Anyway!
    EUROPCAR-AGENT: So what kind of motor *are yee efter*? So
        what kind of motor are you after?

SECOND MAN: Sorry, what was that, *hen*?
EUROPCAR-AGENT (exasperated and extra-slow): What *keind* of car would you *leik*?
SECOND MAN: Er … big one, big one! Four-wheel drive!
GREG HEMPHILL (actor): That's right, it's gotta be a big, big motor, *lassie*!

There are some endearing Scotticisms such as *hen* and *lassie* to address a woman. The Canadian uses *wur* 'our' and *hoose* 'house' that shows that Scottish English has not participated fully in the Great Vowel Shift of early Modern English and has no *h*-dropping. The long /u:/ shifted to a low-rising diphthong there. We see *yee* 'you'. The Canadian does not understand *are yee efter*, *keind*, and *leik* by the sales assistant in Scottish English; *efter* signals a closer vowel than Received Pronunciation and one that starts with a close onset in *keind*. Overall, the passage uses today's Scottish English accent that may count as fairly broad.

Pronunciation

Scots are easy to identify by their accent. It has often been suggested that their vowel system is simpler than that of Received Pronunciation. It has fewer vowel phonemes that are distributed more harmoniously. It does not have the negative social connotations that the English accent has, is more 'likeable', more 'democratic' even, as it is widely spoken across the country. It could well be an alternative in foreign language teaching. However, there are features that make it hard to learn: it varies a lot across the country so that descriptions end up being complicated and unusable.

As for vowels, there is no distinction between long and short vowels. Where Received Pronunciation has pairs, they merge such as *feet* and *fit* merging in /fɪt/. Though not a phonological feature, vowels can be long phonetically before the fricatives /v, z, ʒ/, before /r/, and at the end of a morpheme as in *breeze, bee* or *new*. The mid-rising diphthongs in *late* and *load* are replaced by the monophthongs /e, o/. There is no distinction between *Pam* (proper name) and *palm* as both are articulated like *Pam*. *Cot* and *caught* are not differentiated. A particularly consequential feature is that Scottish English is rhotic and has not done away with the /r/ after vowels. The vowel in words like *fern*, *hurt* or *bird*, for instance, has multiple realizations such as /fern/, /hʌrt/ and /bɪrd/. Scottish English lacks, in other words, a number of vowels of Received Pronunciation and has a system of its own.

As for consonants, rhoticity avoids centring diphthongs but the kind of /r/ is quite different from that in American English, the most widely-known rhotic accent. Words like *which* and *witch* are distinguished with the first having a voiceless /ʍ/, the second a voiced /w/. Stops are not aspirated in stressed syllables such as *pin* or *tent*. The monster of Loch Ness is not only a famous Scottish icon but has a sound that parallels the German *Loch*.

Scottish English is not a mere variant of Received Pronunciation. There are indications of two systems, of endonormativity. But I have postulated a cline and that suggests that variation is gradual. At the upper end it goes into the direction of Received Pronunciation; at the lower end towards Scots. As there is ample allophonic variation, which is impossible to include here, there is no agreed-upon norm, no standard. The conflict between a regular accent and an attachment to Southern English is left unresolved.

Words, word-formation, loans, etc.

Many Scottish expressions are shared with today's Northumbrian, the north-eastern-most dialect in England. Both go back to their Old English Anglian ancestry. One can find a few relics of Gaelic, Dutch and other European languages in Scottish English. A few examples will suffice:

4.5 Donor languages
North Germanic (or Danish): *houss* 'house', *kirk* 'church', *skraich* 'screech', *ilk* 'each', *gate* 'street', *mask* 'mash', *muckle* 'much', etc.
French: *ashet* 'an oval plate or platter', *cundie* 'conduit', *douce and dour* 'sweet and stout'
Dutch: *loun* 'worthless person', *pinkie* 'small beer', *scone*
Gaelic: *bourachie* 'a band put round a cow's hinder legs at milking', *brae* 'hill', *glen* 'valley', *loch* 'lake', *winnok* 'window'

Like in English in the south the impact of Danish is often visible in the pronunciation of individual words. North Germanic had not participated in the change south of the border that led to *church* but kept *kirk* in Scotland. Words like *ken*, *kettle*, *like*, *get*, *give*, are Norse, and *chen*, *chetel*, *liche*, *yet*, and (the archaic) *yive* in England. There are some doublets such as *muckle* and *much*, *breeks* and *breeches*, or *mask* and *mash* that distinguish Scots and Standard Scottish English. These pairs can normally be explained by the period that they were borrowed. Thus, /k/ had long become /ʃ/ in *mash* in the south, while it stayed *mask* north of the border. The originally velar sounds are spelt as *-ch-* or sometimes *-dge*, if voiced in the south and as /k/ in Scots

There are words used on both sides of the border but one is preferred in Scotland, the other in England (Scottish English comes first):

4.6   aye – yes   to stay – to live, reside
       folk – people   to mind – to remember
       through – across

Those familiar with American English will recognize some similarity. As so much variation can be seen in contemporary speech and writing, it has always been hard to assign words (and features of grammar) to either Scots or the wide range of manifestations of Scottish English. The problem was partly resolved when John Aitken suggested a scale that would connect broad Scots with Standard Scottish English. Speakers, he believed, would choose from within this scale to express their allegiance to either end of the scale. Often the outcome is a mixture that is difficult to make sense of. The scale is from Johnston (2007: 111) and reproduced in Leitner (2009. 109) (*see* Fig. 4.1).

The five columns represent a scale from Scots in 1 to Standard Scottish English in 5. *Bairn* and *kirk*, for instance, are broad Scots, *child* and *church* are Standard Scottish English. *Wee* would probably be in column 3, like *auld* 'old' and *hame* 'home'. Whether the whole vocabulary can be arranged in such a tabular form is arguable but even a partial solution is attractive and can be of use with other varieties. Since "the linguistic difference between the two is greater than between any English Standard / vernacular pair," says Aitken, "many speakers have a distinct sense of possession of two linguistic codes, each with its own grammar, and they feel they code-switch between the two." Like Johnston, Aitken fluctu-

1	2	3	4	5
bairn	hame	hame	home	child
brae	hale	hole	whole	slope
kirk	mate	before	more	church
ken	puir	soup	poor	know
darg	main	room	moon	job of work
suit	yuis n.	miss	use n.	ankle
kenspeckle	yaize v.	raise	use v.	conspicuous
girn	auld	young	old	whine
mind	coo	row (= fight)	cow	remember
sort	hoose	winter	house	mend
ay	pey	bite	pay	always
gey	wey	tide	way	very
gead	two (w)twae	agree	two	went
ben the hoose	no (= not)	he	not	inside the
	-na(e)	his	-n't	house

Figure 4.1: Modern Scottish lexis on a scale

ates between a scalar representation and one that builds on distinct codes.

Grammar

Though Johnston (2007) said that Scottish English is becoming more markedly Scottish throughout Scotland, this is not obvious in the public domain and not in the media where one finds reports like this:

4.7 "Aiden Owens was left trapped in the inferno as his mother, Laura, and older sister Chloe, 11, escaped by jumping out of a first-floor window in the *early hours* of yesterday. Neighbours who saw the family at the window screaming were forced back by the intensity of the flames and billowing smoke as they attempted a rescue." (*Herald Scotland*, 27 June 2011)

There is not a trace of anything Scottish. If the time reference were 'wee hours' instead of *early hours* it might divert from the seriousness of the topic. The Scottish element can be found in more informal writing or the deliberate literary reproduction of speech. Once again, one would place it along a scale like the one for lexis. While the 3rd person singular -*s* can be found as in Standard British English, it may be generalized to plural nouns like in English dialects. Here is an example, which also uses *aye* as a kind of marker that is similar to the tag questions in Standard English:

4.8 The weeds cum*s* throu the fence aye

There are irregular nouns such as *ee/een* 'eye(s)', *shae/shuin* 'shoe(s)' or *oax/owsen* 'ox/oxen'. Only the last one is irregular in Standard English. A crucial difference can be found in demonstrative pronouns. Scottish English has a three-way distinction between *this* and *thir* and *that* and *thae*. The first pair refers to something near the speaker, the second to something near the hearer. *Yon* and *thon* is something remote from both.

As in Northern English generally, the definite article is used with diseases, institutions, etc. So one would have

4.9 I shall see you in the summer *or* I shall see you in the morn

The auxiliary *have* is often a main verb as in the contexts of 4.11 and 4.12:

4.10 *Had* you a good time?	Yes, we *had*.
We'*d* a good time.	We *hadn't* a good time.
4.11 I *have* coffee with breakfast.	*Have* you coffee with …
4.12 I *haven't* coffee with breakfast.	

Modal verbs are particularly significant. In Scottish English they share properties with the northern type of English. Thus, modal *will* replaces *shall* in most cases:

4.13   *Will* I put on the light? *for* Shall/Should I put on the light?

A very Scottish feature is the way negation is expressed in questions. A typical question would be

4.14   Is he *not* going?   *for* Standard English   Isn't he going?
4.15   He'll *not* go   *for* Standard English   He won't go.

Negation can also be expressed with *-nae* which is attached as a clitic to a preceding verb in speech, though it can appear as a separate word in print; here are two examples:

(i)   I was nae liking it
(ii)   We were nae really wanting to go last year

To close, we have seen that contemporary Scottish English is extremely variable and that the question of whether there are two clearly distinguishable varieties, (the descendants of older) Scots and Standard Scottish English is hard to decide – at least not from this side of the North Sea. Scottish and English experts and institutions like the BBC or the British Council, though, are quite certain that there is a Standard Scottish accent. And the Standard

Scottish dialect may well be quite similar to that of England if one allows for a small number of lexical Scotticisms and some influence of grammatical constructions.

English in Ireland

Leith (2007) thought that the Celtic regions were colonized in the Middle Ages. Ireland may be a clearer case than Scotland, I said above. It was colonized for the first time when English "was taken to Ireland with the settlers from Britain who arrived in the late twelfth century [in southern Ireland]." (Hickey 2007: 135) McCafferty (2007: 122) talks about a second case, when "English was established in the north of Ireland by the British colonisation of Ulster from the late sixteenth century onwards." Four hundred years separated the two settlements and they occurred in different regions. Yet even here the claim of colonization is controversial. One should not forget, for instance, that there was cross-migration from and to Scotland, which Leith excludes from 'colonization'. What is clear is that today's English has a lot to do with the origins of the inputs from the settlers and with Gaelic, which is called Irish today.

There is an Irish speech style, the *brogue*, that is practiced on both sides of the border. It refers to the great love of good Irish talk. The concept is also used for the accent of the descendants of Irish migrants in the United States. President Barack Obama alluded to the brogue amongst Irish descendants in the United States in a speech in Dublin (24 May 2011):

4.16 "My name is Barack Obama (of the Moneygall Obamas). And I've come home to *find the apostrophe that*

we lost somewhere along the way … Some wise Irish
man or woman once said that *broken Irish is better than
clever English.* So here goes: Tá áthas orm bheith in
Éirinn – I am happy to be in Ireland! … It turns out that
people take a lot of interest in you when you're running
for President … They check out your place of birth …
Now, I do wish somebody had provided me all this evidence earlier because it would have come in handy back
when I was first running in my hometown of Chicago
because *Chicago is the Irish capital of the Midwest.* A
city where it was once said *you could stand on 79th
Street and hear the brogue of every county in Ireland.*"
[Italics added, G. L.]

In Australia the brogue was used to excuse the somewhat
aggressive verbal skills and capacity to entertain people
of the former Australian Prime Minister Paul Keating.
This section will discuss some of these themes and the
timeline below has the main historical dates.

Timeline 3: Ireland

1170	Invasion of Anglo-Norman descendants and set-tlements from Dublin to Wexford ("The Pale")
1366	Statutes of Kilkenny, forbidding the English to adopt Irish customs and language
1541	King Henry VIII proclaimed himself King of Ire-land
1603	King James I inherits title of King
mid-17th c.	Cromwell's plantation system brought Scots to the north-east and Midland English to rest of Ireland
1801	Act of Union with United Kingdom
early 19th c.	Catholic Church shifts to English

1831	National schools replace 'hedge schools'
1840s	Famines depleted the Gaelic-speaking regions leading to language shift to English
1893	Gaelic League promotes Gaelic
1905	Foundation of Sinn-Féin Party
1912	Acquisition of limited autonomy from Britain
1920/21	"Government of Ireland Act" allows Irish Free State and Northern Ireland
1937	Éire (Ireland); 1948 Republic of Ireland
2002	Devolution in Ulster

The story of English in Ireland

Ireland was unaffected by the West Germanic invasion of Britain. The first to invade it were the Vikings in 9th century and the Normans in the 12th century. They built fortified settlements, founded towns and boroughs and introduced English law to secure their dominance. But the Gaelic character of the country and the attachment to a Celtic version of Christianity were so strong that Norman settlers were absorbed, just like the Viking invaders had been by the 10th century. To counter assimilation, the Statute of Kilkenny was enforced in 1366, but to little effect. English was ultimately reduced to the Pale, a small coastal strip of land south of Dublin. Yola, as English was called, was still visible by the 17th century, when the second, successful settlement started. It was well prepared by Henry IV, who had forced local leaders to accept the supremacy of England. He gained the title of Lord of Ireland, which he held from 1399 to 1413. King James I assumed the title King of Ireland in 1603, a title that had been created by an act of the Irish parliament in 1541. England had the nominal supremacy.

It was Cromwell who enforced practical supremacy. He exploited the weakness of the Irish in the middle of the century and established plantations. He also forced thousands of Irish to work as indentured labour in the Bermudas. The Union with England in 1801 was a blow to the Irish and so was the shift of the Church to English. As Irish lost most public domains, the adoption of English was inevitable. Poverty, the famine in 1740/41 and the Great Famine from 1845 to 1852 forced many thousand people to emigrate to America, Australia and New Zealand. That was a natural incentive to acquire English. Gaelic was pushed to the west but made a modest recovery during the Celtic Renaissance at the end of the 19th century. The European Union's language policies have been instrumental in its recent growth. But even the requirement that, for instance, civil servants had to know some Irish did not lead to a successful recovery.

There was, as mentioned earlier, a historical division between the north and the rest of Ireland. The real political separation came with the foundation of the Irish Free State in 1922, which remained a British dominion until 1937. The country was renamed Eíre or Ireland.

Features of English in Ireland

Given that the Republic of Ireland is an independent nation and Ulster a part of Great Britain, it is unavoidable to speak of Irish English in the south and Ulster English in the north. The two are separated by different inputs, with the north acquiring Scots and the south the dialects of the Midlands. There were mixed settlements and shifts so that the current political boundary is not identical with a linguistic one. The broad divisions in Ireland are well represented in Hickey's map (*see* Map 4.1).

Experts like John Kirk and Jeffrey Kallen (2006) are convinced that there is an educated variety of Irish English in the Republic of Ireland. They caution by adding that Irish English is internally highly variable and that endo-normativity has only been reached recently. Irish English still looks fairly unstable and comparable perhaps to Early Modern English in the 17th century. The issue about a standard variety in Ulster is even more difficult as there are competing varieties of English, and in particular Ulster Scots. In both parts of Ireland internal variation correlates with urban or rural environments, with age and the role of the younger generation. Religion plays a role in Ulster. There is an additional complicating factor in the Republic of Ireland that Raymond Hickey (2007: 36) has summed up in this way:

"Because the interface of Irish and English has been a permanent feature in the history of Irish English the weighting of contact in its genesis is the single most controversial issue in this field. Older authors accorded considerable weight to the contact factor ... but studies in the 1980s attached much more importance to the retention of archaic or regional features. In recent years the pendulum has swung back somewhat with contact and retention accorded approximately equal weight."

The patterns are so complex that I can only hint at what could be general or educated Irish English (*see* Britain 2007).

Pronunciation

Like the Scots the Irish are fairly easy to recognize. The task for us would be to identify Irish English as such and distinguish, possibly, the north and the south. I will begin with some remarks on the first issue.

There are some common features. The lateral consonant /l/ is 'clear' in all environments, e.g. *feel* /fiːl/ , *milk* /mɪːlk/; there is no *h*-dropping, and the clusters /hj/ and /hw/ are regular in words like *human* and *where*. Some of these features overlap with Scottish English. Some features distinguish the north from the south. Rhoticity occurs in Ulster English and not in Irish English in the south. The dental fricatives /θ, ð/ are typically replaced by dental stops /t̪, d̪/ in the south. Ulster Scots of the north has retained the /x/ in *thought*, which is the same as in German 'dachte'. It can be replaced by [k] in *lough*. The "rising intonation" in statements is a prosodic feature that differentiates the north from the south (*see* Map 4.1).

Words, word-formation, loans, etc.

There are collections of Irish English words, says Raymond Hickey (2007: 149). As in other varieties, there are words that have retained an older, now defunct meaning in British English. For instance, *mad* and *bold* still mean, says Hickey (*ibid.*), 'keen on' and 'misbehaved'. Others are old and have become regional such as *cog* 'cheat' and *chisler* 'child'. Converses like *give* and *take*, *rent* and *let* or *borrow* and *lend* are often used interchangeably. "I'll *learn* you" for 'teach' is common. Code-mixing with Irish words is a regular stylistic feature.

It is not easy to find Irish lexical items in the formal do-

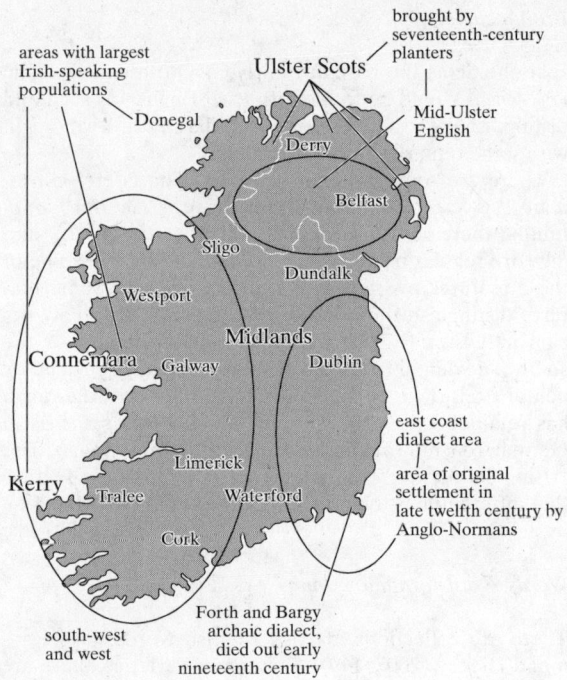

areas with largest
Irish-speaking
populations

Donegal

Ulster Scots

brought by
seventeenth-century
planters

Derry

Mid-Ulster
English

Belfast

Sligo

Dundalk

Westport

Midlands

Connemara   Galway   Dublin

east coast
dialect area

area of original
settlement in
late twelfth century by
Anglo-Normans

Kerry

Limerick

Tralee   Waterford

Cork

south-west
and west

Forth and Bargy
archaic dialect,
died out early
nineteenth century

Map 4.1: Dialect divisions within Ireland

main such as in Irish papers. There is no large national
paper but the ones that there are report very local events
like crime in Standard English. Here is an extract from a
report on a theft from a police station:

4.17 "A man who made off with the official *Garda* stamp from the *barracks* in Enniscorthy …" (*Enniscorthy Guardian*, 22 July 2011)

The word *Garda* has been chosen as it is the Irish word for police; *barracks* designates a police station, which would not be used in that sense elsewhere.

Grammar

The English in the formal public domain is very much like elsewhere in the Anglophone world. More signs of Irish English can be found at the level of colloquial, informal speech. There are different constructions, different frequencies of use, and non-standard forms creeping into the standard. And there are constructions that can be traced to Irish (Gaelic).

I will survey some of them. The examples 4.18 to 4.20 come from the novel *The Emperor of Ice-Cream* (1965) by Brian Moore, which is a useful school text. The story is set during the first part of World War II, when preparations were made for a civil defence force against German bomb attacks. As adults had been sent to war, young children were conscripted. Here are excerpts of scenes where the children are introduced into their tasks:

4.18 "He looked up at Gavin. He screamed. 'Stand up straight. How old are you?' – 'Seventeen.' – '*Childer*, they're sending me. And cheeky *childer*." (Moore 1987, p. 17)

4.19 [two men are lifting another on a stretcher] "But this sod, Price, weighed a ton. Of course, *Wee* Bates collapsed at his end of the stretcher … '*Youse* are not lifting right,' Craig said. '*Youse* have to lift together.'" (*ibid.*, p. 24)

4.20 "'Fair enough, then. ... You, Hargreaves, and you, Burke, clear up the sand. *If youse wants* to be cheeky. *I'll give youse* cheeky.'" (*ibid.*, p. 128)

The word *childer* is the plural of *child* and shows the effect of Old English *čildru*. In English it underwent secondary pluralisation when a weak ending was added, so it became *children*. In Irish English the Old English form was retained. There is a slight phonological change as the strong vowel /u/ became weak (like in English generally). *Youse* is plural and means 'you two' in 4.19 or 'more than two' 4.20. Number was lost in the second person English pronoun system but was retained in Irish English. In "youse wants to be cheeky" we see that the 3rd person singular -*s* was generalized to second person, indeed to all persons.

The present perfect is an ideal area to illustrate the uniqueness of the contact situation Irish English was in. There are three forms to express the meanings associated with perfect, i.e., the *have* plus -*ed* (past participle) construction, the *after* -*ing* construction and the simple past. Here are some examples (Kirk/Kallen 2006):

4.21 So she *has* her schoolbag *packed*.

4.22 A new fella *is after taking* over one of the pubs at home.

4.23 After I coming here, I *wasn't long here*, and an old woman died down here in the cottage.

The construction in 4.21 mirrors an older form of the present perfect in English. It would indicate today that the speaker made someone else do what is in question. The example shows the conservatism of Irish English. Example 4.22 can be traced to Gaelic, where such a construction is used. It clearly reflects the impact of language contact and signals the so-called 'hot-news' perfect or else the perfect of 'ongoing activity'. The simple past is typical of Northern and of American English. Three forms for one (in Standard English) suggest there is no present perfect in Irish English at all. The semantic spectrum is just expressed in different ways. The three expressions can be considered alternative expressions of the perfect as they can be used variably with the regular perfect form of Standard English.

There are many smaller differences. The reflexive is used in coordinate subjects and indirect questions use the word order of direct questions:

4.24 *Mum and myself* are still hoping a separation will not take place.

4.25 Like Tommy's going to ask this printer at work *does he have* any.

So-called measure phrases such as *five mile* or *five year* use the plural in English, while they do need the plural in Standard English; one can say "he ran five mile" or "his work here lasted five year". A feature that will be found in African and Asian varieties is that the progressive is used with stative verbs like *to know*. One might well hear "I was *knowing* your face". There are quotations like 4.26 that indicate that the uninflected *be* expresses a meaning of 'habituality'. The writer usually or frequently gets letters from A in 4.26. In 4.27 the referent has to get up several times during the night:

4.26 When I *be* long getting A letter I have nothing to plie to but the likeness (letter from 1860; *from* Johnston 2007: 129).

4.27 He *bes* up 3 or 4 times a night With Her (letter from 1861; *from* Johnston 2007: 129).

The examples date back to the 19th century but such examples still occur in colloquial Irish English. Experts like Johnston suggest that they are owed to the contact of Irish with English and Scots (http://www.uni-due.de/IERC/misconceptions.htm). 'Habitual *be*' can also be found in African-American English.

Summing up, Irish experts such as John Kirk argue that Irish English (especially in the south) has acquired the patterns of variation that allow one to speak of an educated or standard variety and to argue it has become endonormative. It is up to Irish scholars and the public to decide that issue. There are no substantial Irish dictionaries as yet, let alone grammars to support such claims. Kirk and Kallen (2006: 108) add that the impact of Gaelic is significant even though Celticisms occur at very low frequencies. They maintain that "Celticity manifests itself accumulatively at more than one level" and that any feature will support another one.

What is uncontroversial is that Irish English has had an impact on varieties of English worldwide. African American English came under the influence of the Irish on the Bermudas by the middle of the 17th century. English came to North America at its formative period and American English agrees in a number of points with the northern type and with Irish English. Australian and New Zealand English too contain some features that can be traced to or related to Irish English.

5 Periods of the Expansion of English

We have finished dealing with the English in the British Isles. Before we move on to the expansion of English outside, we must turn to some overarching developments that get out of sight easily in a survey that is based on geo-political entities rather than the political contexts in which English was spreading (*see* Leitner 2009).

The Tudor and Jacobean periods witnessed an unprecedented expansion of English to the New World, the Caribbean and Asia. Standard English was still in its infancy so that the main input abroad came from regional and social varieties. But it developed quickly and came to be used throughout Great Britain, in Ireland and Wales in its written form. There was no spoken standard, but one that acquired prestige despite its feudal base. Both began to influence the English of the colonies. The further expansion from the middle of the 18th centuries had much to do with European wars such as the Seven Years' War (1756–1763) (Grataloup 2007). Britain acquired most of the French possessions in the New World and India. The conflicts during the French Revolution and the Napoleonic Wars made Britain take control over Dutch possessions in South Africa and Malacca.

The independence of the American colonies was a cornerstone that changed the spread of English fundamentally. English became bi-centric and American English increasingly played a separate role in world affairs. Of course, some developments remained closely linked to British interests. The foundation of the Australian and New Zealand colonies between 1788 and 1830; the control over South Africa; the colonization of and indirect rule over South-East Asian sultanates; the Anglo-Burmese Wars; the occupation of parts of New Guinea are cases in point that were meant to enlarge and stabilize the British Empire. The scramble for Africa towards the end of the 19th century and the formalization of outcomes during the Berlin Conference in 1884 was mainly of European concern. But other activities such as the Opium Wars and the forced opening of the ports of China and Japan involved both Britain and the United States. The United States were sole agents in the North Pacific and the Caribbean at the end of the 19th century and the beginning of the 20th.

The beginning of the 20th century saw the emergence of the first global institutions such as the League of Nations and the International Labour Office (1918). The trusteeships in the Middle East and over former German colonies followed World War I; they too were largely a European issue. Britain reached its territorial zenith. English was the language of its colonies and had an impact even in non-colonies. If one includes the United States, Canada and Australia, which were independent nations, it is clear that English was on its way towards a quasi-global language. The English of all persuasions could now be heard around the world, as Arnold Zweig described in this passage set in Palestine:

> "No-one noticed that the two gentlemen spoke German to each other, while all imaginable forms of the English worldwide could be heard around them – coming from Indian, Scottish and South African lips, in London's Cockney, which predominates in Australia, and in the Oxford or Cambridge variety of educated King's English" (*see* Leitner 1990: 191).

The growth of American English to the most dominant variety of English was a matter of the period after World

War II. The United States remained the sole functioning world power. The Cold War ensured its spread as the Western world depended on America's defence. The role of British English also diminished during decolonization and the creation of nation-states. There emerged two opposing pressures. For one, there was the gradual localization of English in new nations, and, secondly, the pressure from American English and of internationalization (or globalization). The communicative configuration of the world was shifting towards the United States.

Inside the West there was highly sensitive social change, such as the shift towards a less rigid class society, a more open society based on merit and a more consensual and colloquial language. American English might have become the major force anyway but these changes sped up the process. British English still remains important to education systems worldwide but American English tends to be the model that spreads more forcefully through popular culture, business, the military, science and technology. It sounds "in", more democratic even.

6 The New World

English came to the New World in 1607, seven years after
it was taken to Asia. Most experts refer to Jamestown as
the first permanent settlement and the beginning of
American English. But Newfoundland was visited by
John Cabot in 1497 and 1498 and claimed for England in
1583. Other forerunners of English-speaking Americans
were sailors and companies that participated in the slave
trade. There was the "Lost Colony" of Roanoke in 1584
though no original settler was found in 1590 when relief
ships arrived. That amount of evidence led some experts
like John Dillard to conclude that some Native Indians
will have used an English pidgin, a contact language, before the Jamestown settlement and that American English owes more to language contact than is generally assumed. That controversy will not be resolved here, but it
is worth knowing about it to remain critical of the power
of the research consensus. This chapter retraces the development and stratification of American English on the
background of historical data (*see* Timeline 4).

Timeline 4: North America

1492	Discovery of New World by Christopher Colum- bus
1497	Newfoundland, claimed by John Cabot for Eng- land
1607	Jamestown, Virginia, established by British settlers
1620	Plymouth (Massachusetts), by Pilgrim Fathers
mid-17th c.	Bermuda: Irish indentured labour and slaves
1763	Territories east of Mississippi acquired from France

1773	Boston Tea Party, leading into independence
1776	Declaration of Independence of the Thirteen Colonies
1783	End of American Revolution, recognition of independence
1803	Louisiana Purchase (area west of Mississippi) from Spain
1840s	China: participation as non-military party in Opium Wars
1848	Californian Gold Rushes
1861	Civil War, ending in 1865
1898	Dominion of Canada (remained part of British Empire); Hawaii finally part of US; USA acquires the Philippines after Spanish-American War
1918	League of Nations; USA a signatory power
1941	Participation in Second World War (to 1945)
1945	United Nations, seat in New York
1959	Hawaii and Alaska become last states of USA
1960s	Civil Rights Movement
2009	Barack Obama becomes first coloured president

The story of American English

The story of English in America is best told in three stages. The first one is appropriately called 'colonial' and covers the period to the Declaration of Independence in 1776 or 1783, the year when Britain accepted it. This period spans the development of American English away from the variety of inputs from Britain and on to the rise of a general American English. It is followed by the period from independence to World War II. That long period might be sub-divided into the decades up to the end of the Civil War (1861–65), the end of World War I and to the end of World War II. English developed its own American standard, the general American English (a still disputable term) and accentuated its range of dialects. It became a variety widely known in East Asia and the Pacific at first, after World War I in the world at large. Black American English developed from a pidgin into a creole in the south and to an urban ethnolect in the north. The 20th century saw its rise as a powerful variety in popular culture. The decades since represent the third period, when American English has truly become the most important variety of English worldwide. Some details will be presented below.

England had for long wanted to participate in trade in the New World and in Asia, but was unable to do so because of the sea-power of Spain. An attempt was made when Sir Walter Raleigh was granted a Royal Charter. He sailed to Roanoke in today's Virginia in 1584 but the story ended tragically. Relief ships were held up until the defeat of the Spanish Armada. When they arrived in 1590, not a trace of any settler was found in the "Lost Colony".

It was easier to move west after the defeat of the Armada in 1588, but it took to 1606 before the London Company, a company of merchants, could send three ships to establish a settlement. They founded Jamestown, in 1607. The colony was called Virginia. The Pilgrim Fathers arrived in Plymouth in 1620 and established Massachusetts. That colony differed from Virginia in terms of religious orientation, aspirations, and regional origin. The regional background of the Mayflower settlers was East Anglia, while the settlers in Virginia had a strong component of south-western England. The next colonies to be founded were New Hampshire (1679), Maryland (1632), Connecticut (1635) and Rhode Island (1636). With the foundation of Georgia in 1732 the Thirteen Colonies had been set up along the Atlantic coast. At the end of the Seven Years' War (1756–63) Britain acquired the territory east of the Mississippi from France, a vast stretch of land from today's Canada down to Louisiana.

As the dialects transplanted to the New World merged, they levelled out numerous characteristics within some 40 years – the *foundation period*. They developed away from its British parent, but the backgrounds of the settlers and the fact that they had settled in different communities gave rise to three broad dialect regions: the North-East or New England, the South, and a small strip that separated the two, but expanded like a balloon the further west one looks, i.e., the Midland. Like English in England, American English started out as a set of dialects that slowly developed an overarching American layer. That base would develop further throughout the period to independence. The contact with American Indians (or First Nations, as they are called today) introduced several hundreds of loan words into American English (*see below*).

Natural dialect formation overlapped with deliberate actions to make American English different from British English. The relevant segments of American society had enough self-esteem to feel no need to follow British practices and attitudes slavishly. The colonies had been granted self-governance on internal matters, while Britain retained control in the international domain. The two domains overlapped and there was enough ground for conflict. One example was the *Stamp Act* of 1765, which imposed a tax on newspapers, etc. The *Tea Act* of 1772 excluded American wholesalers from dealing in tea and was intended to resolve financial problems of the East India Company. Both were perceived as going against American interests and protests led to what has gone down into history as the *Boston Tea Party* in 1774. A group of protesters threw a shipload of tea into the Boston harbour, which was followed by punitive actions by Britain. Several *Continental Congresses* were convened to articulate common interests and to create a pan-colonial political structure. The Declaration of Independence of July 4, 1776, spelt out a solid consensus of where the colonies wanted to go. With Independence being rejected by Britain, the American Revolution or the War of Independence was inevitable. It ended in 1783 with the Treaty of Paris that settled differences. Britain ceded the land east of the Mississippi to the United States. The English language had already become a political issue in the context up to the federation of the colonies. It was felt to be too British. As an independent nation required a language of its own, there were calls for a *Federal English* by Noah Webster, George Washington, and the first president, Benjamin Franklin, and others. It would have to be viable nationally and need to be codified to develop the standard required for the nation.

The second period thus started with the strong feeling that English needed to become American. Subsequent developments are strongly associated with Noah Webster, whose political activities are less well-known than his linguistic role. He initiated change or, to put it in terms of standardization, codification that will be mentioned below. The War of Independence accelerated another development, i.e., the separation of Canadian English away from that of the USA. The expansion of the United States westward gained further momentum, when the land west of the Mississippi was acquired from France in the so-called "Louisiana Purchase" in 1803. Most of Texas was annexed in 1845. Oregon was acquired in 1848 after an agreement with Britain. In the same year Mexico ceded a large part of today's California. By the middle of the 19th century the USA had acquired its continental possessions, which permitted new waves of immigrants to move to the Far West.

A change closely related was the development of different economic profiles of the regions. The North-East with its big cities like Boston, Plymouth and New York became heavily industrial and trade-oriented. New York, for instance, rose to the status of the largest city of the USA and a global metropolis. The states in the Mid-West were agricultural with huge farms. And the South remained class-divided, small-scale agrarian, and dependent on slavery. These discrepancies had to create problems between the states and more so with their economic profiles. There were controversies about import tariffs on goods, states' rights as opposed to those of the federal government. But none of them was as conflict-laden as the slave issue. Southern states wanted to expand it to new states, the northern states wanted to abolish it. The Civil War was the consequence, though the underlying reasons were more complex and interests changed in the course of the war. Its outcome had a significant impact on English. Black English, an ethnic language, had mainly been in the agrarian south. With the abolition of slavery a massive stream of free slaves began to move into the cities in the north and created ghettoes. Black English became an urban language with a network of features that connected it nation-wide. It became more visible but did not play a big role in the public arena.

The most visible aspect was that American English was firmly established as national language, it was being codified and accepted nationally. But the legacy of linguistic authoritarianism of the 18th century continued to flow from Britain. It crystallized in an interesting mix of American chauvinism and moral arguments about correctness in language. The class heritage that was linked to the accent in England was replaced by a more democratic one that found its expression in *general American English*. Instead of the accent being divisive, Americans focused on correct spelling, the rejection of non-standard words like *ain't* as morally corrupt, etc. There were of course forerunners to the explicit attempts to codify English and one of them was Hugh Jones' *An Accidence to the English Tongue* (1724), the first English grammar printed in America.

A third cluster of developments towards the third quarter of the 19th century facilitated the mobility of goods and information. The improvement of communication technologies such as the telegraph helped the spread of information on an almost global scale. America now participated in events taking place in Asia. Loan expressions due to language contact elsewhere in the world made their way into American English just like into British English. The big railway lines helped internal mobility. The Eerie Canal connected New York with the Great Lakes and enabled quick access to the northern hinterland. Regular shipping lines between Europe and North America followed. Words like the Malay *amok* were known worldwide. That period saw American English "going international". The major events that involved the United States in East Asia and the North Pacific were mentioned in Chapter Five and need not be repeated. The impact of American English was beginning to be felt in Britain and intensified attitudes against American English.

During the following decades the internal texture and the standard or general dimension stabilized so that H. L. Mencken's book *The American Language* (1919) can be seen as an adequate expression of its independence. Externally, it became the model of English in the Philippines, Guam and Puerto Rico, which were acquired from Spain in 1898 and in Hawaii, which was 'handed over' to the United States by the Hawaiian king in 1898. Thousands of Chinese migrant labourers built the trans-Pacific Railways, worked on goldfields, etc. They naturally acquired American English and made it known across the North Pacific. The United States had a history of involvement in China and Japan by then when it helped build schools, colleges, and universities. After World War I American missionaries worked with European, African and Asian missionaries in Africa so that it would be known globally. At the end of World War I global institutions such as the League of Nations and the International Labour Office were established in 1919. The United States assumed a leading role.

Modifying one of David Crystal's assertions somewhat, American English was the variety that was at the right place at the right time; but it was there much earlier than he assumes. An overlooked aspect is that global institutions propagated technical registers from Anglophone and Francophone countries in international communication worldwide. Programme exchanges in broadcasting, film, popular culture and music were other factors that became important in the 1920s and 1930s and promoted American English and American broadcast formats. Black American English, too, was carried worldwide in the context of popular culture. The 1930s saw several conferences on applied English linguistics in New York and Great Britain that aimed to develop policies and teaching materials for foreign language teaching (*see* Leitner 2009). American English was an indisputable element in this context.

The USA remained as the sole fully functioning power after the World War II. Its supremacy in technology and science, in trade, its military power, and its success in popular culture made it the most important crystallizing centre. American English turned into a competitor of British English, which itself felt ever more strongly the American impact. The weight of the development of English gradually shifted to the United States.

American and British English in contrast

It is natural that the transplantation of a language or a set of dialects to new surroundings opens new paths of development. Peter Trudgill sub-titled one of his books with *The Inevitability of Colonial Englishes* (2004). The different composition of a population with its linguistic heritage, he says, creates different contact scenarios. In America, the mixing was more extreme as settlers from the south-east of England suddenly lived next to Northerners, Scots and Irish. There was a richness of expression for much the same purposes. *Autumn* and *fall* were synonyms that were bound to be reduced as a new system emerged. (One may be reminded of the early Modern English period when English borrowed heavily from Latin and French.) While England had largely lost the /r/ sound after a vowel, as in *beard*, the West Country and Scots had retained it. It had been a formative element and was reinforced in most American dialects except New England. There was bound to be reduction, levelling and regularization in other areas.

The differences between the two varieties began to be noticed. George Bernard Shaw, for instance, said that Britain and America were two nations divided by a common language. A former editor of the *Oxford English Dictionary*, Robert Burchfield, believed that the two varieties would end up as distinct languages (*see* "Divided by language", http://news.bbc.co.uk/2/hi/uk_news/1445564. stm). An American said that "The gulf between American and British English is more pronounced than a mere difference of pronunciation", and that "We don't have the same language. We use the same words, but they are often used in different ways. You say one thing, but we mean another." A *scheme* is a plan one may follow in Britain but is found suspicious on the other side of the Atlantic.

Before embarking on a comparison of British and American English, it may be good to make two points. The first is that Canadian English often follows practices of both British and American English. That is increasingly being seen as a 'third path' as the options need not reflect simple, but compatible options. When monophthongs rise in American English but become more open in British English, they have to go one way in Canadian English. The second point refers to the concept of a 'standard' in American English for a moment. Schneider (2011: 81) calls it "a difficult and problematic one any how" and adds that there is no single accent (like Received Pronunciation) that signals formality and a speaker's social and educational status and that ignores regional origin. All American accents show traces of origin. The term *general American English*, which was so familiar in the past, he says, has been replaced by *Standard American English*, which implies "that in formal and supraregional contexts speakers deliberately avoid using marked regionalisms" (2011: 81). That characterization makes some interesting points. For one, the focus on the avoidance of regionalisms reminds one of Quirk and Stein's claim that Standard British English avoids drawing attention to itself. Secondly, being defined negatively, it permits regional expressions that are not "marked". The same is true of contemporary Received Pronunciation where some regional traces are permitted, too. I will use that concept of standard American English in the following survey. The features mentioned belong to the stable core of Americanisms.

There are some "evergreens", to use a Germanism, in American and British English. *Tomatoes* is one of them: it has the vowel of *fast* [æ] in America and that of *pay* [eɪ] this side of the Atlantic. A word that created confusion and some anger in post-war Germany was *corn* which does not mean 'Korn' or 'Weizen' as assumed, but 'maize' in America. The standards of British and American are different but the differences are, as such examples show, more subtle than, say, between educated Indian and American English. An excellent example is the Declaration of Independence, a masterpiece of American plainness and rhetoric.

6.1 "When in the Course of human events, it becomes necessary for one people to dissolve the political bands which have connected them with another ... a decent respect to the opinions of mankind requires that they should declare the causes which impel them to the separation.

We hold these truths to be self-evident, that all men are created equal, that they are endowed by their Creator with certain unalienable Rights, that among them are Life, Liberty and the pursuit of Happiness ..."

The style of the declaration signals the utmost formality and one cannot find a trace of a colloquialism. The expression *pursuit of happiness* has become an icon of American English and especially of the rhetoric of the nation. This style can also be seen in the speech of President Barack Obama in front of Capitol Hill in 2009, the Clinton affair in 1998 or, in a different context, the "Sorry Speech" by the former Australian Prime Minister Kevin Rudd in 2008. There are sharp contrasts with other types of speech in the public domain.

American English was described in dictionaries and grammars since the early 19th century. Nevertheless, grammars like those by Lindley Murray or Bishop Lowth continued to be used on both sides of the Atlantic. By the beginning of the 20th century American English had reached endo-normativity, if one goes by H.L. Mencken (1919). Separate developments in pronunciation had begun earlier and were well fixed, as Wells (1982: 36) explains, adding that it is "perhaps only since the convulsion of the Second World War that GenAm [General American] has entirely ceased to look over its shoulder at RP, i.e. that Americans have resolved that Americans, not the British, set the pronunciation standard for America."

Pronunciation

Who would not be able to tell an American from a British person, when they pronounce the letter *r* in words like *girl*, or articulate the "t" in *continen**t**al* as if it was a very brief "d". When these features accumulate as in *wa**t**er* [wɔːtə˞], they have that distinct *Americanness* that many find so 'cool'. American and British English differ (i) in the phoneme systems, (ii) the articulation of phonemes (allophones), (iii) the distribution of phonemes, and (iv) the pronunciation of some words.

There is a number of differences which make the phoneme system of American English simpler than that of Received Pronunciation. The most prominent one is the post-vocalic /r/ in words like *mere*, *far* or *bird*. American English has /mɪɹ/, /fɑːɹ/ and /bɝd/ and lacks centring diphthongs. The back vowels are difficult to generalize as they are tied to distinct dialect areas in American English. British English distinguishes the vowels in *caught*, *cot*, and *calm*, i.e. /ɔː, ɒ, ɑː/. Many American accents have only two vowels, i.e. /ɔ/ in *caught* and /ɑ/ in *cot* and *calm*. Some and especially those in the Mid-West merge the two so that *caught* and *cot* sound the same. But before /r/ they are kept distinct so that *store* and *star* sound different.

There is an abundance of allophonic differences. A large class of words like *tune* or *news* are pronounced as /tuːn/ and /nuːz/ in American and as /tjuːn/ and /njuːz/ in British English. The short front vowels in *bet* and *bat* are raised, which makes them sound like /ɪ/ and /e/, respectively. The phoneme /æ/ can indeed rise so as to sound like /ɪə/. Vowels may acquire a nasal quality next to nasals. Thus, *man* is very much like /mæ̃n/. The so-called flap in *continental* was mentioned above.

A number of differences are tied to the pronunciation of individual words. The hero in the film *The Man of La Mancha* (1972) is *Don Quixote*. In older British English it was pronounced as /ˈkwɪksət/, in American English as /kɪˈhoʊti/. The British pronunciation was consistent with the adjective *quixotic*, which is not the case in American English. Quite clearly, the American pronunciation sounded modern, the British one archaic. The word led to a kind of class and age war in Australia until a compromise form was accepted. The country was spared the consequences of that 'war' as the hero has sunk into oblivion.

Turning to word stress, there are some systematic differences. There are suffixes that retain a secondary stress as *-ary* in *library*, while others are reduced like *-ile* in *fertile*. There is a large number of lexical differences. A few examples, with American English coming first, are *atta'ché – a'ttaché, ca'fe – 'cafe, rather* /ræðəɹ/ – /rɑː ðə/, etc.

Spelling

There are a number of eye-catching differences that are attributed to Noah Webster. Looking at the variation that could be found on both sides of the Atlantic at the time, he suggested one form for American English. His suggestions were based on some principles that were to make spelling regular, simpler and closer to pronunciation. Most of his proposals were systematic, but some were tied to individual lexical items or small classes of items. And there are areas that have been, and continue to be, variable. The following paragraphs will briefly survey this area which is well covered in most dictionaries.

To begin with regular differences, there are the well-known ones like the British *-our* and the American *-or* in *humour/-or*. Many British academic publishers like Cambridge University Press have shifted to the American practice. American English is more regular, but some words like *donor, creator* or *terror* had shifted to *-or* even in British English. *Terrour* was still a spelling in this American quotation: "diffuse a *terrour* among the people" (http://www.law.gmu.edu/assets/files/publications/working_papers/09-01%20Second%20Amendment.pdf).

Webster's reform avoided irregularities between derived words like *honour* and *honorable*. Words like *computerize* and *emphasize* are written like this in American English. British English would have *computerise*, but *emphasize* would be like in American English. The reason is that the latter is of Greek origin, not the former (or, better, was introduced after that rule was applied). But there is a lot of fluctuation.

The ending *-er* was widely used in British English up to the end of the 19th century but disappeared then. There are traces such as in *arbiter*. Generally *-er* is considered American. Consonant doubling occurs mainly in British English and was simplified in American English, e.g., *counselor*, *jeweler*, *leveled*, and *worshiping*. Doubling is retained in *skilfull*. The ending *-ence* is spelt as *-ense* in *defense*, *offense* and *license*. This too introduces derivational uniformity (*see defense/defensive*).

Loan words from Greek and Latin included combinations like *-ae* or *-oe*. Such double letters have disappeared in American English: *anaesthetic – anesthetic, orthopoedic – orthopedic, mediaeval – medieval* and *foetus – fetus*. *Economics* was spelt with the double letter *oe* as *oeconomics* to the end of the 18th century, but British English followed Webster's proposal. The same principle was applied to words ending in *-ick(s)* such as *physicks*. Words like *acknowledgement* retain the silent *-e-* in British English to signal the sound quality of *-dg-* and *-g-*.

A number of differences are, as I have said above, connected with lexical items. I will list some with the American variant coming first: *mom – mum, ax* or *axe – axe*; *percent – per cent; peddler – pedlar, plow – plough, gage – gauge*. Some of Webster's proposals have not been accepted. The deletion of *-gh-* in *night* or *right* to make them *nite* or *rite* was not adopted. It is occasionally used in advertising. *Theater* may be used to differentiate the popular ones from the classical *theatre*; *program* has caught on but began as a computer program. *High* and *low* are often spelt *hi* and *lo*.

While American spelling has simplified and regularized some idiosyncrasies, many oddities remain. Why is *debt* spelt with -*b*? Only because some doctrinaires insisted on etymological spelling, overlooking the fact that this word came from French and never had the sound in question. American English also shares the spelling of compounds as single words such as *policymaker or wordformation*.

Words, word-formation, loans, etc.

Words may betray one's social or regional background. Talking about the *fall* for the period of September to December is a sign of American English. The seventh President of the United States, Andrew Jackson (1829–37), was nicknamed *Old Hickory* for his stubbornness as president. Literally, *hickory* refers to a native tree with very hard wood. The *White House* is a cultural and political icon just like *Downing Street 10* or *Number 10* in Britain. The *Big Apple* stands for New York, the *Bible belt* for the conservative religious states in the south. Words come to be known as *Americanisms* if they have been coined or borrowed in American English first. The term Americanism is also applied to those words that have undergone semantic processes such as the addition of a new meaning, the reduction or loss of meanings, the shift of connotations, etc. that have occurred first in American English. Such -*isms* are often a matter of pride as they show the vitality and adaptability of a variety to its new environment. The retention of a word that got lost in the parent variety may signal the conservative nature of the American variety. The American word *fall* is an old dialect word in British English today.

Apart from the words mentioned, many others reflect American realities. *Government*, for instance, has a wider, more abstract sense than in Europe and includes in its designation the Congress, the federal court system and other federal bodies such as the trade commission. A particular government such as that of Barack Obama is referred to as an *administration*. The word is now used for the governments of Malaysia and other countries. The president is not elected directly by the people but by *electors* that are tied to a particular candidate. Presidential decisions can be *overridden* by Congress with a two-thirds majority. Congress can *impeach* 'seek to depose' a president. That nearly happened to President Richard Nixon, but he resigned in time in 1974. What are called *Ministers* in British government are *Secretaries*. The *Secretary of State* is the Foreign Minister. As elsewhere in the world the names of political parties are tied to their history. The *Democrats* might be compared to *Labour* in Britain while the *Republicans* are similar to the *Conservatives*. The party structure is, as readers will know, never static so that this information is more related to the parties' history than to current policies. To just name a few more concepts of the language of politics: *primaries* or *primary elections*, *run for president*, *endorse a candidate* 'approve of a candidate publically', *platforms* 'a candidate's programme', speeches are referred to as *stump speeches*, which refers to the tree stump from which speeches were made in the past. Candidates *barnstorm* the electorate, etc. There is no scope to look at other domains, but a good collection is in Tottie (2002).

There are many colloquial expressions in the context of

politics. *Rollback* for 'reversal' is one that appeared in *The Washington Post* (29 July 2011):

6.2 "But reversal – rollback, in Cold War parlance – is simply not achievable until conservatives receive a mandate to govern."

An interesting contemporary example is *Tea Party*, which also occurs in *tea party patriots*, *tea party express* or *tea party movement*. It shows how political language can use the country's history as a resource:

6.3 "The Tea Party movement has become a platform for conservative populist discontent, a force in Republican politics for revival … But it is also about the profound private transformation of people like Mrs. Stout …
　　These people are part of a significant undercurrent within the Tea Party movement that has less in common with the Republican Party than with the Patriot movement, a brand of politics historically associated with libertarians, militia groups, anti-immigration advocates and those who argue for the abolition of the Federal Reserve." (*The New York Times*, 15 Feb 2010)

This passage from an opinion article in *The New York Times* amounts to a political science definition but makes it clear that, while it refers to conservatives, it does not necessarily refer to the Republican Party. It includes a broad right-wing patriotic movement of civil disobedience with hardly a homogeneous agenda. The word itself derives from the Boston Tea Party on 16 December 1773, a cornerstone in the American War of Independence.
　To return to the origin of American English, one can note a mixture quite different from that of British Eng-

lish. The contact with local American-Indian languages
was less pervasive overall and restricted to a period of
probably around 200 years. Most Native American words
come from the areas of fauna, flora, material and social
culture. Some words have developed a life of their own
and have become significant cultural icons of American
English. A few examples will suffice:

6.4 <u>Native American words</u>
   bayou, Choctaw *bayuk*
   caucus, Algonquian *caucauasu* 'counselor'
   chipmunk, Algonquian *chitmunk*
   hickory, Algonquian *pawcohiccora*
   opossum, Powhatan *aposoum*
   tomahawk, Algonquian *tamahaac*
6.5 <u>Caribbean slave words</u>
   barbecue, Carib *barbricot*
   canoe, Caribbean
   hurricane, Carib *huracan* 'his one leg'
   maize, Carib *mahiz*
   potato, Taino *batata*
   tobacco, Arawak *tzibatl*
6.6 <u>Native Mexicans loans directly or via Spanish</u>
   avocado, Nahuatl *ahuacatl*
   chile, *chili*, Nahuatl *chilli*
   chocolate, Aztec *xocolatl*
   tomato, Nahuatl *tomatl*

African and, by implication Caribbean languages too
have provided some words:

6.7 <u>Words from African languages</u>
   juke 'cheap bar'
   voodoo 'Caribbean religious cult involving witchcraft'

As mentioned earlier, European languages, too, were sources for American English lexis. Once again a short list must suffice:

6.8 <u>Words from European donor languages</u>

Spanish: *canyon*, *coyote*, *sierra*

French: *bayou* 'a body of water, small river', *crevasse* 'break in river embankment', *prairie* 'treeless grassy plain'

Dutch: *boss* 'employer', *coleslaw* 'cabbage salad', *cookie* 'small, flat, sweet cake', *dope* 'a narcotic, drug'

German: *verboten*, *angst*

The impact of German and other languages often goes deeper because some word-formation pattern or the use of some word becomes generalized. A case in point is *customer-friendly* which is derived from 'kundenfreundlich'. The word *-friendly* has become so productive in American English and other varieties that one can find dozens of compounds like *user-friendly*, *eco-friendly* or *crash-friendly*.

The final category is words that show modern creativity especially in the sciences, the technologies, commerce, and popular culture. The American book supply dealer Amazon, for instance, has its *Kundenzentren* worldwide but one finds the technical term *fulfilment centre* in quite different forms in Britain, as these examples show:

6.9 Amazon currently operates ten *fulfilment centres* worldwide, including six in the United States and one each in the United Kingdom, Germany, France and Japan.

6.10 Amazon.com … Headquartered in Seattle, Washington, USA, we also have offices, *fulfillment centres*, customer service centres … (http://www.amazon.co.uk/Locations-Careers/b?ie=UTF8&node=203040011)

6.11 Amazon.ca will establish a *fulfillment center* in Canada

One can expect confusion in Germany. The Deutsche
Post, the logistics concern Hermes, and other major companies have located customers' orders, deliveries, complaints, etc. in *fulfillment centres*. One finds *fulfil<u>l</u>ment
centre*, *fulfil<u>l</u>ment cen<u>ter</u>* (German Baur) or *fulfil<u>l</u>ment
cen<u>tre</u>* (Australian LeisureCom travel). Similar variation
can be found with *skilful* and *skilfull*. With variation and
mixing being everywhere, one can notice national trends
at best. American English has always been productive in
word-formation. One particular rule is that verbs can easily be derived from nouns but the productivity or the
number of new coinages is large in American English.
Here is one example:

6.12 "He also correctly recognized that no matter what he
    says, those who want *to demagogue* this issue will con-
    tinue, and the evidence bears him out." (*Washington
    Post*, 24 July 2011)

Grammar

Robert Burchfield, former chief editor of the *Oxford
English Dictionary*, once argued that American English
would become a different language altogether. Being in
the position he was in, his views were discussed – and rejected. The amount and diversity of contact is too high
for any one variety to develop too far away from the other. If they did, they would endanger the global status of
English.

Whether the differences are big or small is a matter of
perspective. They are not insignificant and may betray an
American or a Briton – just like spelling, pronunciation

or words do. There is a number of features that American English shares with Scottish, Ulster English and the north of England (= Northern [type of] English). The use of the definite article with nouns referring to institutions, illnesses etc. (*see* 6.13) is a case in point. In Standard British English a definite article would refer to a specific university, hospital, etc.

6.13 My son is at *the* university.
      My daughter is in *the* hospital.
      John plays *the* guitar.

Collective nouns are problematic and there has always been a great deal of variation. In general, American English prefers the singular, British English the plural in the verb or a following pronoun (British English is in parenthesis).

6.14 The government has (have) decided that it (they) have to launch a campaign.

There is a lot of inexplicable variation, which shows that we are almost concerned with the grammar of words rather than the grammar of sentences. *Police* and *staff*, for instance can take the plural or the singular in both varieties with little difference. Words like *audience* are said to be more appropriate in the plural if a communal action such as applause is referred to.

Turning to prepositions, there is a number of American usages:

6.15 "That would give Geithner enough borrowing authority to cover the nation's bills *through* the end of this year" (*Washington Post*, 24 July 2011).

British English would have *till*. Verbs can be classified in terms of their complements. The verb *to sleep*, for instance, has none, *to read* ('a book') and *to give* ('John a present') have one and two, respectively. There is a complement after *to become* ('a teacher' or 'interested'). A large group of verbs are followed by a preposition or adverb like *to go on* or *to back out*, etc. As verbs are full of idiosyncracies (*see* Chapter Two), it is not surprising that varieties differ from one another. American English, for instance, deletes the preposition after some verbs. Where British English *vetoes against a decision* American English has *to veto a decision*. In many cases a following preposition is changed. Instead of saying *to speak to*, Americans *speak with*. One could make a case out of *to speak to* and argue it expresses a hierarchical situation, while *to speak with* is more democratic. But that interpretation was made possible only once there was choice.

Modal verbs like *shall*, *will* and *would*, *may* and *might*, *can* and *could*, etc. are an area full of special cases. In a traditional form of Standard English one would use *shall* if one predicted something that would happen or where one committed oneself to some action:

6.16 "I *shall* not die, but live, and declare the works of the LORD." (King James Bible, Psalm 118:17)

6.17 "... but of the truth of what I *shall* relate, I can summon more than one witness of undoubted veracity ..." (Jane Austen, *Pride and Prejudice*, Ch. 35).

6.18 I *shall* certainly see better days soon.
I *shall* definitely come around.

The first two examples are older but *shall* may still occur in the contexts of self-commitment. In other contexts, such as in the other example, it has become rare. It has almost disappeared in both varieties outside legal and formal writing and tends to be replaced by *will*. Still, it has been found that this change is more frequent in American English. Even in sentences like 6.16 American English prefers *will* where one finds *shall* in British English:

6.19 What *shall* I do?

The verb *must* expresses two very different meanings:

6.20 (a) I *must* really stay in to do some work.
(b) John *must* be at home as the lights are on.

In the a. example it expresses obligation, in b. an inference that the speaker makes, seeing that the lights are on. Problems turn up when these sentences are negated so that an obligation or the inference are denied. In British English *must* in a. has to be replaced by *don't have to* while b. is rendered with *can't*. American English, in contrast, permits *mustn't* in b. and a. would be like British English.

The present perfect has very difficult restrictions put on it. Learners will know you cannot use it in the a. version below and have to replace it by the b. version.

6.21 (a) I *have seen* that film last week/yesterday.
(b) I *saw* that film last week/yesterday.

In contrast to 6.21 you have to use the present perfect in British English though the event is clearly in the past:

6.22 (a) Did John come home yet?
(b) Has John come home yet?

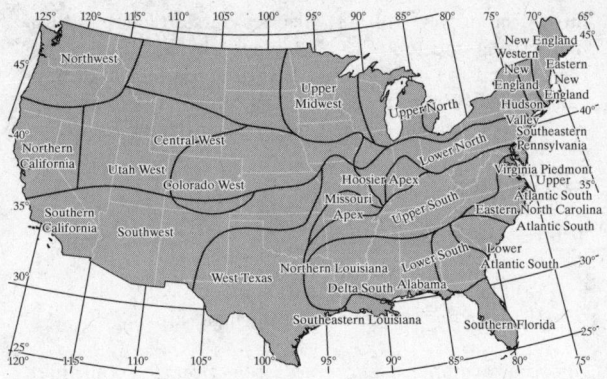

Map 6.1: Dialect areas of the United States

American English allows the b. version. The present perfect is the formal variety in American English, the simple past the informal one.

Internal variation: dialects and ethnolects

I have said earlier that standard or general American English had a much broader demographic and regional base than Standard British English and, above all, Received Pronunciation. I also said that general American English refers to a regional dialect. It is important therefore to have some understanding of the regional texture of American English and of on-going developments. I also said that the dialects of American English reflect early settlement patterns and the mixing that was going on in the West. The following map has the broad regional details.

The term 'general American English' thus has two meanings. It can refer to the standard or educated variety or to a very large dialect region. No wonder that many experts either deny there is an American Standard and argue that there are regional variants across the continent (*see* Map 6.1).

Ethnicity and non-standard English

Ethnicity has always been an important dimension. Settlers came in contact with Native Americans from the beginning. Slaves were imported from the 1630s to work on plantations or in households. They mainly settled in the South until slavery was abolished after the Civil War in the 1860s and ex-slaves moved into the northern cities. The early French and Spanish settlers were close neighbours to the colonies up to the mid-19th century. Germans and other Europeans immigrated from the beginning but in large numbers in the 18th and 19th centuries. Asian groups had been imported in the 19th century. While there emerged an anti-Asian sentiment at the end of the century, a small community stayed in the cities. Spanish and Mexican settlers were, of course, strong in the west and south but their presence today stems from large-scale migrations in the late 20th century from different South and Central American countries.

Most of these groups had created ethnolects, but many assimilated to American English generations ago. Only few have maintained ethnolects or are creating new ones. The African Americans have formed the strongest ethnolect, a variety that has had and continues to have an important role in popular culture. That of the Hispanics is still forming and its direction is as yet unclear. I will turn to ethnolects in Chapter Ten so it is enough to have alerted readers to that dimension of variation in American English.

7 The Southern Hemisphere

The Great Southland, the Antipodes, as this large continent was called, was 'discovered' relatively late. It had been a theoretical construct in Antiquity, when the earth was considered flat. There had to be a land mass to counter-balance the weight of the known world, it was believed. Centuries of exploration did not yield any evidence but the belief in some such *terra incognita* persisted. When it was discovered accidentally at the end of the 16th century explorers were unaware that this was the continent they had looked for (Leitner 2006, 2009). It was finally known at the turn to the 18th century. New Holland, the south-east, was claimed for Britain by James Cook in 1776. The wider region was known as *Austral-Asia*, which included New Guinea, New Zealand and Melanesia. The region in the north was the *East Indies*. Though a geo-political term, Austral-Asia was common in book titles. The timeline below has some important dates.

Timeline 5: Australia and New Zealand

1768–79	Captain Cook's voyages to South Pacific, incl. Australia and New Zealand
1778	First Fleet, setting up New South Wales as a convict colony; other territories claimed were Victoria, Tasmania, Norfolk Island
1836	Foundation of South Australia
1840	New Zealand; Treaty of Waitangi turning NZ into a colony
1850s	Gold rushes and end of convictism in Australia
1901	Foundation of the Commonwealth of Australia

1907	Dominion status of New Zealand; independence in 1947
1973	Great Britain joins European Union, leading to Australia and New Zealand to redefine their geo-political position in Asia
1976	Referendum on Aboriginal citizenship; Land Rights' Act
2008	"Sorry Speech" by the former Australian Prime Minister Kevin Rudd, apology to Aboriginal peoples

Like North America, Australia and New Zealand were settler colonies, though there were whalers and sealers before settlement. Native populations were subjected to extensive repression that decimated their numbers within decades. Both nations have maintained strong ties with Great Britain even though they gained full or *de facto* independence during the first decades of the 20th century. They have shifted their geo-political orientation to South-East and East Asia after Britain's entry into the European Economic Community. Today they see themselves as middle powers in world affairs.

This chapter will embed the development of local varieties within the broad geo-political history and illustrate the variety of Australian and New Zealand English.

The story of English in Australia and New Zealand

No one would mistake an Australian for an American, said the Australian amateur linguist Sidney Baker in the 1940s. The acute listener will detect the [z] for "zz" in words like *mozzies* 'mosquitoes' or *prezzies* 'presents'. If someone has "kangaroos in the paddock" he is somewhat mad. No one would see such colloquial expressions as an obstacle to communication, two American observers, Greenough and Kittredge said in 1902: "The slang of the United States differs in many particulars from that of Great Britain ... Yet the lively intercourse of trade and travel, the newspapers ... and the 'dialect sketch' have kept the different English-speaking peoples tolerably familiar with one another's latest coinages." (*see* Leitner 2004a: 93) Australian English expresses an identity of its own, New Zealand English does to a lesser extent.

It is best to divide the story of Australian and New Zealand English into three periods. The first ranges from the beginning of settlement to the formation of the Commonwealth of Australia or, in the case of New Zealand, to the end of World War I, when it could start to act as an independent nation. The second period goes from there to the end of World War II when both countries became targets of massive waves of immigration and had gained in national independence. The local varieties of English were widely seen as unavoidable. The last period covers the post-War period. One cannot fail to see some similarities with the growth of American English. The historical development of the two countries is not entirely parallel. In general New Zealand lags behind by a generation; it also retained ties with Britain for a longer period. That must be borne in mind.

A stable base of Australian English emerged by the 1840s. The varieties transplanted had developed away from their formative input. It was seen as Australian, though it had a very low prestige inside and outside the country. What struck most was the accent, which was likened to London's working class Cockney. There were long lists of convict jargon, of slang and, at best non-standard English. Logically, one looked to the mother country for guidance on what was 'good' English. That exo-normative attitude seems to have been ineradicable and could still be seen in the 1970s (Leitner 2004a). The norm of pronunciation was Received Pronunciation and in lexis and grammar it was Standard British English. Despite that perception, the strength of the 'base' persisted and ensured that, when migration gave rise to a second accent by the 1860s, it was close enough to what now could be called 'broad'. For a number of reasons a third accent, the 'cultivated', emerged by the 1880s when education became obligatory and when socio-political infrastructure formed in the advent of Australia's nationhood. New Zealand was lagging behind. The dialect, i.e., the lexis and grammar, too departed from the British model, but they did so mainly in the colloquial domain, in speech and at the lower end of the social spectrum. It was, after all, developed by a convict population, settlers and administrative personnel that came from the lower middle classes at best. A shift in the social composition of migrations from the 1860s produced the general accent and ensured that the dialect at the upper level of society, in bureaucracy and the public domain in general followed the path of British English.

The second period up to World War II saw a greater awareness and acceptance of the local variety as the genuine sound of the Antipodes. Australian English had replaced Cockney in the depiction of local characters in poetry and fiction at the end of the 19th century. Though an educated level, the cultivated accent was emerging, it went unnoticed and the perception of Australian English continued to be negative. A new phase was heralded in when Sidney Baker, an Australian amateur linguist, published his book *The Australian Language* (1945). The nationalist tenor of this book provoked controversy. Alexander Mitchell, a London trained phonetician, propagated a version of the cultivated accent in the 1950s that hardly departed from the Received Pronunciation. Australian English, he argued, should not depart much from British English as that might endanger its intelligibility (Leitner 2004a). The double perception of English in Australia as broad and cultivated was firmly placed on the cards.

The third period saw the slow acceptance of the cultivated accent in the public domain. A particular angle was that many words could not be pronounced other than in an Australian way. That was particulary obvious with place and personal names. Educated or standard English, too, incorporated a number of low level Australian usages. Australian English was also beginning to be codified in dictionaries and usage manuals. By the end of the century it was the sole target of teaching English as a native language. Australian English has become a full epicentre with some outreach into the Asian sphere. New Zealand, too, has reached that stage.

What is worth adding is that Australia and, to a lesser extent, New Zealand have defined themselves in relation to their varieties of English (Leitner 2004a). The double self-perception that I alluded to above was especially stereotyped in Australia and used as an asset in cultural politics inside and outside the country. It was typified, for instance, in the film *Crocodile Dundee* (1986) that features the broad, little educated, rural character. *G'd day mate* 'hello' or *fair dinkum* 'true, genuine' are widely known examples. The image that such expressions convey is well-known. Australian English is well liked abroad and seen as pleasing, for instance, by most Americans, as a study on foreign attitudes on Australia before and after the Olympics in 2000 has revealed:

"As a country of English speakers, Americans are fascinated, amused, and a bit confused by that 'funny' (male respondents) and 'cute' (female respondents) Aussie 'accent' … close to a quarter of all respondents … associated Australia with the unique accent of its inhabitants. The frequency of attention to Australian language was consistent … despite the fact that the US media also clearly enjoyed Aussie speak. … all media outlets provided frequent 'lessons' in Australian English, defining such diverse terms as barracking, pokies, flat white, going to Atlanta, schooner, perving, and footies for American audiences." (http://www.crctourism.com.au/wms/upload/Resources/bookshop/Rivenburgh_Olympics-foreignAttitudes.pdf)

Nevertheless, the Australian Tourism Board is not alone in wanting to replace that cute but essentially questionable image by one that reflects modernity, diversity, and high 'world-class quality'. The linguistic expression of such an image would be a flexible standard of Australian English.

The broad and the standard allow Australia to project a double perception. The Malaysian *Star* carried an interview with the former Prime Minister Kevin Rudd on his first visit to Malaysia that illustrates this ambiguity. Its headline was "Malaysia has found a new mate down-under" (17 July 2008). The colloquialisms *mate* and *down-under* count as linguistic icons. The interview itself did not have a trace of informality and was in Standard English. Instead of suppressing the broad, Australia propagates the two varieties to present itself as down-to-earth, friendly, and yet competent. A similar example is a headline that refers to the author who admitted he did not understand nor care about, cricket, a national sport: "Professor feels the *strine*". The word *strine* is a pun that could mean 'strain' as well as 'strine' – a jocular expression for an Australian play on words (*see below*).

The varieties of English in Australia and New Zealand share some characteristics with South Africa that derive from their settlement history. All three are sometimes called *Southern Hemisphere Englishes*. I will highlight it with history and detail. The centre of presentation is Australia (Leitner 2004a; 2009).

Features of Australian and New Zealand English

The strongest input into all varieties of Australian and New Zealand English came from the working class dialects of London and East Anglia. There were migrants from the north of England, Scotland, Ireland, and Wales but their influence was less pervasive. In Australia, for instance, the Irish influence came after the formative period of the accent. A Scottish influence is noticeable in New Zealand as the Scots created cohesive communities on the southern island, but not in Australia. Nevertheless, there are traces of non-south-eastern English in lexis, grammar, and pragmatics. I will now illustrate the breadth of Australia and New Zealand features and its sub-varieties.

Pronunciation

There is a well-known joke about Australian English. An Australian visitor arrives in London and takes a city taxi. The taxi driver asks when he arrived and gets the answer "I've only come here 'to die'". The onset of the vowel in (*to-*)*day* is shifted to a lower position, so that /ei/ sounds like [aɪ]. This pronunciation is similar to popular London or Cockney and makes the point that the input into the accents of Australian (and New Zealand) English came from south-eastern English. The influence from American English is noticeable, but limited, that of contact with Aboriginal and Maori, and non-English migrant languages is nil.

Both varieties are noticeable by their vowels. The pronunciation of *(to-)day* as if it was *die* is part of a chain shift that affects the diphthongs in *late*, *light*, and *load* such that /ei/ shifts to [aɪ], /aɪ/ to [ɒɪ], and /əʊ/ to /æɪ/ (the slashes are used to signal the phonemic form of a word which is common to British English, while the angled brackets stand for what the phonemes sound like in Australian English). What this means is that words like *day* sound like *die*, *late* like *light*, while *light* sounds like (the non-existing word) *loit* (which one knows as a syllable in 'loitering').The greater the extent of the shift the broader the accent! There are concomitant changes that increase the broadness such as the lengthening of the onset or the nasalization of the vowel. Long and high monophthongs in *feed* and *food* participate in that shift and develop an onset that ranges from [ɪ] to a low [ə]. *Feed* may sounds approximately like [fəɪd] or [fəʊd]. Some linguists refer to this regular change as the Second Great Vowel Shift. An equally noticeable characteristic is that the short monophthongs in *bit*, *bet*, *bat*, or *pot* are articulated more closely. A foreigner may well mishear *bet* for *bit*. A bit of training will make sure one can identify an Australian accent. A third and more important feature is the pronunciation of *hut*. In Received Pronunciation this was a back vowel /ʌ/ but it has moved forward to a front position. In Australian (and New Zealand) English it is quite front or [a]. The reason why this is so interesting is that [a] can be heard as a short version of the long vowel in *chance*. If one were to change the transcription practices of /ʌ/ to a symbol that is more accurate phonetically, one might see that Australian and New Zealand English have a new pair of short and long vowel phonemes /a, a:/. The /ʌ/ in *hut* is re-classified. This reflects accurately what it means for a variety to become endo-normative: to develop rules of its own!

There are other characteristics worth mentioning such as the unaccented vowels in *effect*, *begin* or (*he*) *boxes*. They are pronounced as schwa [ə], rather than with [ɪ], as in (older forms of) Received Pronunciation. This shift leads to homophony as *effect* and *affect* and (*he*) *boxes* and (*the*) *boxers* sound the same. Modern forms of Received Pronunciation are gradually shifting the same way. Very noticeable is the speech melody (= intonation) in declarative sentences that really are assertions. A sentence like "I worked in a supermarket" can have a (high) rising pitch "I worked in a ´supermarket" and then sounds as if it were a question. But that cannot be the case. It is a statement. This feature emerged only some forty years ago and can also be found in Ulster English, many English and American accents. Its communicative effect is that statements do not sound as if the speaker is 'telling' something or 'talking down' to the addressee. The speaker sounds as if he was 'sharing' information.

An American influence can be found in the pronunciation of /t/ in words like *letter* or *continental*. It may be articulated as a flap [ɾ]. It is interesting that in Southern English accents and increasingly in Received Pronunciation /t/ tends to be replaced by a glottal stop [ʔ]. As the glottal stop signals working class associations and the flap a more classless, modern association there is an interesting conflict.

I have presented the two Antipodean accents as if they were very similar. Historically speaking, they have the same origin but increasingly New Zealand English takes a path of its own. Thus, the short /ɪ/ in, say, *fish* and *chips* shifts to [ə].

Words, word-formation, loans, etc.

Bloody was called the most typical swear word, though it occurs in all varieties worldwide, of course. It stands for the broad or non-standard image of Antipodean English. Words, word-formation and loans are the area that betrays the Australian and New Zealand character most clearly. I have already mentioned the word play called "strine". The underlying 'rules' or blueprints that it is based on are well illustrated in this comic speech in broad Australian English by Austen Tayshus:

7.1 Sitt*in'* at home last Sunday morn*in' me* mate *Boomer rang*. Said he was hav*in'* a few people around for a *barbie*, Said he might *cook a burra* or two. I said, "Sounds great, will *Walla by* there?" He said "Yeah and *Vege mite* come too". So I said to the wife "Do you *wanna Go anna*?" She said "I'll go if *Din gos*". (http://www.justsomelyrics.com/546229/Austin-Tayshus-Australiana-Lyrics)

Strine relies on the re-segmentation of words so they can mean something else, while retaining the original meaning as an association. Re-segmentation is most effective when Aboriginal loan words like *boomerang*, *wallaby*, *goanna* and *dingo* 'wild or domesticate dog' are used. It also occurs with names like the bread smear *vegemite*. Strine is naturally an art form that rests on mutual background and stands for the informality of the broad dialect and accent. It is not used much in colloquial conversation. The following video "Nobody likes a bogan" by Individuality Lyrics shows other features of non-standard English (http://www.youtube.com/watch?v=qA8gJoT5yl4):

7.2 Well he's the king of fashion in his neighb*or*hood
   With his ripped blue jeans and a flannelette shirt …
   His *mates* will all tell *ya* he's a *real* top bloke.
   His real name is Barry, but his mates call him *Bazza*
   and his girlfriend's name is Sharon, but *ya* call her
      Shazza …

Bogan is a word whose meaning is vague, contradictory even (http://en.wikipedia.org/wiki/Bogan). A *bogan* is typically a young male person who is not liked much by many; he is urban, fashionable, working class and easygoing. The lyrics explain he is "the king of fashion in the neighbourhood"; he is dressed informally, etc. The lyrics contain a series of colloquial expressions such as *real* as an adverb or *ya* 'you'. The inherent association with Australianness seems to go hand in hand with connotations of xenophobia, as in this example:

7.3 So let them, and the world, know we're not all insensitive pricks. Stop the boats? Nah. Stop the *bogans*. Speak up.

Formations like *Shazza* are not unknown in British English and other varieties but are comparatively frequent in Australian English. There are a variety of modifications of personal names to evoke some emotion in English. *Tony*, formerly from 'Anthony', is abbreviated (or 'clipped') as 'Tone'. But complex formation as *Maz* 'Mary', *Baz* 'Barry' or 'Basil', *Shaz*, *Shazza*, or *Shazzer* 'Sharon' or

Caz 'Caroline' or 'Carolyn'(*see* 7.4) are different. (The "z" is always pronounced as [z].) Here is another example:

7.4 "My cat died on New Year's Day. I got home from work and mum stopped me in the hall, grabbed my hands and looked into my eyes. '*Caz*, I've got bad news.'... 'Tina died today.'" (*The Age*, 23 Dec 2001)

Names like *Caz* express, some experts say, contradictory emotions. The person referred to is admired and seen as tough ('you can do this') and are called 'depreciatives', an emotional stunt.

While not unknown elsewhere, Australian English is famous for words that end in *-i/-ie/-y* and *-o* like *Barbie* or *compo* in this headline on an ABC News programme (31 Aug 2009): "Apology to abused 'won't help compo claims'". *Compo* means 'compensation', for the wrongs done to Aborigines up to the late 1960s.

Particularly interesting are items that are due to language contact. The most famous ballad "Waltzing Matilda" is a good starting point, but there are other examples:

7.5 Once a jolly swagman camped by a *billabong*
    Under the shade of a *coolibah tree*
    And he sang as he watched and waited till his *billy* boiled
    You'll come *a-waltzing* Matilda with me

7.6 "Two men were stabbed and died while drinking with friends ...
    Mr Dixon said he knew *white law* did not allow *payback spearing* of the accused. Immediately after the deaths, hundreds of relatives and friends arrived ... at Laramba to attend *sorry camp*, a period of group grieving staged

over several days and nights." (*Northern Territory News*, 2 Jan 2010)

There is not a large number of Aboriginal loans in Australian English but they are highly symbolic of the nature of cultural contact, a symbolism that may also be due to the ill-feeling about their persistent mistreatment. Some have made it into the common core of English and most languages of the world: *boomerang*, *kangaroo*, *didgeridoo*, *koala*, etc. Many have remained confined to Australian English such as *billabong* 'small lake' or *coolibah* 'eucalyptus tree'. The famous *swag* 'itinerant worker' was alleged to have stolen a *jumbuck* 'young sheep', a word that comes from the Aboriginal creole. Most loans refer to fauna, flora, material culture and only a few to social practices like *corroboree* 'religious dance'. Recently some such words have been borrowed in an effort to understand Aboriginal mythology or religious beliefs (Leitner 2007). The word *cooee* 'a shout or call to attract attention' has become a colloquialism in rural Australian English. The expression *be within cooee* means something like 'be in hearing distance' or 'be close'.

Some Aboriginal concepts have been translated into English or been formed in English, which is the dominant pattern today. *Dreaming*, for instance, illustrates loan translation, *women's business* 'secret knowledge confined to (some) women' the other. Words like these are open to deliberate misinterpretation and trivialization. There is a number of 'common' words in both Aboriginal and white English to refer to each other or the colonial hierarchy. *Master*, *blackfellow* and *whitefellow* (with multiple spelling variants) are some of the prominent ones. *Blackfellow* cannot be used by white people and *whitefellow* would not be used, but is used by Aborigines. The social conventions are quite serious, but hidden to the outsider.

There are many more native or Maori words in New Zealand English than Aboriginal ones in Australian English. I will just mention *Pakeha* 'New Zealander of non-Maori descent', *Aotearea* 'New Zealand', *kiwi* 'a bird that is active at night', or *haka* 'a traditional dance'. As in Australia, the majority of words come from fauna and flora, and topography, but there are others related to cultural practices. Some are deeply embedded in New Zealand. *The Kiwi* is the name of the national New Zealand rugby league team.

Grammar

Until not so long ago there was a consensus that Australian English was barely distinctive at the level of grammar. What there might be would be found in broad or nonstandard speech. Here are some statements from widely acclaimed experts (*see* Leitner 2004a: 135ff):

"At the level of educated speech and writing, there are very few obvious grammatical differences between Aus-Eng and EngEng. It is, for example, usually not possible to tell if a text has been written by an English or Australian writer." (Trudgill/Hannah, 2008: 19)

"Australian English is undoubtedly the dominant form of English in the Antipodes and by reason of Australia's increased wealth, population, and influence in the world affairs, this national standard (though still by no means fully institutionalized) is exerting an influence in the northern hemisphere, particularly in Britain. Much of what is distinctive in Australian English is confined to familiar use. This is especially so of grammatical features like adverbial *but* or the use of the feminine pronoun both anaphorically for an inanimate noun (*job … her*)." (Quirk *et al.*, 1985: 21)

I have quoted these statements at some length as they have also been made about New Zealand English and many other varieties of English. The statements by Trudgill/Hannah (2008) and Quirk *et al.* (1985) are somewhat outdated but can still be found. They are often made by looking at Australian English from without. In the 1960s Robert Eagleson, an Australian scholar, had labelled them an obstacle to genuine empirical research (*see* Leitner 2004a). He called for detailed empirical research, which is now done. Yet differences are still typically found in speech and are stated in terms of observed frequencies rather than significant general rules. Collective nouns, for instance, tend to have plural concord in standard British English but singular in mainstream Australian English:

7.7 The government at the same time *are* also not, *is* also not …

There is change in the use of *who* and *whom*. It has been found that *whom* is commonly replaced by *who* when a preposition precedes it, as in 7.8 and 7.9:

7.8 and who's sensitive *to who* (Leitner 2004).
7.9 "It was a distinctive tribute to the guts and determination of a small number, *many of who* had little interest in the issues and *some of who* might as easily have been on the other side …" (*The Canberra Times*, 15 Apr 1992, p. 2, F. Cronston on "Malta's unique flag …")

The phrase *mob of* 'many' is frequent in newspaper usage but quite rare in British English: ·

7.10 There's *a mob of* islands in the area ... (Leitner 2004).
7.11 "Yeah, when people write to me, Chris, and say things like uh 'we're losing our language' and stuff but when you say things like 'mobs of trees' and stuff I think it's still pretty safe, isn't it." (Leitner 2004)

A pattern that Australian English shares with Scottish, Irish and American English is the use of definite articles with nouns that refer to institutions, sports, days of the week and the like:

7.12 ... *the Parliament* itself doesn't have a great influence (Leitner 2004).
7.13 I've been down with *the flue* (Leitner 2004).
7.14 "he was sentenced ... to be confined to six months in *the jail*" (Governor King to Lord Hobart, *Historical Records of Australia*, vol. 3, 1801–03, p. 584).

Australian English is also similar to American, Scottish, Irish English and other (northern) varieties in that *of* can be missing after verbs like *look out*:

7.15 ... looking out my window and I have the most beautiful view through the window.
7.16 I'm going out the paddock (Leitner 2004).

Turning to the present perfect, we find contrasts with standard British English. It is increasingly used with adverbials of time that locate an event in the past:

7.17 "He *has* now *met* with Ayres this morning" (96 FM Radio, Perth; afternoon news, 24 Aug 1999).

7.18 "Police confirm that at 16.30 hours yesterday the body of Ivan Jepp *has been located*" (92.6 FM Radio, Perth; news, 17 March 2000).

7.19 "Between the arrival of migrants in Cohort 1 and those in Cohort 2, migrants … *have been excluded* from access to social welfare payments for a period of two years after arrival." (*quoted from* Leitner 2004b: 139)

Style, colloquialisms, slang

The double perspective of Australian and, to a lesser degree, New Zealand English was mentioned at the beginning of this chapter. I will now show how the two can mix in public discourse. Both varieties are known for their lack of formality and for their ease of 'dipping into' a colloquial style and slang. In the first example the interviewee, the chief executive of a large company, encourages Australians to spend more money. In the second one a judge offends a young defendant (Leitner 2004: 241):

7.20 "Australians should be '*as happy as pigs in shit*' with low unemployment and a resources boom, but instead they're scared to spend money, retail king Gerry Harvey says." (*Sydney Morning Herald*, 30 Sep 2011)

7.21 [Judge to a defendant at Magistrate Court in Adelaide] "You're a *druggie* and you'll die in the gutter … I don't believe in the *social worker crap* … I'm sick of you *sucking us dry* … *We dicks* pay for your life. It's your choice to be a *junkie* and die in the gutter. No one *gives a shit* …" (*The Australian*, 2 May 2003, "Magistrate condemned for abuse")

Offensive speech could be cited abundantly but there is also a fair amount of colourful colloquiality, as in these examples:

7.22 "In all his shouted, grinning pronouncements about the program that has killed four installers ..., Garrett resorts to impersonal lawyerly gobbledygook. That's when he's not pretending to have more urgent business inspecting angle-headed geckos in national parks. When asked why he went bush this week, instead of attending a meeting ..., Garrett glibly replied: 'I don't go to technical experts' meetings in the normal course of events – my officials go to those meetings.'" (*Sydney Morning Herald*, 18 Feb 2010)

7.23 "The government has characterised the levy as a '*mateship tax*', equating public support for the measure with compassion for disaster-hit Queenslanders. Mr Abbott said taxing someone was the exact opposite of mateship. '*Mates help each other*; they *don't tax each other*,' he said. 'Mateship comes from people, it doesn't come from governments. Mateship is what people choose to do, it's not what they are forced to do.'" (*The Australian*, 23 Feb 2011)

The colloquial nature of Antipodean English extends into the ways people interact with one another or, to use the technical term, into pragmatics. The level of respect or social distance can be quite small amongst Australian speakers – not with outsiders though. Farewell congratulations such as "You've cut yourself a pleasant career" might be seen as somewhat offensive, out of place at a formal and public event. But such interchanges are common when interlocutors know each other reasonably well and have respect for each other. The public conventions permit that, just like they permit offensive language. A politician was once quoted as threatening a female journalist by saying "I'll screw your tits off if you report that" (*from* Leitner 2004). These rules of linguistic behaviour are almost inaccessible and such utterances are better avoided by foreigners.

Ethnicity: Aboriginal English and Kriol

For most people who spend only short periods of time in Australian cities Aborigines may be a theme in the press but nothing they encounter in real life. What they see is alcoholics, down and outs. That peripheral role does injustice to Aborigines, who, with all their well-known social problems, represent one of the oldest cultures in the world. It is important here to show the linguistic reflections of Aboriginality (*see* Leitner 2004b). To do that, I will use this passage from an Aboriginal hip-hop group:

7.24 Ha ha I'm back all with South West Syndicate so make your call
Slappin' high fives everywhere I go with my lyrical flow that I know, so –
Our nation of residence is getting hesitant
They can't do shit cos' they got no evidence
200 years of this bullshit us kooris have had enough …
Keep an eye on them drunks in the park
Time for us to raise up outta the dark …

South West Syndicate is quite a prominent pop group and these lyrics show the protest of Aborigines against the white domination. There is but one clearly Aboriginal word, *koori*, which refers to the Aboriginal people in the south-east of Australia, i.e., to Victoria, Tasmania and parts of New South Wales. There are other terms for Aborigines elsewhere such as *Murries* 'South Australia' or *Noongar* 'South-west Australia'. In general, the text uses common non-standard English such as "they can't do shit" "they can't do anything". *Shit* means 'nothing'. Some expressions clearly come from American English, e.g., "slappin' high fives" 'a greeting'. The expression *our nation of residence* is a sarcastic reference to Australia.

Here are some more contemporary words. *Brothers* or *bros* means 'fellow Aborigines', *black fuckers* is a non-deferential expression for 'black people' (*fucker* is often used in extreme slang for 'person') that could only be used by Aborigines themselves.

8 Asia

Some of the the most populous countries in the world such as India, China, Indonesia and the Philippines are located in Asia. English plays a significant role in this large continent and the largest number of users of English comes from there. In a radio programme for the Australian Broadcasting Corporation in 2005 David Crystal referred to an Indian survey that allegedly found that "about a third of the population had the ability to carry out a conversation in English." He supposes the figure to have risen to more than 350 million in a population of some 1.2 billion inhabitants (according to 2011 Census). Some 65 per cent of 90 million Indonesians are said to know some English. English is the number one foreign language. China has some 1.3 billion inhabitants and, Crystal says, up to half the population know some English (*see* Schneider 2011: 180). There are large numbers of users in Japan and Korea. Estimates like Crystal's have been circulated widely though their basis has never been made explicit. Crystal does not reveal whether levels of competence, especially in speech play a role in defining 'knowing English'. He ignores the attrition rate of learners when English is barely used, as in China. One cannot escape the impression that such estimates are motivated politically and commercially. This becomes clear if one reads, in the context of the Philippines, that the 1980 Census estimated that 65 per cent of the population had some ability in English, which ranges "from a smattering of words and phrases through passive comprehension to near-native mastery" (McArthur 1998b). Experiences in China show that such estimates are vastly inflated. It is unlikely that the growth of English has outstripped the population growth in Indian in 30 years. The figures for

China imply a growth from almost zero in the 1990s to 600 million today. But any estimate would have impressive figures. It is clear that the majority of users of English come from Asia and that most publications such as books and newspapers are of Asian origin.

Britain's involvement is a part of a long history of European contact with Asia (Grataloup 2007). Ignoring privateers who fought against the supremacy of Portugal in Asia, contact began in the 17th century. It was spurned by England's desire to participate in the spice trade that Portugal and, somewhat later, the Netherlands had managed to engage in.

Timeline 6: Asia

1600	Foundation of East India Company (with Royal Charter)
1600	First trading post in Surat (Gujarat) in 1612; later in Madras (1639), Bombay (1668), and Calcutta (1690)
1711	China (Guangzhou) (e. g. Hirado, 1613)
1757	Acquisition of Bengal from France
1786	Acquisition of Penang (Fort Conwallis); Malacca (1795)
1819	Raffles' trading post in Singapore under East India Company
1826	Straits Settlement linking Singapore, Malacca and Penang
1830s	East India Company has political power over Straits Settlement
1835	Macaulay's "Minute on Education", essential to the Anglicist-Orientalist debate on the role of English
1857	Indian Rebellion; India becomes a Crown Colony

1885   Foundation of Indian Congress; Muslim League
        (1906)
1947   Indian Independence, separation of Pakistan
1963   Federation of Malaysia (incl. Eastern Malaysia, not
        Singapore)
1971   Bangladesh leaves Pakistan

Before I turn to the three regions, South, South-East and
East Asia, it may be good to add a note on the Middle
East and to make five generalizations. The Middle East is
a part of Asia geographically, but was a hub in the west of
a commercial network that extended from China to East
Africa up to the 16th century. The British East India Company opened up some *factories* in the Middle East and
Britain engaged in diplomatic contacts with Oman in
1800. After the collapse of the Osmanic Empire in 1918
Britain (and France) acquired protectorates over some of
its former parts, including Egypt. While that gives some
ancestry to English, the important period begins after
World War II. But Islam and Arabic were instrumental in
forming an Arabic-Islamic bond to as far as Morocco and
the Western Sahara in the west and to as far as Indonesia,
where Arabic is a restricted religious language. Any dis-
cussion of the role of English must therefore include Arabic and, by implication, this vast geo-political area (*see*
Al-Issa/Dohan 2011). That cannot be achieved here, but
passing remarks will be made here and there.

The first general remark is that the spread of English in
Asia began with trade colonialism, but that its active use
only reached a level worth mentioning when the Company and Britain assumed a political role around the middle
of the 18th century. We will talk about its Indianization later. Its current standing, in contrast, is mainly owed to its
position as a world language, not to the colonial heritage.

The second generalization is that former colonies (unlike non-colonies) are caught in a linguistic dilemma. How are they to go about their linguistic heritage, i. e., the localized varieties when a globalizing world demands internationally viable varieties of English? The third one is that colonialism has had repercussions beyond the colonies. Kirkpatrick reports that the Thai King Rama IV was keen to modernize the country and encouraged the learning of English so as to access Western learning (2010: 48ff). Initiatives like these have had no sustained effect, of course, but they show the positive reaction to English during the 19th century and help understand why the local demand for English should have grown in real colonies like India. Up to the late 18th century British administrators often used local or contact languages such as a Portuguese or a Malayan pidgin. In today's Pakistan, to give one example, the British used Urdu and Sanskrit. The use of English was increasing at the end of the 18th century. By the late 19th century English had definitely become the language of the political opposition to Britain. Colonialism was thus the driving force in much of Asia that led to second language varieties in India or Singapore. It also led to (defunct) contact varieties in East Asia (like it did in some parts of the Middle East). However, its current growth is due to quite conflicting historical circumstances that merge in the period of globalization. In Japan, Korea and some other areas it was driven by the security needs during the Cold War period. In China it was promoted after Mao Tse Tung's death and the phase when the country opened itself up to the world. In Hong Kong it was a perpetuation of its old colonial standing.

The fourth generalization is that English is deeply embedded in multilingual languages habitats in most of Asia. Kirkpatrick says "the majority of speakers are multilinguals who have learned English as a second or later language. They use English as a common language with fellow multilinguals. This lingua franca use of English is prevalent throughout … the Association of Southeast Asian nations." (2010: xi). The *lingua franca* function cuts across the status of English as second, foreign, and native language and increases the conflict about the colonial heritage in young populations. Middle class parents invest heavily in the future prospects of their children, as English is the icon of participation in a never-before-seen social transformation process in modernization. Nation-building, globalization and regional bodies are making significant communicative demands to keep a balance between traditions, the linguistic heritage and the need of modernization.

The last point is that English in Asia has two different sources, which overlap regionally. The dominant one is British English in South and South-East Asia. The other one is American English, which predominates in the Philippines and the North Pacific. Both overlap in China, Korea and Japan. American English is the preferred choice in business and banking, amongst adults and university students, and amongst those who expose themselves to popular culture. There is a layer above intra-national communication which is supported by businesses, large regional and global institutions mentioned earlier. It is here that English as a *lingua franca* has such an important role.

Closely related is the fact that English has become the language of many domains such as the sciences, technologies, international communication, etc., and plays an increasing role in creative writing. The lively literary world of India is well-known. There is a growing literature in English in Malaysia and Singapore and, most interestingly, in former non-colonies such as Thailand and China. English is the language to articulate national and Asian voices.

I will focus on India, Singapore, Malaysia and the Philippines. Pakistan, Bangladesh and Hong Kong are mentioned in passing (Kirkpatrick 2010). China and Japan are included as they challenge Kachru's classification of native, second and foreign language.

South Asia: India and Pakistan

The beginning of English in South Asia goes back to 1600 (*see* Timeline 6), when the East India Company was granted a trade monopoly to and from Asia. From a cultural angle one cannot reduce the story to the implantation of English after 1600. It is well-known that the tomb of St Thomas is supposed to be in Chennai, former Madras, and that the West Saxon King Alfred the Great is reported to have sent an emissary there (Bragg 2003: 250). There were trading relations since the Middle Ages and ample scope for words to be transported from India into Europe's languages. Words like *bungalow*, *dungaree*, *polo*, *jungle* and *swastika* have made it into English. From a commercial angle India was no more than "a launch pad" during the first decades after 1600, as Bragg (2003: 251) put it.

The story of English in the region

The relevant story of English in South Asia can be divided into three periods (Leitner 2009). The first one extends from 1600 to 1857, when India became a Crown Colony. English started out as the language of the Company and their staff (*Anglo-Indian English*) and slowly became the language of the Indian elite (*Indo-Anglian English*). The second period reaches to Independence in 1947. It is characterized by the process of enforcing English, a British education system and institutions but is also marked by the growth of an Anglophone Indian opposition that is connected with names like Mahatma Gandhi, Jawaharlal Nehru and others. The third period covers independence and the language policies in nation-building. Though choices had been made to manage the high level of multilingualism nation-wide, English continues to play a crucial role.

The beginning was, as I have said, purely commercial. Like the Dutch East India Company before, the English East India Company established trading posts along the coastline from India to China and Japan and participated in a trade network within Asia and with Europe. While the Company had trading posts in the entire region, its main interest was the Indian sub-continent. Towards the 19th century its interests expanded to the Burma and the Malayan Peninsuala and Borneo. Turning to India, the Company had trading posts in Madras, Bombay and Surat at the end of the 17th century. A significant transformation took place when the Company chose Kolkata, formerly called Calcutta, as its administration centre in 1690. A further transformation took place in 1763, when the Company gained political control over West Bengal. Great Britain was now increasingly confronted with questions about the objectives of its colonial empire and various forces slowly pushed it into a policy of strict Anglicization. A debate between the so-called Orientalists and the Anglicists that had begun in the 1790s was resolved. The Orientalists had advocated restraint and the support of local languages, i.e., Sanskrit and Persian, local education, and the respect for religions, the Anglicists had called for the imposition of English, an English education system and the propagation of Christianity. The repercussions of this debate were felt in all colonies from Australia to South Africa.

Though the Anglicists had won the debate, there were financial constraints. An Anglophone education system for the masses of India was out of reach and undesirable. Decisions had to be taken and what became the consensus is spelt out in this excerpt from the so-called "Minute" (1835) by Thomas Macaulay, a prominent politician and member of various bodies to do with India:

> "… it is impossible for us, with our limited means, to attempt to educate the body of the people. We must at present do our best to form a class who may be interpreters between us and the millions whom we govern, – a class of persons Indian in blood and colour, but English in tastes, in opinions, in morals and in intellect. To that class we may leave it to refine the vernacular dialects of the country, to enrich those dialects with terms of science borrowed from the Western nomenclature, and to render them by degrees fit vehicles for conveying knowledge to the great mass of the population." (http://www.mssu.edu/projectsouthasia/ history/primarydocs/education/Macaulay001.htm)

That formed the foundation stone of education reforms after 1835. While that view might be comprehensible, it was Macaulay's disdain of Indian cultures and languages that has made him more than a controversial figure. He wrote this:

> "I have conversed, both here and at home, with men distinguished by their proficiency in the Eastern tongues. … I have never found one among them who could deny that a

single shelf of a good European library was worth the whole native literature of India and Arabia." (*ibid.*)

This view was widely accepted within a political climate of the Industrial Revolution that emphasized solely economic gain. English was seen as the door to access European knowledge.

English had been used for decades by those Indians who had been in contact with missionaries, had worked in households and similar occupations, been the company's employees or been involved in other contexts with the British administration. An old contact language, an expanded pidgin, which was known as, for instance, *Butler English*, was being replaced or supplanted by a learner English, as more and more Indians acquired English at school. It Indianized within decades and developed into what is known as *Indo-Anglian*, a name given to contrast with the *Anglo-Indian*, the variety of English developed by British expatriates. Attitudes towards English fluctuated after independence. Many saw it as an imposed colonial heritage that should be abolished as soon as possible. Others thought of it as an unavoidable means of inter-Indian communication and, ultimately, an asset. Here is a typical statement from the late 19th century·

"The defeatism of wearing the chains of English – which is more foreign to us in its essence than Chinese and even French – has to be thrown out of our mentality" (Melchers/ Shaw 2003: 135).

All leaders of the opposition, i.e., the Indian Congress and, somewhat later, the Muslim League, opposed English. But they expressed their demands through English. Gandhi's success would be inexplicable without English and, one should add, telegraphy. English not only stayed on but deepened its roots in the political culture.

The third, the independence period thus inherited a dilemma. The Indian constitution stated that English was to be abolished within fifteen years at the level of the Union of India. The period was extended and, for a variety of reasons, English was maintained at Union level as one of three official languages. To overcome a series of language riots, the state structure of India was re-drawn and the so-called "Three-Languages Formula" agreed upon. It stipulated that Hindi, English and a South Indian language will operate at the federal level and that states could decide themselves what languages to use internally. Only Kerala in South India abolished English (Leitner 2009). That formula is still consensual, but English is now widely accepted as an asset.

David Crystal believes that Indian English is one of the most powerful varieties of English worldwide today. Its advance since the 1980s was indeed spectacular. Next to the USA, e. g., India is the major book-publishing country in English. Its film industry is renowned and influential even in English.

An important condition to become independent in 1947 was that India agreed to the division of India and Pakistan (both East and West). Bangladesh separated from Pakistan in 1971. Many of these modern nations had been under British control late so that the implantation and the depth of English were recent. Sindh in Pakistan, for instance, was annexed as late as 1849 and Punjab in 1879. These regions were much larger than today. Bengal, whose eastern part is now Bangladesh, was made a Presidency as early as at the end of the 18th century. Frictions between Hindus and Moslems in the east led the British government to divide the country into two provinces in 1905.

Features of Indian English

"What is your good name Sir?" is a polite question at hotel receptions and formal meetings. "Can I leave now Sir?" is a polite way of closing a conversation. A somewhat older form is "Have I your permission to leave, Sir?" Indian English is a medium of expression in fiction and poetry and I will quote from the poem "The Patriot" by one of the major Indian poets, Nissim Ezekiel:

8.1　All men are brothers, *no*?
　　　In India *also*
　　　Gujaratis, Maharashtrians, Hindi*wallahs*
　　　All brothers –
　　　Though some *are having* funny habits.
　　　Still, you tolerate me,
　　　I tolerate you,
　　　One day Ram Rajya is surely coming.

The poem is about the tolerance of Indians despite major cultural differences, the *funny habits*. Sandeep Thorat (2009) writes that "Tolerance of diversity is an essential feature of Indianness ... At the same time, Indians are also given to making fun of others' habits, including food, dress, manner of speaking, music, and so on ... And so, Nissim must make a statement: 'Though some are having funny habits.' If this statement is not included, one can surely state that the poet's assertions are not truthful." The Indianness is not only in the message but in the language that portrays Indian communities "Ezekiel very artistically reflects the Indian attitude towards Indian national integration", Thorat says. There are a number of (italicized) features that illustrate the Indianness of the language. The tag *no* in the first line would be a tag question like "aren't

they", if this were British English. There is *also* that serves
to highlight the message. The progressive *having* would be
replaced by the simple present tense, etc.

A variety that has gained such a high literary profile
must have reached the stage of self-determination, of endo-normativity, and be an epi-centre of English similar to
American and British English. To illustrate the scope of
Indian English, this passage from *Baumgartner's Bombay*
(1987), a novel by Anita Desai, shows the pidgin English
that can be found abundantly:

8.2 "Eventually a woman appeared, seemingly from the
cracks of the floor above, sidling down the staircase, ad-
justing her hair and her cotton garments as she did so,
with a wet, dripping hand.
    '*Wanting room*?' She screamed at Baumgartner …
'One upstairs – *room fourteen free*.' Following her up the
wooden stairs, Baumgartner cleared his throat again, this
time to ask, hesitantly, '*This Taj* Hotel?'
    She turned upon him like a jungle cat, spitting. 'Yaiss,'
she screamed, '*this Taj* Hotel. Why not Taj Hotel, *heh*?
Only one can be Taj Hotel? Ten, twenty Taj Hotels in
Bombay – no one can tell me *this no Taj* Hotel, this Bombay Hotel, Goa Hotel, Hindu Hotel, *I no listen*!' she
screamed. 'I say Taj Hotel, then *this* Taj Hotel,' and she
marched on down the dark passage to a door at the end
that she flung open. 'Wanting?' she challenged him, cross-
ing her arms to wait for an answer." (Desai 1988: 84f)

There is no subject, the progressive is used in "Wanting
room", the verb *be* is deleted in "room fourteen free" and
in "This Taj Hotel". The negation in "I no listen" is
placed before the verb. Clearly, the basilect or pidgin differs vastly from the literary acrolect in Nissim's poem.

The survey that follows will largely focus on what could be called Standard Indian English.

Pronunciation

Given the long history of English in the country, one can be sure to find a fairly stabilized variety of pronunciation. One will also expect regional differences that are tied to particular languages. One will indeed find that Bengal shows interference effects that differ from those of Hindi and other languages. But as English is widely learnt in school, one may see it as an effect of teaching. It is interesting also that there is still no comprehensive description of Indian English – clear sign of the negative perception of localized English.

The pronunciation of Indian English varies considerably in relation to the level of competence and exposure. A pidgin was used up to the mid-20th century. The variety that forms the centre of the description is the English of educated speakers in relevant domains such as (higher) education, business or administration. Even here one will find considerable variation and clear characteristics of Indian English.

The vowel system is considerably reduced. Unlike other varieties that we have discussed (e. g., Scottish English) or will turn to (e. g., South-East Asia), vowels can be long and short. The vowels in words like *bath* or *goose* are /ɑː/ and /uː/ respectively. The rising diphthongs in Received Pronunciation are long monophthongs /eː/ and /oː/, while the vowel in *price* is /aɪ/. As most varieties of Indian English are non-rhotic, there are diphthongs that end in schwa (= centring diphthongs) or /ɪə, eə/. There is a considerable amount of variation that must be ignored. To just give two examples, *near* could be pronounced as [eə], *square* as [æ]. Unstressed vowels can be reduced as in *horses* (where it represents part of the plural ending). But a word like *comma* is unreduced and has /a/.

Turning to consonants, the complexity of Indo-Aryan and Dravidian languages – the dominant language families in India – makes itself felt. Readers should recall the difference in the stops in *potato*, where /t/ in *-ta-* carries considerable aspiration (= puff of air) as it is stressed, while *po-* and *-to* hardly show any. Indian languages have a phonemic distinction between aspiration and non-aspirated consonants. There is also what is called retroflex /t/, similar to some articulations of /r/ in American English. Words like *London* or *certificate* give away a distinct Indian flavour.

The greatest difficulties may arise because words are stressed differently. A word like *development* comes out as 'dev*lop*, where the first syllable is stressed and the one that would carry the stress in British English is lost. The absence of the reduced vowel in *-lop* creates an additional problem. Often words are stressed on the first syllables such as 'animation, 'dramatic or 'terrific. Add to this that *-ation* has /e/, but *-atic* has /ə/ and the "t" in *-atic* and *terrific* are retroflex, one can guess that the accumulation of differences produces problems of intelligibility to a non-native European speaker.

Comprehension problems increase because Indians do not use the kind of speech melody or intonation as in British English. Loudness is often used to express meaning. The result may be that Indians are seen to sound aggressive, which is not what is done in Indian English.

To briefly turn to regional differences, Bengali English may replace /s/ and /z/ in *sit* and *breeze* by "sh" or /ʃ/ and "dg" or /dʒ/. The result is this:

8.3 "The Bengalis like to 'shit outside' in the cool 'bridge'."
(*from* "Flavors of Indian English: Hindilish", http://www.
fortunecity.com/campus/books/845/heyyaar.htm)

Words, word-formation, loans, etc.

As in other varieties, the vocabulary reflects the history
and cultural embedding of English. Older words and meanings may have been retained but, at the same time, English
may have been altered creatively. On-going contact of
English with local languages has and will continue to have
an impact. The younger generation draws on American
English, which would make an interesting study of its own.
Some of these phenomena will now be illustrated.

Some older words have been retained but have undergone shifts of meaning and typically of connotations:

8.4 "Regarding a mosquito plague: 'The residents of the
nearby Nutan Nagar, a *colony* of seven residential build-
ings, are full of ire. ...' They don't *entertain my requests*."
(Cybernoon.com, 8 Jan 2001)
8.5 "The *travails* of passengers do not end here." (*Navhind
Times*, 8 Jan 2002)

The word *colony* refers to an apartment complex of some
size; access is typically controlled by a guard. To mention
a related common word in English, *station* too has a different meaning in Indian English. It refers to an office
(e.g., *be out of station* 'be away from one's office, work-
place'). In Australian English it refers to a farm, and to
many things in Anglo-American English. The following
passage from the same narration in 8.5 illustrates the formality of a complaint:

8.6 (a) I *recount* my experience of my *rail journey* as this.
(b) I *got* 5 berths *reserved* … for Ø self, wife, nephew and
two maid servants. … (c) The journey was to *commence*
on June 1. … (d) The *first trouble* we experienced was
that, there was no light in the compartment. (e) (i) The
second trouble started at the first *stoppage* at Kanpur,
(ii) when *unaccountable number* of *unreserved ticket-
holders* entered the compartment …

Indian English has often been characterized as being
enormously formal, often old-fashioned. The phrase "entertain my requests" in the speech of an expert in 8.4, the
verbs *recount* 'tell', *commence* 'begin', the adjective *unaccountable* 'large' and *unreserved ticket-holders* 'passengers with no reservation' in 8.6 are typical of a very formal register and show the desire of objectivity and precision. The passage departs significantly from British
usage. Sufferings of the passengers are described as *travails* in 8.5, which is a very strong word to describe work
that wears one out physically and mentally. It has acquired different connotations in Indian English. The opposite kind of semantic development can be seen in *mis-
hap*, which can describe very serious accidents, while it
refers to minor misfortunes in English. Such examples
represent, one might gather, an old-fashioned Indian
English that may come out of use with the younger generation. But the impression of informality is not the only
one. There are many colloquial expressions in spoken
English like "I'm damn busy" that leave the foreigner
perplexed. Are they offensive or merely colloquial?
Eve-teasing is an Indian, or perhaps a South Asian, expression that describes serious offenses and even crimes
against women in public. Here are two quasi-definitions
that reveal what it refers to:

8.7 "Short of rape, all these violations of women's persons and sensibilities are glossed, by Indian newspapers, under the quaint and even ludicrous label of '*eve-teasing*'." (*The Hindu*, 11 Apr 2004)

8.8 "*Eve teasing* is a complex social problem that will not vanish until the mindset is changed. Apart from law, it is also about education and respecting women." (http://www.eveteasing.org/eve-teasing-problem.html)

I will turn to loan expressions, but should say that, given a history of over 400 years, there will be thousands. Quite a few have entered the common core of English, while others have disappeared or become archaic. Some have been fully established and others, younger ones, may begin to characterize modern Indian English. The poem by Nissim contained the word *Hindiwallahs* (*see* p. 181). The second element can have several meanings but in general it refers to a person that is associated with some kind of activity. A *Hindiwallah* would be someone who promotes Hindi. Other examples can be found in Indian literature such as the short story *Breathless in Bombay* by Murzban F. Shroff (2008). The main character is a *malishwalla* 'a massage therapist'. A *ticket wallah* would be a 'sales assistant in book store', etc. *Wallah* is a very productive compound element whose origin is Hindi. Two other fully integrated words are *lakh* '10,000' and *crore* '10 million'. With the currency, the Indian rupee, large figures are very frequent in economic texts. (This is a good website on the Indian counting system: http://en.wikipedia.org/wiki/Indian_numbering_system.) The following passage has loans for festivities or institutions:

8.9 The autumnal blossoming of *shiuli* [official glower of West Bengal] and *kash* [reed-like plant with white

blooms], frenzied *puja* [Hindu ceremonial offering] *shopping* and Birendra Krishna Bhadra's magnificent *chandi-
paat* [a collection of ballads relevant to Hindus] on radio
– these convey the advent of the *Durga Puja* [Hindu festival to celebrate the goddess Durga]. When I was a child I
looked forward to it mainly because I got presents. In the
mofussil town [suburb; small country town] where I grew
up Durga was worshipped with a simple piety lacking in
Kolkata pujas [most famous ceremony].

But then Kolkata pujas are designed to be crowd-pull-
ers where each tries to rival the other in *pandal design*
[tent-like design imitating the tent that is used to house
the holy images for five days], the representation of
Durga and electric illumination. You may ask: "Haven't
we seen it all before?" Have we? Far from having a
sense of *déjà vu* I still look forward to it. I still *love to
hog* [to eat like a glutton] *the consecrated bhog* [usually
vegetarian food offerings] of delicious *kedgeree* [Indian
dish]. (*The Statesman News*, 11 Oct 2001)

8.10 For this purpose, the main focus will be on strengthen-
ing the newly elected *panchayats* [local councils] and related institutions at *Block and Zila level* [administrative
units] which combinedly comprise three-tier *panchayat
system* … (*Daily Excelsior*, 11 Oct 2001)

8.11 "Shyam's glance swept over the figures of his three
friends. Gopal's bright yellow *dhoti* [a man's cloth worn
round the waist] and *tikka* [oval mark on forehead to
mark caste], the *fez cap* [head cover typical for Muslims]
and Shehriyar's head and the *turban* [head cover typical
for Sikhs] worn by Gurdial [typical Sikh name] seemed
to mock at him. They seemed to be the symbols of all that
was odd, inferior, all that separated him from the sahibs
… [content] 'It's because of people like you!' Shyam's re-
sentment burst forth! 'You ancient, pre-historic people,

who *stick to your silly customs like leeches* [Indian meta-
phor]! ... It's because of you that they have bad impres-
sions of Indians.' Gopal ... tossed his *chutia* [pigtail]
proudly upwards. 'What's wrong with me?' he asked."
(S. Panandiker, I. Saxena, N. Sinha, 1990, *Together We
Marched*, Ministry of Information and Broadcasting,
Govt. of India: Publications Division, p. 31f)

Such texts show the deep embedding of Indian English in
the cultural and linguistic contexts or habitats of multilingual India. Loans are used to add authenticity, express
loyalty or connectedness, quite apart from the fact that
they are often used because there is no alternative or
none has been coined. In literature they project the flavour of Indian realities, especially when metaphors or
similes like "stick to s.th. like leeches" are used. Though
there is no large Indian English dictionary, smaller glossaries have appeared in abundance.

Grammar

There is a large number of differences from Anglo-American English in grammar. Given the lack of a grammatical
description of Indian English it is not clear what would
count as educated, spoken or written. The following examples are typical of educated Indian English.

The first one illustrates the extension of the progressive *are rushing* to situations where habitual actions are
referred to. Often it occurs with verbs of cognition, i.e.,
are liking, which would be ruled out in Anglo American
English. The simple present tense would be necessary
(*see* Chapter Two). Note again the use of *also* to foreground the communicative status of 'their wives'.

8.12 "Day by day our Jullundhar graduates *are rushing* to this
country and minting lakhs and lahks of rupees. They *stay*
in nice houses with 24-hour electricity and no load shed-
ding. They have running hot and cold water. They and
their wives *also are liking* to work. They enjoy all manner of comforts and amenities." (*from* Meyerhoff 2006)

The lack or 'false' insertion of articles is a major feature
of Indian English (and of other varieties). It was noted
above in "when Ø unaccountable number of …" (8.6).
The novel *Baumgartner's Bombay*, too, had examples
(*see* 8.2). The following excerpt from a crime story in *The
Times of India* uses the indefinite article *a* twice in interesting ways.

8.13 "The 33-year-old Amit Jogi was attacked when he was
going in *a* vehicle in a village, some 40–50 km away from
Madhya Pradesh's Jabalpur town. A mob, mainly of
youths armed with iron rods …, torched *a vehicle carrying Amit Jogi* …" (26 June 2011)

The first *a* is somewhat unexpected as one assumes the
vehicle was the man's own car. In (ii) it would have to be
replaced by *the*, because the vehicle is the same as in (i)
and because it is identified by "carrying Amit Jogi". The
example below is from the same paper and illustrates the
omission of the definite article (*see* Ø) and the expected
the in a running story. Such features are typical though
their origin, meaning and regularity are a matter of debate.

8.14 "The Mamata Banerjee government seems to be inching
towards Ø return of land *from* the disputed site in Sin-
gur, *even as* it fights a legal battle in Calcutta."

Even as is an emphatic marker which might translate as "wo es *doch*" in German.

At the end of this section I should add that English in India is deeply embedded in local and multilingual cultures and that Indians do not define their linguistic identity in any one language but as their ability to participate a multicultural society.

South-East Asia: Malaysia, Singapore, Philippines

South-East Asia consists of a continental part and thousands of islands that have experienced a succession of colonial powers. European colonialism involved Portugal and Spain at first. The Netherlands followed from the early 17th century and the British at the end of that century. There were conflicts of interests between European powers but they were resolved at the beginning of the 19th century. Britain focused on the Malayan Peninsula and northern Borneo, the Netherlands on the spice islands, today's Indonesia. The French occupied what was called Indo-China. Portugal was forced to relinquish its colonial possessions in the region but maintained control of Macao and Goa in India.

The history of English in the region is thus shorter than in India and begins at the end of the 18th century in the west and at the end of the 19th century in the east. The input came from Britain and the USA. Yet, English has been localizing all over the region and there are signs of it developing epi-centres. The following sections focus on Singapore, Malaysia and the Philippines.

The story of English in South-East Asia

Given the colonial history, the region is divided into the British part in the west and the American one in the east.

The British East India Company took control over Penang in 1786 with the consent of the sultan of Kedah, acquired Malacca from the Netherlands in 1824 and Singapore from the sultan of Johor that same year. That island had already come under some form of British control when Thomas Raffles established a free port in 1819. Given its location at the entrance of the Straits and its proximity to Burma and east India, Penang became a thriving cosmopolitan town that attracted even German writers like Karl May. In 1895 it was made a Presidency and raised to the same level as Bombay or Madras.

The three ports, Penang, Malacca, and Singapore, were federated into the Straits Settlement in 1826. The Federated Malay States were established in 1895 and the Unfederated Malay States in 1909, which assembled the remaining sultanates. The acquisitions in the northern region of Borneo, the location of Malaysia's Sarawak and Sabah, and of Brunei, go back to 1882. Given the indirect methods of gaining control over the various sultanates, the question of whether Malayan sultanates were ever colonialized is debated today. Former Prime Minister Dr. Mahatir, for instance, argues they were not.

Peninsular Malaya formed the Federation of Malaysia in 1957. In 1963 it was renamed Malaysia when North Borneo and Singapore joined. Singapore left Malaysia in 1965 and went a path of its own.

The majority of the population in Malaysia are Malay, followed by Chinese and Indians. Indigenous tribes form a marginal community. As a result of decisions taken at the time of independence Islam is the national religion;

other religions are given protection in the constitution. Bahasa Malay (or Malaysian, as the language is called) was made the only national language and English was reduced to a language that was taught in schools. There have been continuous shifts in policy that cannot be reiterated here (Azirah 2009) but it is fair to say that English has retained a significant role in government, business, the higher courts, or tertiary education. There is a large English language press and a growing local literature. Given the desire of government to raise Malaysia to developed nation status, English will acquire a higher status. What is less clear is the fate of its localized forms that will be illustrated below.

With no hinterland Singapore could not be an agricultural and industrial nation. Its success rested on service industries, science, research and education and the capacity to act as a political and commercial hub in regional and global affairs. The composition of its population was a factor that made it different from Malaysia. The major ethnic group is the Chinese, followed by Malays and Indians. Its geo-political location and its demography have had repercussions: Singapore could not be an Islamic nation, Malay not be the dominant language, Arabic was negligible. There was a need for a cross-ethnic language and it was English that was to adopt the integrative national language for all citizens. Chinese, Tamil and Malay are languages of ethnic communities. All communities are minimally bilingual, but as many speak other languages as well, multilingualism is typical. Yet, the national policy caters for only English, Malay, Mandarin, and Tamil and imposes serious constraints on the choice of language.

The Philippines were in the possession of Spain since Magellan's arrival in 1521. It was lost to the USA during the Spanish-American War in 1898. When the Philippines became independent in 1946, the proportion of English users was around 26 per cent. It will be well over 40% now. English shares with Filipina, a standardized version of Tagalog, the status of official language.

Differences between the three countries aside, the educated public and politics do not see English as a threat to other languages, as it promises access to global participation.

Features of Malaysian, Singaporean and Philippine English

There is a growing segment of functional native speakers of English, whose English shows signs of localization. The level of English competency differs between these countries and is related to degrees of localization. All of them maintain an exo-normative attitude that manifests itself in the widespread rejection of localized expressions. To take an example, *Singlish*, the variety at the bottom, leads to continuous controversies. A public row occurred when a 19-year-old Singaporean of Mandarin descent was elected beauty queen and spoke English. "In her interview," the Malaysian *Star* (10 Oct 2009) reported, "Low spoke in a mix of local pidgin English that was splattered with slurred or mispronounced words. ... She would say 'preens' instead of prints, 'rad' (for red), 'pis' (piece) and 'begini' (bikini), and used a distorted word 'boomz' to describe a glamorous outfit." But a community representative admitted that "Most of us are competent in neither English nor Mandarin. We have become a nation of half buckets, as the Chinese saying goes." "We only have to open our ears in food centres, shopping malls and school canteens, and we get a constant aural assault of sub-standard English and Mandarin," a letter stated. Similar complaints are made of *Manglish*, the localized variety of English. The Malaysian *Star* carried a column entitled "Let's Communic8", written by a British expert in the country. He defined *Manglish* as a "unique blend of English and a number of other languages spoken in Malaysia as well as old fashioned language left behind from colonialism." He gives these examples:

8.15 Next week I'm going *outstation*.
8.16 Can you *slow* the volume?
8.17 Sorry I'm late, I *met an accident*.

Outstation, a colonial remnant, means 'out of town, any-where outside Kuala Lumpur'. Its reference is vague but it refers to a branch of an organization somewhat away from its main base. The *New Oxford English Dictionary* refers to a part of a farming estate in Australia and to a working place of a journalist away from the main office. It has no such meaning in British English. *Slow down* (the volume) for 'lower (the volume)' is informal and can perhaps be expressed by 'turn down', the author says. *Meet an accident* means 'have an accident'.

Officially, these countries favour British English. But a former Prime Minister of Singapore argued that students should be made familiar with American English. The *Straits Times* and other papers carry blogs on 'good English', and the Education Ministry has a permanent committee on English (http://www.podcast.sg/radiopodcast/938/MDC060201_0001211/audio/MDC100205-0000015.mp3c).

There is evidence of English developing regularities no longer compatible with the English Received Pronunciation. Like in South Asia I will focus on the English of the growing educated elite that was trained at schools and can count as a guide to today's educated English. The lower end of the linguistic and social spectrum will not concern us much. But it is important to recall that the two varieties have been described in terms of a polar or *diglossic* situation whereby native-like English would occupy the 'high' position, while the localizing forms of English were demoted to a 'low' position. But I will turn to the other model that goes back to Platt *et al.* (1983). They suggested that Singaporean English, their prime example, was best described as a cline from a native-like form to one close to a pidgin (*see* Chapter Two) or as ranging from an acrolect to a basilect. The social segment selected would speak an upper mesolect.

Pronunciation

The social or stylistic patterns of pronunciation or phonology are not easy to describe as there is no agreed upon yardstick. The features attributed to the upper mesolect differ somewhat between accounts of Malaysian and Singaporean English and it is not quite clear whether they reflect a real difference or different choices in what has been selected as a baseline (Azirah/Tan 2012; Baskaran 2008).

The essential point is, however, that the vowel systems are reduced, if compared with Received Pronunciation. There are some common characteristics such as the absence of the vowel length distinction. The long vowels in *heart* and *sport* merge with the nearest short vowels, i.e., with *hut* and *hot*. A somewhat different development is the merger of the vowel in *bat* with that in *bed*. Rising diphthongs in *late* and *load* are realized as monophthongs. The result is a Malaysian five-vowel system. Some more complexity remains, as the vowel /ɜː/ in *bird* and other words is realized by different phonemes. Singaporean English is described as somewhat more differentiated with nine monophthongs and four diphthongs (Wee 2008: 267). A remark on consonants, dental fricatives /θ, ð/ are replaced by /t, d/.

A closer look at vowels reveals that modifications are not mere reductions. A stable system emerges in Singaporean English. Deterding (2005), for instance, has looked at how Singaporeans of Malay, Indian and Chinese descent pronounce the vowels in *egg*, *bed* and *dead* on the one hand and *beg*, *peg* etc. on the other. He found that the majority of speakers in his sample had three front vowels, i.e., /i, e, ɜ/, which differ from the ones in Received Pronunciation, i.e., /ɪ, e, æ/. Deterding concludes that "a standard Singaporean pronunciation is emerging, a style of speech that is quite independent of any external standard [such as the English one]" (2005: 249). The phonology of Singaporean English is, one might say, on its way towards forming an epi-centre. He says that the standard is a matter of the last decades, which implies that it developed since independence.

There are countless allophonic processes that render Malaysian and Singaporean English different from Received Pronunciation. For instance, the plosives in *key*, *tea* or *pea* are not aspirated. Voiced consonants at the end of a syllable or word become voiceless. One might think of the German *Auslautverhärtung* when one notices that *give* is pronounced as /gɪf/, *move* as /mʊf/, and *does* as /dʌs/. The sibilants /s, ʃ/ may be voiced in some words like *nice*, *fierce* and *wash*. The *h* in *house* never disappears, but it would be hard to prove that this is due to the impact of Scottish or, more generally, Northern English.

Words are often stressed differently from British English. Thus, nouns and verbs like 'import and to im'port are not differentiated by stress, both are stressed on the second syllable. The stress in ca'mera shifts to the syllable before the last. In 'insurance it shifts to the first one. The compound *English* 'teacher 'teacher of the subject English' and the phrase 'teacher from England' are not differentiated as in British English. The stress is on 'teacher and the differentiation of meaning is carried by context. As unstressed vowels are not reduced, the rhythm of Malaysian and Singaporean English is syllable-timed.

The final syllable of words with several syllables at the end of a sentence can be lengthened noticeably. For instance, the last syllable of *carefully* is stressed and lengthened in "She did it carefully". Foreigners will easily notice this pattern and wonder what it means. Some experts (Wee 2008: 275) argue that the speaker implies that nobody can really disagree that the woman did something 'carefully' and expects confirmation, if at all. In Standard English one might think of a tag question with a falling tone: "She did it carefully, didn't she".

A particularly audible feature is the reduction of consonant clusters. Local languages do not have clusters and so they are reduced in English and create an effect in the grammar. The plural in *kids* or *grants*, for instance, disappears.

There are few studies on the cumulative effect of such characteristics on intelligibility. But experience shows that reduced systems, different realizations, different word pronunciations, reduction of consonant clusters, and intonation lead to comprehension difficulties.

Philippine English is similar in many respects. It has a

reduced system of five monophthongs with no distinction made between long and short vowels. Vowels in unstressed vowels are not reduced so that its rhythm is like that of the other South-East Asian varieties. The consonant system, however, is different as there is no distinction between voiced and voiceless fricatives. *Sink* and *zinc* are pronounced with [s]. The American impact can clearly be seen in it being rhotic. And yet, one cannot fail to see that over and above the different types of British and American input are overlaid with local features.

Words, word-formation, loans, etc.

What is the origin or etymology of *ketchup* and *amok*? Both words are part and parcel of the core of the English vocabulary and of many languages world-wide. Yet, few people and even Malaysians are unaware that they come from South-East Asia and may be related to Malay or Chinese. They are deeply embedded in the taxonomy of deviant behavioural diseases in psychiatry and criminal law or the registers of cooking contain them, respectively. Equally deeply embedded are loans in fauna and flora but few of them have entered the public registers. As elsewhere, one can find archaisms, shifts in meaning or reference, new creations, and, loan words. I will provide examples of each but focus on loan words as they reflect the deep cultural embedding. Here are a few examples:

8.18 "Girl dies while trying to save brother from burning *shophouse*" (headline, *The Star*, 24 Feb 2010).
8.19 "Since it is the harvest festival, the state of Kerala is *a riot of* colours as the fields are golden and full of fruits

and flowers." (*The Star*, 2 Sep 2009, "Malayalese celebrate Harvest Festival …")

A *shophouse* is merely a 'shop'. But the word-formation
pattern is related to a very common older English one.
There were (or occasinally are) words like *schoolhouse*,
government house, *coffee house* or *bakehouse*. Today, this
pattern has a tinge of the 'good old days' in, say Australian English, and lends itself to tradenames. *A riot of*
means 'many', a metaphorical expression. To illustrate
the shift in class membership, one can point to the fact
that *alphabet*, a collective noun in native English, can be
used to refer to individual letters. But one might entertain a different idea when one reads G. B. Shaw's *Pygmalion* (1913). Professor Higgins wants Eliza to "say her
alphabet".

To return to loan words, English has benefitted from
the input from Malay, Chinese and Indian languages.
Arabic too must be mentioned as a source. *Amok* was
said to be a Malay loan. It was first attested in English in
the 18th century, according to the *Oxford English Dictionary*, if we ignore its translation from Spanish:

8.20 "There are some of them [the Javanese] who … go out
into the streets, and kill as many persons as they meet.
… These are called *Amuco*." ("The Book of Duarte
Barbosa: An Account of the Countries Bordering on the
Indian Ocean and Their Inhabitants", ca. 1516, English
translation)

In this case it is an agent noun and refers to the person
committing or 'running' amok and comes from Spanish.
In *running amok* it is an adverb like *afar* is in *going afar*.
As a kind of folk etymology, it became common to write

a muck, 'to run a muck', which can even be found today. In the past there were words like *amoker* or *an amok* for 'someone who runs amok' or *an amok* 'a case of amok'. That use has survived in medical or criminal registers. Nowadays, the most frequent meaning is for acts of multiple killings done under some presumed mental illness. Its use can be trivialized so that occurrences like these are common across all varieties of English worldwide:

8.21 "If a man be mad enough to scatter fire balls amongst a crowd, shall we increase his power to do mischief, by clapping a poisoned sword and loaded pistols into his hands, to 'run amuck and tilt at all he meets'?" (*The Sydney Gazette* and *New South Wales Advertiser*, 16 June 1829)

A prominent area in Malaysian English is loans from Arabic. They have a lot to do with religion but, given the pervasive impact of Islam on public and private life, they can be found in many contexts.

8.22 "Najib and delegation perform *umrah* [minor pilgrimage] ... performed the role of *motawif* [guide] ... The Malaysian leader is scheduled to perform Friday prayers and *tawaf Wida* [farewell, walk around the Kabah, G.L.] later ..." (*New Straits Times*, 15 Jan 2010)

8.23 "The wedding [that was called off, G.L.] feast was turned into a *kenduri doa selamat* [thanksgiving] feast instead." ("Groom calls off wedding ...", *The Star*, 9 Feb 2010)

8.24 "The management of University Putra Malaysia (UPM) has been urged to resolve issues surrounding the university's campus election, which triggered a scuffle between two groups of students two days ago. Deputy Prime

Minister Tan Sri Muhyiddin Yassin also advised its student affairs department to conduct a *musyawarah* [dis-
cussion] with unhappy students for an amicable solution
over the problem." (*New Straits Times*, 25 Feb 2011)

Here are some words from Malay:

8.25 "The extravagant buffet line stretches from the Coffee
House ... to Golfers' Lounge. To enhance the mood, the
place has been given a *kampung* [homely] touch." (*The
Star*, 31 Aug 2009)

8.26 "Malaysians should discard the attitude of being *lebih-
kuran* [more or less; italics sic!, G.L.] or they will degen-
erate into a nation of *sloths* instead of becoming a precision society ... 'We have to create a precision society
where terms like *lebih-kuran* are not used anymore,' he
[Prime Minister, G.L.] said ..." (*The Star*, 21 July 2010)

Some Indian and Chinese words:

8.27 "... a unique *Kolam* [colourful design] made from fresh
flowers called *Pookalam* is placed in front of the house.
... The women and the men wear an interesting costume
called the *Mundu*. The *Mundu* is two pieces of white
material with interwoven gold threads and the women
wear them with the auspicious gold, red or yellow blous-
es. ... Some of the most important dishes are rice, *samb-
har, avial, pulicherry, kalan, olan, upperi, meerku varati*
and savoury *inji puli*. There must also be two sweet des-
serts called *payasam* which come in two colours, the
dark payasam (*prathaman*) and white payasam (*velethe
payasam*)." (*The Star*, 2 Sep 2009)

8.28 "While the *Hungry Ghost Festival* – which is also known
as *Poh Thor* in Hokkien and *Yu Lan* in Mandarin – is

sometimes compared to *Qing Ming* [the Chinese All Souls' Day], Wan is quick to point out that Qing Ming is an occasion when families would all go to the graveyard to clean the tombstone and surroundings and pray to the deceased ... 'The Hungry Ghost Festival, on the other hand, is about praying for suffering spirits that are unable to reincarnate, so that they'll be able to experience rebirth,' he said ... a four-day celebration of the festival ... with a *kai kuang* [a Buddhist ritual, G.L.] ceremony to invite *Da Shi Ye* [the God of Hades] to come to the world of the living." (*The Star*, 2 Sep 2009)

Some social tendencies such as gender-neutrality in language use are not always visible:

8.29 "Malaysia must *man up*, subsidies on the way out." (*The Star*, 8 Feb 2010) [quoted from Prime Minister]
8.30 "Currently, there are 1,126 beds available at the hospital but only 925 can be used because there are not enough *nurses to man* operations at full capacity." (*The Malay Mail*, 14 June 2011)

A few comments on Philippine English must suffice. Some words have undergone a shift of meaning or have derived words that are not available in American English. Thus, *folk* associates with 'provincial' and there are derivatives like *concretize* or *conscientize*. Loan words can come from Spanish like *delicadeza* 'sense of propriety' or from Tagalog and other languages like *bibingka* 'rice cake'.

Grammar

"We don't have grammar" or "We don't speak English properly" are frequent responses to a foreigner's difficulty in understanding Malaysians' talk. Lack of self-confidence, perhaps? But it is also true, if we go by a very prescriptive grammatical angle. We have seen in many varieties that inflections get lost. Local varieties are treated with suspicion. Yet, many characteristics in grammar are low-level, like in American English. There are some that point to more crucial departures in the mesolect or in colloquial style in speech and writing.

One should begin by saying that educated speech and formal writing is similar to Standard British English. One only needs to read the front pages in newspapers and online editions to find that confirmed. In informal speech, too, there are pervasive stretches of no differences. For instance, it has been said that the modal *shall* is decreasing in frequency in most native varieties. It might be still somewhat more frequent, pending detailed corpus studies, but its use does conform with native English, as this example shows:

8.31 Now *I shall* get going to visit my mum. ... another [sister] busy so she must have been left on her own quite a bit.

Shall expresses first person singular and signals self-imposed obligation; the continuation explains the reason for the obligation. In less educated or less careful speech, there is a variable but consistent absence of inflectional endings. It would be wrong to attribute that merely to the avoidance of consonant clusters. It is more likely to be due to the grammar of local languages. Here is an example:

8.32 Yeah do you know that Thursday I *work* very hard …
you know I cut the cardboard box then I cut *two cardboard box* and I *join* together and then it *become* one
dustbin like that.

Only the lack of past tense marking in *work* and *join* and
the plural *-s* in *two … box* can be explained (away) by
phonological rules. The use of *become* for 'became' cannot be. There are more radical departures still, such as
the deletion of constituents, code-switching, and the non-
use of articles (data mainly from Azirah/Tan 2012). 8.33 is
from a tape-recording:

8.33 S1: shall I offer you Ø banana but …	no article
S2: oh so good	no subject, verb
S1: *pai seh pai she*	code-switching
S3: can I have one	[like native English]
S1: oh Ø can	no subject, object
8.34 Ø Been out most of the day	subject, auxiliary deletion
and Ø am tired. It's still	subject, auxiliary deletion
very cold but Ø not really complaining	
8.35 The data that M. and I, and also that of my student, have would be quite suitable …	
Ø can talk about social positioning of self …	subject deletion
8.36 She knows your writing	subject deletion
and Ø won't open Ø.	object deletion
8.37 Ø always talk like a *tawkey* [owner of a business],	subject deletion

One cannot escape the impression that these multiple deletions are regular and not aberrations from native English. The following is a radio commercial that uses grammatical features of Malaysian English humorously to convey its message:

8.38 (Telephone is ringing)
    A: Hello, "Anything Can" auto repair.
    Customer: Ah ... I like to *send in* my car in for *a* service.
    A: *Can.*
    Customer: My car is Ø Toyota, you know.
    A: *can.*
    Customer: You use original parts?
    A: *Can can can can ...*
    Customer: You know how to repair a Toyota *meh*?
    A: *Can can can can ...*
    Customer: Eh, hello, can you say anything besides *can ah*?
    A: *Can lah.*
    Customer: Eh, do you offer a warranty ah?
    A: *Cannot.*
    (A hangs up)

The modal verb *can* is used to agree or say 'yes' in most cases. There are some other features. *Send in*, for instance, means 'bring', articles are absent in a number of places, etc.

The influence of non-standard native English makes itself felt on occasion:

8.39 "Go: *ain't no* optical illusion" (headline, *New Straits Times* 22 Jan 2010).

It is interesting to notice the regularization of certain irregular verb patterns in the written and formal mode.

Some verbs have become regular as in American English but there is a lot of variation:

8.40 "'might get burn*ed*,' he said." (*New Straits Times*, 7 May 2011)

8.41 "and in the Mid Valley cab rank I learn*ed* an important lesson" (*New Straits Times*, 7 May 2011).

One can also find *burnt* and *learnt* of course. This minor pattern seems to be extended sometimes to words like *earn* which can have *earnt* for the past tense and past participle.

To turn to other characteristics of syntax, the structure of questions contrasts significantly with British English. Information or *wh*-questions omit the *do* support and lack inversion:

8.42 What book you want to read? (omission of *do*)

8.43 How they are going? (lack of subject-verb inversion)

Another common feature in colloquial Malaysian English is the way questions that require a 'yes' or 'no' as an answer are formed. Instead of the usual Yes/No question construction with the inversion of the subject, they are expressed as a declarative with an appended 'or not' phrase (Baskaran 2008: 616):

8.44 She can come or not?

8.45 She can come, yes or not?

8.46 Don't so *kiasu* can or not! [Can you stop being so anxious about something!] (www.urbandictionary.com)

When such questions are reduced to "Can or not (lah)" where all but the auxiliary verb remain, they become incomprehensible unless one knows the context. Malaysian English is enormously context-dependent. There is more to that. The alternative construction sounds like a challenging in native English and is remote from being polite. It is impossible to know that a Malaysian speaker is polite, though it can be seen in direct contact.

The deletion of major constituents, the reduction of structures like questions, tags, etc., and the reduction of intonation contrasts affect the expression of politeness. Malaysian and Singaporean English may come over to Europeans as fairly, not to say, bluntly direct. Examples 8.44 to 8.46 sound very direct, a style avoided in British English.

Some particles are similar to German particles like *ja*, *doch*, *ne* etc., which are used to guarantee an easy flow of communication, soften the force of utterances, but also to structure the weight of information contained in utterances. Here are some examples:

8.47 Why Ø the girl so shameless *lor*?
8.48 Yeah that's why ah that's why your fan is so fast *lor*.
8.49 "No *lah*, I'm not a celebrity. I've just been very lucky." (*New Straits Times*, 12 Sep 2010)

Adverbs are often used in a similar manner to Indian English to signal emphasis:

8.50 One indication of this is that the Chinese school leavers are *even* not keen on teaching …" (*The Star*, 27 Oct 2003)

To close with two examples from Philippine English, the passive in 8.51 is attached to "the yearly event", which would be impossible in British English (as it is a time adverb). We also see loan words from Tagalog such as *parang* 'a kind of long knife'. Example 8.52 shows clear reflections of American spelling and its affinity to common English patterns of word-formation in *boomlet*:

8.51 "The yearly event *is participated in* by Filipino Catholics who see it as a form of penance ... When asked why foreigners are now banned from joining the traditional crucifixion re-enactment on Good Friday, the officials said tourists 'made fun of the rites' last year. '*Ginawa nilang parang shooting* [they have imitated this for fun]...,' an official here said." (*Manila Bulletin*, 29 March 2010)

8.52 "For example, the Paris metro trains are notorious for pickpockets not by Frenchmen but by gypsies and migrants from Bulgaria, Romania and *neighboring* Balkan countries as well as from North Africa. ... Philippine tourism is enjoying a *boomlet* ..." (*Manila Bulletin*, 29 March 2010).

As indicated before, South-East Asian varieties show very similar patterns without disguising the input from British and American English. Some of these patterns have pragmatic implications on politeness and the identification of emphasis that will espace the foreigner without a deep enough familiarity with the cultures.

China, Hong Kong and Japan

Who would deny that English is a major language learnt in East Asia? According to figures mentioned earlier, hundreds of millions of users of English come from East Asia and there is a particular controversy about whether English is an (East) Asian language or a transplanted set of varieties that show relatively stable Asian learner features, but are still seen as a foreign language. The *Asian Englishes* camp maintains the one, the *English in Asia* camp the other position. The debate has significant implications on what we consider English to be today. I will survey some of the claims made by either side, and then look at what is considered so typical of English in the region.

Many experts working in the region have argued that English is an Asian language (Kirkpatrick 2010). Braj Kachru and his school have even abandoned the crucial distinction between English as a second and foreign language. They now maintain that China and other countries are developing what they call *Englishes* with features and norms of their own. It is hard to find firm evidence that points to stable and widely accepted norms. European scholars like Schneider (2011; ch. 6.4) are cautious and refer to the need of stable features before one can and should speak of Chinese, Japanese, Korean or, in an adjacent region, Thai and Vietnamese English. "Claims about the existence of a 'Japanese English'", he says (2011: 178), "lack substance." Even the stability of features is not enough. Germans have made the same 'errors' in English for centuries. They replace /θ, δ/ in *think* and *then* by /s, z/ or say "I've meet her five minutes ago". These are stable errors, not features of "German English". What is needed is the acceptance as genuine English in some nation. We are far from that.

Yet, the idea of Asian Englishes has been propagated widely and has caught on. Asian experts are taken aback if the belief in a Chinese (or China) English is question-marked. It is as if their pride in 'owning' a variety of English is being hurt. There are indeed reasons to assume that English may stabilize in a localized variety in East

Asia in the future. The millions of learners, the sparseness of teaching facilities, and the lack of native models may speed up the process of 'localization'. An excellent study by Kirkpatrick (2010) compares varieties of English in Asia and includes features from Africa. There is a good number of common ground, which will be mentioned in the final chapter. There is the first dictionary of Hong Kong English by Hans-Georg Wolf (2011), which contains a considerable number of lexical items that are identified with Hong Kong. One would expect that words and concepts are easier to stabilize and be accepted inside the country. Will they appear in future text books?

The fact that tens of thousands of parents send their children to schools in the USA, Australia or Great Britain to acquire native English is a clear sign that the outcomes of localization are not fully accepted. The academic practices of calling any *de facto* manifestation an instance of *Englishes* may be premature. There is ground for debate and one will have to observe what is happening in the future.

The story of English in East Asia

The story of English in East Asia is a long one, as I have pointed out on several occasions. It is best told in three phases. The first one is set within the context of the early period of the East India Company's activities in the late 17th century that gave rise to Chinese Pidgin English. It ends when European colonial powers and the USA attempted to force the opening of ports on the South Chinese coast, started the Opium Wars and succeeded in forcing Japan to open its ports. It ends with the post-World War II period. The third period is marked by English being accepted as the language of access to, and participation in, an ever more globalizing and networking world.

Given the role of the East India Company and the commercial interests of colonial powers, it is unsurprising that a Chinese Pidgin English or China Coast Pidgin emerged by the 17th century. It was mainly spread through maritime trade and the major parts across Asia and the Pacific. It was used also by a growing number of stranded Chinese shipping crews in London. By the 19th century it became a factor in the rise of Australian Aboriginal pidgins in the Northern Territory and Melanesian pidgin in the South Pacific. It was used now in Singapore and other places. It disappeared more or less when English began to be offered in a more organized way in the 19th century but may left some kind of active trace in Hong Kong and some other parts. It is doubtful that it has had more than a peripheral effect on today's Hong Kong English and it certainly had none in the interior and on the current status of English.

A more consequential type of the spread of English and language contact followed around the middle of the 19th century, when Britain and the United States set up schools and a small number of universities. The mid-19th century saw waves of migration to Malaya, especially Singapore and many Chinese went to the United States and Australia. Their English could have been important as they kept in close touch with their native country and returned during the racist white-only policies.

The third phase covers the post-war period. The spread of English at that time is closely related to the Cold War. Countries associated with the West, i.e., Japan, South Korea, Taiwan and the entire North Pacific, came under the influence of the United States and, by implication, of American English. The only exception is Hong Kong, which was and remained British. In China the uptake of English began with the post-Mao period and the opening up of the country to modernization. The growth of English since then has been massive. English has become a compulsory school subject nation-wide. The success and the maintenance of English, however, need better scrutiny. The story of English in (South) Korea and Taiwan is connected with the support from the USA during the Cold War period, while the current demand is stimulated by globalization. Japan's history is broadly similar to China's as it begins in the mid-19th century.

Features of East Asian varieties of English

Given the arguments about the status of English in East Asia, I will confine myself to the one country where they have been discussed in the most controversial manner, i.e., China. English in China ranges from a near native command to one that is negligible at best. We have related this spectrum to one that ranges from the basilect to an acrolect and the diminishing impact of local languages. English shows features that can be related to the learning situation, the influence of Chinese dialects, and the acquisition process. Formality, loans and simplification or the generalization of rules can be identified across all levels of language. The following examples come from Tian (2011) and Hung (2004).

There are numerous loans from Mandarin or Hokkien or other dialects. Some words are *dimsum* 'tidbits, delicatessen' or *fengshui* 'geomancy'. Less known is *laisee* 'a red envelope containing money as a gift'. There are institutional names that cannot be replaced by common English words.

The role of Chinese can be seen in, e.g., the absence of agreement between the subject and the verb in 8.53 and 8.54 or the lack of the subject in 8.55 and 8.56:

8.53 It *help* produce mucus.
8.54 A super carrot *have* been produced by plant breeders.
8.55 Beside Ø can *enhance* my English standard.
8.56 Ø felt angry with people.

What is worth noting is that *have* in 8.54 is not typical elsewhere as irregular verbs are often learnt well enough to use the required form 'has'. The learning context might be behind *enhance* for 'improve' and in *English standard*, a technical academic word in 8.55.

To close this brief section, I might recall the impact of Chinese on English in South-East Asia and especially the discourse particles such as *lah*. Such particles are also used in China.

9 Africa

Europe and most of Africa have been closely connected as the "Old World" since Antiquity (Grataloup 2007). The Mediterranean was the geopolitical centre in Antiquity. The names of towns like Tripolis show their Greek past. Africa ceased to be of interest until the explorations set in in the 14th and 15th centuries. Africa was back on the map, but merely a stopover to reach Asia (*see* Leitner 2009). The Iberian nations maintained a natural interest in exploring the West African coastline. With the rise of the Osmanian Empire in the middle of the 15th century the land route to Asia was blocked. Two new routes were discovered. The Portuguese Vasco da Gama sailed around Africa and reached India in 1498. Under Spanish flag the Portuguese Ferdinand Magellan sailed west and reached the Philippines where he was killed. One ship continued to sail westward and returned in 1522. Decades later Francis Drake circumvented the earth (1577–80) and opened up perspectives for England. Asia could now be reached from around Cape of Good Hope to the east or past West Africa westward to Cape Horn.

Timeline 7: South Africa

1652	Arrival of Dutch settlers, Dutch East India Company; also French and German settlers in Cape territory
1795	First (temporary) British occupation of Dutch colony
1806	British recapture the Cape; first wave of settlers
1814	South Africa becomes a British colony

1820	Second wave of immigration; settlements in eastern frontier to form a defensive buffer against the Xhosa
1850s	About 4,000 British people migrate to Natal
1860	Labour import from India to Natal to work on plantations
1860s/70s	Discovery of gold etc. leads to new wave of immigration
1910	Union of South Africa; Dutch (from 1924 on "Afrikaans") acquire co-official status with English
1934	South African Independence
1948–94	Apartheid Era
1990	Legalization of African National Congress (ANC); release of Nelson Mandela
1994	ANC wins election: end of Apartheid
1999	ANC wins second democratic elections

The Portuguese set up trading posts on the climatically favourable islands such as Cape Verde, São Tomé and Príncipe in the 15th century and colonies in Angola and Mozambique. The Dutch established a settlement colony at the Cape in 1652 which attracted settlers from Europe and Asia. The British involvement began with the slave trade and continued with the take-over of the Cape colony in 1795 in the context of the Napoleonic Wars.

East Africa and the interior were barely known until the 19th century. The discovery of minerals and gold and Germany's attempts to create a colonial empire led to the scramble for Africa and to its partitioning amongst European nations. Competing interests were formalized at the Berlin conference in 1884/85. Decolonization started in the late 1950s.

The scramble for Africa created a mosaic-like pattern of colonial languages. There were English, Portuguese,

French, German, Dutch (Afrikaans), and Italian colonies. The major heritage clusters survived decolonization, i.e., the Anglophone, Francophone and Lusitanophone nations. One should add Arabic in North Africa as a fourth block (*see* Map 9.1).

The story of English in West and East Africa

Britain's involvement in Africa is best told in two stages. The first one is connected with slavery when the Royal Africa Company began to set up forts and trading posts 1672. It was equipped with a Royal Charter that spelt out its task to trade in gold, silver and slaves. It succeeded another company that went bankrupt and by earlier activities still associated with Francis Drake. Slavery became a most profitable enterprise by the end of the 17th century but peaked in the 18th century. London's rise to a metropolis has largely to do with slavery. The trade led to a black community in Britain, whose number increased when freed slaves were brought to Britain from America in 1783. Slavery was abolished in Britain in 1807 and thousands of slaves were emancipated. Before that, the Poor Black Society had acquired Freetown in 1787, the capital of today's Sierra Leone. Ex-slaves were 'repatriated' on the assumption that they had an ethnic or race relation with black peoples. Freetown was chosen because it had a major role in the slave trade. It became a British colony in 1808. Slavery was a much more important aspect of the history of America that led to the Civil War of the USA (1861–65). In 1822 Liberia was set up by American humanitarian bodies for the same purposes. The inhabitants of Freetown and Liberia were Christian. The slave trade was instrumental in producing

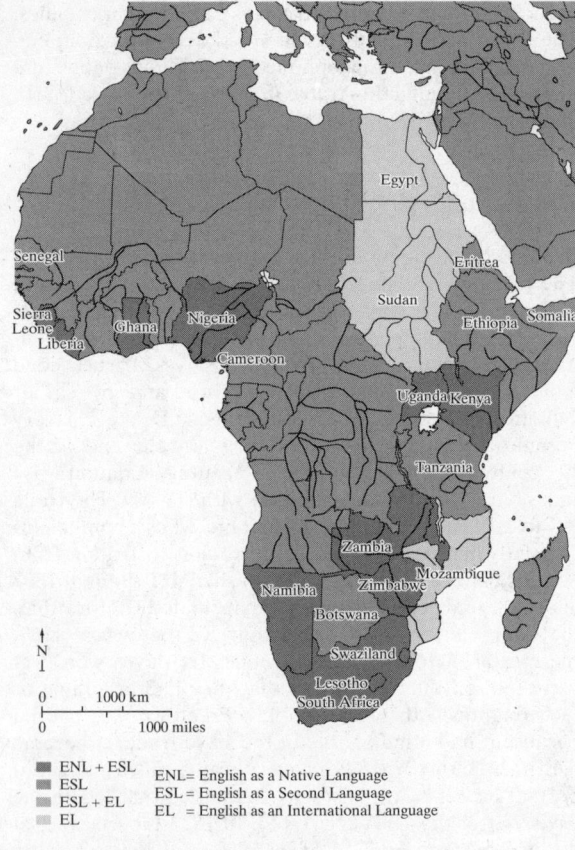

Map 9.1: *Anglophone areas of Africa*

ENL + ESL
ESL
ESL + EL
EL

ENL= English as a Native Language
ESL = English as a Second Language
EL = English as an International Language

a pidgin which was transported to the Caribbean, the Bermudas, the American colonies, and even to England. The trade was triangular and linked British ports with West African and Caribbean ones. As a result its development was as much influenced by American Black English as the African pidgin until a strong base was formed in the colonies. The ex-slave settlement in Liberia brought the Black English that had originated in the slave trade back to Africa. It was now spreading across coastal West Africa as a *lingua franca* and became known as Krio. It was the first contact variety ever to be used as native English in a settlement colony.

The second period was, as I said, connected to the European wars of the 18th century and started when the Dutch Cape colony was taken over in 1795 to stop France from controlling the passage to Asia. The first British settlers arrived in 1806, larger numbers came after the Cape had become a British colony in the Congress of Vienna in 1815. The colony was extended in the north and included most of Bechuanaland. Today's Botswana remained under direct British control. South Africa was the first country English was transplanted to as a settler language. It was declared the official language in the 1820s, which forced Dutch settlers and Coloureds to learn English. It became an additional language that many black people learnt. Ethnic diversity became a major differentiating factor in internal varieties. While Schneider would argue that differentiation is the main factor at the final stage of endo-normativity, this is not so. It is rather the desire to merge varieties of English and to form a national South African umbrella. Today South Africa has eleven official languages but English is undoubtedly the most influential national *lingua franca* and the language of access to the world. Its heritage is an asset to the nation. A word in passing on Botswana, Botswana English was the language of the colonizers and has become the state's official language.

East Africa is a completely different story. The transplantation of English only began in the 1860s, when the fertility of the land and the moderate climate in the hinterland were discovered. That triggered migrations of native speakers from South Africa and Britain. They kept themselves away from the African tribes, so that English was hardly spreading beyond the settlers. English was only adopted by Africans on a large scale in the 1920s and came to be used as a kind of *lingua franca* and developed into a low, basilectal form. It is still used amongst the black African population but is learnt increasingly in the education system.

To return to West Africa, while Krio was spreading, varieties of native English were brought by the Christian missions. They had begun to proselytize across Africa and set up schools in various locations such as in the Congo or Nigeria and East Africa during the mid-19th century. That kind of English had more official support and was used in the administration of the colonies since the end of the 19th century. The two 'native' traditions of English thus met in West Africa and created a sociolinguistic texture that today's West African nations struggle to exploit as their resource. The dual heritage is more accentuated than in Asia. As English and French have co-existed in some regions such as the Congo there are sub-varieties that include the influence of French.

The end of the First World War and the collapse of the Osmanian Empire enhanced the role of European nations and their languages in Africa and the Middle East. Britain and France acquired protectorates. Lesotho and Egypt (and Middle Eastern areas), for instance, became

British. The period of protectorates did not last long enough to implant English deeply in the public and private domains. The Second World War followed and led to decolonization and nation-building. The 1950s and 60s raised the issue of what language to choose for independent nations. The linguistic Africanization was not an option or not the sole option in many nations. English and French remained and localized. Both languages are seen as vehicles to access knowledge in the sciences, technology, tertiary education and work mobility.

There is no one African English. English is best seen as the aggregate of different traditions and a highly heterogeneous entity. It has become a literary language that reflects important aspects of African identities. The creation of pan-African organizations such as the African Union (2002) and its fore-runners have given a boost to localize English and the perception of what is appropriate African English.

Features of English in West and East Africa

There were crucial differences between the growth of English in West and East Africa, as we have just seen. The slave trade was the major factor in the west and created a pidgin that was the predecessor of African American English. It inherited words such as *pickaninny* 'small, esp. black child' from earlier pidgins or *savvy* 'do you know' from French 'savez-vous' that made it into English worldwide and appeared in the pidgins of Australia, to mention two examples. When Freetown and Liberia were set up for freed slaves their native English was introduced and was spread to trading posts such as Lagos (1861) and the Gold Coast (1874). The 'true' version of native Eng-

lish was taught in schools that mission societies opened
up. It became the language of the African elite. Interme-
diate forms emerged in speech and constituted a cline
similar to the one described for Singapore.

Localization is related to influence from native languages. Nigerian English benefitted from such languages
as Yoruba. But, the African expert Ayo Bangbose (*see*
Graddol *et al.* 2006: 149f) argued, not all of Nigerian English can be seen in this light. He prefers what he calls the
'creativity approach' that looks at English from within
the Nigerian context and accepts local usages as a part of
it. Here are some illustrations that cast light on its nature
and on the issue of the best angle to describe it.

Krio is not confined to street talk, markets and the like
either. It can be heard on radio news as it is understood
by a larger number of people than any other variety of
English (*see* Schneider 2011: 144ff). A few illustrations
will make the point:

9.1 "*One hand no* dey *carry* heavy load put for head. Na *im
    make* di Lagos Mainland Government *don set* task force
    wey go follow put eye to monitor how private sector peo-
    ple o wey dey do dirty carry-carry work to do am well
    well and proper proper.
    You can't lift up a heavy load with only one hand.
    That's why he LMLG has set up a task force to supervise
    the work of private waste disposal companies."

This is a media text quoted from Schneider 2011: 144 that
shows the input from Krio. Notice the unmarked instrumental adverb *one hand* 'with one hand', the pre-verbal
negation in *no ... carry*, or the neutral pronoun *im* 'they'.
There are formal English words like *task force* and *private sector people*. The educated level of West African

English is marked by features that show the diminishing role of the British English input.

The following passages from letters-to-the-editor in Nigeria's *The Nation* illustrate educated Nigerian English and its grammatical and lexical characteristics:

9.2 "Students derive joy in speaking this language to confer status on themselves or how '*tushed*' they are. *One is not painting* Ø English Language bad …

I believe if teaching *is been done* with mother tongue, kids *will be* able to ask questions, express their views and learn more. Most things the so-called elite do is to segregate themselves from the locals …

All these ideas don't have any effect on *these* people [= the rural people] neither do they understand all *the grammars* from the borrowed language. We say the world is global but those in the rural areas *are not feeling* it. … Comprehension of language is *the* most important when a state *is aiming* for development …" (*The Nation*, Nigeria, 17 Aug 2011).

The present progressive is generalized in "*One is not painting* Ø English Language bad" so that the difference between the habitual meaning and on-going situation-meaning disappears. The phrases "*are not feeling it*", and "*is aiming for*" too express habituality. Note the lack of the definite article in the passage just quoted. In another letter one reads "made *an* interesting *reading*" (8 Aug 2011), which shows that the avoidance of articles is extended to gerundial nouns. The singular noun *grammar* is pluralized to refer to any of the set of rules in a normative grammar concept. In the *if*-clause "if teaching is been done" the present is used instead of the *were*-subjunctive. It is unclear whether *been* is used for 'being'.

The next example is from an interview with a traditional medicine doctor published in a popular newspaper.

9.3 "Although some herbs are naturally spiritual, but in healing some diseases, there will *be Ø need for certain* spiritual intervention. The example was …, when someone *had Ø headache* and I *did little incantations* and that was the end. Another one is that when people *have Ø mental illness* … We have to go spiritual and call his or her ancestors and ask them what they want from him or her …" (*Osum Defender*, 17 Aug 2011).

The different uses of definite and indefinite articles or their absence is a striking feature that we have seen in the varieties of Asia before. The final example does not stand out for any grammatical features but for its flowery rhetorics to commemorate a deceased comedian artist of national standing:

9.4 Why death now when we are supposed to be enjoying the good luck that flows *from the temple of the high priest* in Aso-Rock? Christy Igbokwe is yet to be buried. Now, we have *lost another giant of the entertainment industry to the icy hands of death*. His death will leave a large void behind for us to fill. Death is often *a mischievous reaper*, not always after the crooked ones and tyrants who dot the entire landscape of our country. No matter their sins against our nation, I do not wish them dead anyway, for we are all humans after all. (*The Beacon* 2 [33], 16 to 22 Aug 2011; http://www.thebeaconnigeria.com/Vol2/NO33/samloco.htm)

One may note the irony following *reaper*.
Cameroon English is a special case as one finds the in-

trusion of French spellings and lexis (*see* Wolf 2001: 252f, 265f). Here are some examples:

9.5 <u>Influence of French</u>
  – Spelling: academi*que* (< académique), appoint*e*ment, ex*e*mple, vehic*u*le, assist at (< assister à), correct (< corriger), mémoir (< mémoir 'dissertation')
  – Loans (direct): *aide-de-champ*, *foyer*
  – Loan translations etc.: *convoke* (< convoquer), *obeisance* (< obéisance), *planification* (< planification)
  – Loan blends (hybrids), calques: *scholarise* (< scolariser), *bilingualise*

It is obvious that the interpretation of these properties as 'creative English' by Bamgbose (*see* Graddol *et al.* 2006: 149ff) is a sensible one. However, the relationship with speech and writing and the cline from formal to colloquial (spoken) English is unclear. Especially West African experts suggest that West African features are quite regular and could become features of Standard West African English. Endo-normativity seems to be on the horizon.

English in South Africa

In South Africa English is only the fifth most widely spoken language. It is one of the eleven official languages but is the dominant one "in government, at higher levels of business, technology, higher education and the media" (Svartvik/Leech 2006; 114). It is being adopted by large sections of the black population for the simple reason to succeed, to give their children the linguistic edge to access information worldwide and to 'make it'. It is a neutral language that avoids conflicts and divisions in the country. Its chequered colonial history cannot but mirror that complexity. One can distinguish a number of sub-varieties:

(a) White South African English of mainly British decent
(b) Indian South African English
(c) Afrikaans South African English by white second language speakers with Afrikaans as a mother tongue
(d) Coloured South African English spoken mainly by second language speakers with a good mastery of English and Afrikaans
(e) (Varieties of) Black South African English by second language speakers with African languages as mother tongues (also in Botswana)

That diversity throws up the question of the choice of norm in post-Apartheid contemporary South Africa. Should norms be based on national usage patterns or reflect native Anglo-American ones? What could a national norm be like? What would have to be done to create a variety that expresses the identities of the nation? These questions are at the centre of language policies. To see why they are so difficult to resolve, I will look at the history of English.

Three waves of immigration led to varieties of White South African English. The settlers of 1806 came with a south-eastern type of English, which was similar to that of Australia and New Zealand and is the reason for including South African English into Southern Hemisphere English. That input was strengthened during the second wave in the 1820s when migrants settled in the eastern province of the Cape. The third wave of immigrants came between 1848 and 1862. They brought an educated middle and even upper class English from the Midlands. (Readers should recall that Standard English and Received Pronunciation were by no means as strong country-wide as later.) These immigrants settled in Natal and in proximity to the Boers. As a consequence there developed two types of English in South Africa, one that goes back to working class English and another one that drew on middle class, regional English. The former was referred to as broad, the latter as general. While the terminology is similar to the Australian one, the two were used in separate regions. In a generally friendly context the general variety borrowed many words from Dutch (or Afrikaans) and African languages. When tensions mounted in the advent of the Boer Wars and the Great Treks inland language contact deteriorated and borrowing declined. The discovery of gold and other minerals led to renewed waves of immigration of non-English-speaking Europeans. Speakers of both working and middle class English moved into the growing towns. In urban environments the Natal variety English became the dominant one and the variety of an urban middle class. The Cape variety remained working class. Especially in towns the regional differentiation was transformed into one based on a social class dimension. White varieties thus have both a regional and a social class connotation.

Though commonly related to ethnicity, the other varieties of English were more mixed and the categories set up above reflect an unrealistic level of ethnic purity. The English of Black African speakers who worked close to the mining industry incorporated the impact of African languages and turned English into a variety with strong links to ethnic background.

On that background it is obvious that the distinction

between native and second language is not easy to maintain. There are speakers of both types in every segment. Today all varieties of English have come under pressure to merge into a South African English variety able to express the identity of a new nation.

Pronunciation

The pronunciation of White South African English has, as I have said before, been likened to that of Australian and New Zealand English and categorized as *Southern Hemisphere English* with them.

The vowels are quite similar. Short vowels are typically closer, the final vowel in words like *happy* is raised to /i/, and rising diphthongs in *late* or *load* tend to have a lower onset. The /ɪ/ in *bit* or *ship* can be raised like in Australian English or centralized to schwa /ə/ as in New Zealand English. But this variety differs from Antipodean English as the vowel in *hard* is not shifted to a front /aː/ but remains a back /ɑː/. As it has shifted to a mid-position even in contemporary Received Pronunciation and other general English accents, South African English tends to be conservative in this respect. There are no noticeable differences with consonants but it is worth remembering that it is a non-rhotic accent.

There are noticeable differences in Black South African English. Similar to other African varieties of English, vowel length is largely abolished. The /æ/ in *trap* may merge with /a/ as in current Received Pronunciation or rise and come close to /ɛ/ as in Australian English. Rising diphthongs in *day* and *road* may be realized as monophthongs. Unstressed vowels are typically unreduced and acquire the vowel suggested by spelling. Articles in unstressed position too are often articulated with the strong form. The impact on the rhythm of English is well-known: Black South African English is syllable-timed.

Variation in consonants is minimal, apart from the replacement of the dental fricatives by /t, d/. Consonant clusters are reduced, and like white English it is non-rhotic.

Words, word-formation, loans, etc.

Language contact makes itself felt most in the domain of lexis and word-formation. I will illustrate the contact with Afrikaans and native African languages. The first excerpt is from a famous story (published in the *London Review of Books* 2002) that was reproduced in parts in the press. It shows the impact of Afrikaans in Afrikaans English.

9.6 *Protocol and Pink Slippers* by Harold Strachan
"*Alle woreld!* A cake appears such as I see again in the furious fantasy of the mind's eye and salivate as I write these words: a coffee cake, iced around with coffee icing and frillies at the rim in a lighter tone of coffee brown … It stands on a silver pedestal, as indeed such a noble creation should, and this pedestal is surrounded by plates of small sausages rolls and home-baked biscuits with chocolate topping and walnuts, and a great plate of heavenly *koeksusters* [kinda doughnut] still warm from the cooking. … I look down and round, and there stands the little girl. We smile. '*Pappie soe die oom ith 'n kunthtenaar?*' she declares. '*Ja, dis waar,*' I say. '*Thal oom vir my 'n kwagga teken?*' she asks. (Am I an artist and will I draw her a zebra?) … '*Ek wil dit ook doen.*' '*Nou ja, dan SAL jy dit mos een dag doen, nee, as jy werklik waar WIL.*'"

The Afrikaans words are not hard to understand. The switch into Afrikaans is typical in bilingual situations and signals a switch from the black African listener to the girl's father.

A somewhat more systematic list of loans is this:

9.7 <u>Loan words in South African English</u>
   (a) Dutch and Afrikaans
      – early Dutch words: *aum* 'unit of liquid measurement', *baaken* 'a post for marking boundaries/territory', *Burgher Senate*, *drostdy* 'a magisterial district', *landdrost* 'a magistrate', *morgen* 'unit of land measurement'
      – topography: *kloof, kopje, krantz, rand, veld*
      – transport: *trek-wagon, transport-rider, the span* 'team'
      – farm life: *hamels, kapaters, kraals, lands, campus*
      – diseases: *blood-sickness, gallsickness, tulp-poisening*
   (b) African languages, esp. Nguni and Xhosa
      – Xhosa (in settler, missionary writings of the 1820s): *indaba* 'tribal discussion', *tagathi* 'witchcraft', *tokoloshe* 'a mischiefous water-sprite
      – Sotho languages, esp. Sesotho, Setswana: *lapa* 'forecourt of a homestead', *morogo* 'wild spinach', *ousie* 'address form for a woman'
      – other Bantu languages: *babalaas* 'suffering from a hangover', *bonsella* 'a small gift, something extra', *daga* '(to) plaster' (from Xhosa *ukudaka*)
      – loan translation: *to eat up* 'to punish ... by confiscating or destroying possessions', *great place/son/wife* 'eminent', *monkey's wedding* 'both rain and sunshine'
      – modern loans: *mbaqanga* 'rhythmical township music', *spaza* 'store run from a township home'

Grammar

Some grammatical systems are simplified. Plural marking is often missing when it can be retrieved from context. Concord in the third person singular present tense is variable. There is confusion between the omission of the definite article and other areas of grammar.

Summing up, South African English is a highly diversified variety of English. It shows the deep contact with Afrikaans within the Afrikaaner variety of English. Lexical items from Afrikaans can be expected to show up in all varieties. The story by Harold Strachan is written in English but the realism in depicting the setting demands the inclusion of Afrikaaner words and code-switching. Other ethnic varieties draw more on African languages. As for the role of English in marking a new, modern national identity, there is a lot of language policy and quite detailed proposals on specific language expressions.

10 Contact Languages

In the short story "The Drover's Wife" by the Australian Henry Lawson (Leitner 2011) the wife recalls an episode where she needed urgent help in her homestead. An Aborigine known to her happened to come by and promised to call his wife, saying "All right, missus, I bring my old woman, '*she down alonga creek.*'" It is not difficult to guess that he meant to say "she is/lives down by the river". The omission of the verb and the use of the preposition *alonga* 'by, near' are markers of Kriol, the creole spoken in the Centre. "Samtaim gud rod get, samtaim, olsem ben get" or "Misi kamesi Arelu Jou no kamu ruki me Mi no ruki iuo" from New Hebrides creole and Hawaiian Pidgin English respectively, can leave readers flabbergasted (Fasold 1990: 181f). They can be paraphrased by "Sometimes, there's a good road, sometimes there are bends" and "Mr. Kamesi, how are you? We haven't met for a long time" or, alternatively, "You haven't come to see me and I haven't come to see you."

Contact, we have seen, has played an important role in the formation of English, its homogenization, the growth of standard varieties and their diffusion. But there are differences in intensity, in length of time, in purpose and in what languages participate in contact. Middle English was the result of intensive and long-term contact based on a dominance relationship. It transformed English. Similar scenarios have occurred elsewhere in the world and some of the outcomes have become proper epi-centres. Others have disappeared or been fully integrated in some 'mainstream' English. Extreme contact situations where interaction is unavoidable pose problems. But "life found a way", to paraphrase John Hammond in *Jurassic Park*. Jargons turned into pidgins, then possibly into creoles. There are hundreds of examples worldwide – not all involve English – up to the present time. A few locations will suffice: The Hebrides, Jamaica, Aboriginal Australia, China or West Africa.

This chapter will look at a few examples to illustrate the context in which such languages arise, how they develop and what their fate is. It will show that contact will trigger universal processes of rule formation that create similar outcomes despite different patterns of contact. There is no timeline as such languages have arisen at different periods of time.

Socio-cultural history and developmental steps

Contact languages spring up in the 'right' circumstances and their development follows a common path. Leaving aside early stages, a division is made between pidgins and creoles. A prototypical *pidgin*, Sarah Thomason says,

> "arises in a new contact situation in which three or more groups of speakers come together for purposes of trade or other limited communicative purposes. The contact among the groups is sufficiently limited that no group has the need, the desire, and/or the opportunity to learn any of the other groups' language ... If there is a socially or economically dominant group, its vocabulary is chosen as the lexical base of the emerging pidgin. If the contact situation is sufficiently stable over time, and if the circumstances of language use remain more or less constant, then a fully crystallized pidgin develops. ..." (1997: 76)

Pidgins serve limited purposes, are reduced and simplified, have a small range of lexical and grammatical re sources, and have no native speakers. Developed creoles are the main language and are learned as a native language. They have an expanded structure, a larger vocabulary, and are beginning to develop grammatical structures that none of the participating languages has. That happened in Aboriginal Australia's Kriol, in Gullah (a variety of African American English), and in Papua New Guinea's Tok Pisin. They have become distinct languages. But often contact languages are drawn into renewed contact, and then they join the mainstream variety and form a cline that ranges from a basilect to an acrolect (*see* Chapter Two). As that happens, they may end up as an ethnic variety, an ethnolect. They are often used as expressions of the opposition to a mainstream society. It is this association that makes them so successful in modern rap, hip hop or theatre.

Case studies

The examples at the beginning of this chapter came from developed contact languages. They still seem simplified compared with native English but reveal underlying regularities, rules. The missing verb in "she down alonga creek" or the absence of *there* in "samtaim gud rod get …" are not chance variation but part of the system of the creoles in question. I will illustrate several contact languages that reflect the extent of linguistic departures and the nature of creole grammars.

African American English

African American English is by all intents and purposes the most well-known and best studied ethnic contact language. And yet controversies about its origin persist. To what extent is it based on contact with African languages? Does it continue patterns of British English dialects such as from Irish or Scottish or Elizabethan English? Could there be universal principles of language development at work?

There is a consensus that it originated as a pidgin that started in the slave ports in West Africa, was transported to the Caribbean and then – in a localized form – carried on on the plantations in the southern states. It is obvious that one expects to find traces of the diversity of inputs. But given a history of some 400 years and the scarcity of written evidence from the late 16th century to the mid-19th century, there is little hope to find the original input that was most important to its base. It has acquired a prestige worldwide in pop culture. In the educational context it has created problems and heated political and ideological debates on whether it should be accepted as a variety in schools or as a transitional vehicle.

The following example is from a conversation between a teacher and two students (*see* Ferguson *et al.* 1981: 100) that shows a number of features (which are underlined):

10.1 JIMMY: Hey Ms. Smith. D'ya evv<u>ah</u> watch Kung Fu on TV wif dat dude ... wha<u>'s</u> his name?

DAVID: He <u>have</u> my name, Jimmy. <u>He David</u>, too.

JIMMY: Yeah, <u>d</u>at's right. <u>D</u>at's <u>duh</u> dude's name.

MS. SMITH: Yes, <u>I've watched</u> it a few times. It's really an exciting show.

DAVID: <u>Did</u> you ev<u>vah</u> see how he <u>throw</u> all <u>d</u>ose dudes
    aroun<u></u>', an' how <u>he use</u> his legs?
JIMMY: Yeah. You know what? He <u>don'</u> really fight to be
    mean <u>dough</u> [though]. He <u>fight</u> to be good, and he
    <u>he'p</u> [help] people. An' he <u>always duh</u> good guy.

The spelling is heavily 'phonetic' to show, e.g., the replacement of the dental fricatives /θ, ð/ by [t, d] in words
like *with*, *that*. That is not done consistently as David says
throw. The final consonants in *wha's* and *aroun'* are deleted and show the tendency of simplification. The 3rd person
singular is left unmarked in "he throw" and "He fight"; irregular forms like "he don'" are used. There are more significant differences in grammar. For instance, David says
"He David, too" and "he always duh good guy", where
the verb *be* is missing (or replaced by *duh*). While African
American English departs significantly from American
English, there are clear signs that it is American. For instance, the simple past in "D'ya evvah" would be rendered by the present perfect in British English.

Here is a stanza from the lyrics "Ain't nut'in personal"
by Snoop Dogg (http://www.metrolyrics.com/aint-nutin-
personal-lyrics-snoop-dogg.html):

10.2 Murda, murda, kill, kill, if you put me danger
    I ain't trippin' on and ain't be needin' no strangers
    I'm a tank representer till I'm history
    Making playas hatas into mother fucking memory ...

This excerpt shows some affinity of African American
English to non-standard English. Like the first text, there
is phonetic spelling to show non-standard features of pronunciation. There is *ain't* and double negation in "ain't
(be needin) no strangers". But there is a significant gram-

matical departure in (*ain't*) *be needin'*. A construction with the so-called invariant *be* has a meaning that is not available in white English, i.e., "always"; together with double negation it means 'never'.

There are lexical features from African languages such as *bogus* 'fake, fraudulent' *cat* 'a friend', *bad* 'really good', and *dig* 'understand, appreciate' that come from Wolof. *Big-eye* 'greedy' is a loan translation from Ibo. Overall, there are mere remnants. Some of the loans look English and may well be misunderstood as mere shifts in the meaning of English words.

African American English has developed systematic rules of its own. From the perspective of English in America one would say that there are multiple norm-setting varieties, there is, one might say, pluricentricity inside American English.

Sierra Leone's Krio

The role of Sierra Leone's capital Freetown was mentioned on several occasions. It started out as a resettlement location for former slaves in Britain. They brought a range of varieties of Black English of the time. It spread along the West African coastline down to Congo over subsequent decades and is known as Krio. This poem illustrates some of its properties; the rightmost column has some more literal transliterations than the literary translation in the middle.

10.3
Sierra Leone creole (*see* Darthorne 1975: 253)

Slip gud o, bebi-gial   Sleep well, my "baby-girl"
open yai lilibit   open your eyes a little bit

en lik mi wan minit	look, just for one minute
bifo yu slip	ere (before) you fall asleep
A wan *fo si* da 'tin' ['to see'; 'thing']	I wish to catch a glimpse
we kin de shain insai ['what, that']	of what peculiar light
insai yu *fain-fain* yai ['very fine, nice']	within in your eyes so bright
en *kot* me *at* ['caught … at']	that stuns me so

The spelling is phonetically close to pronunciation. As it
is not standardized, there is a lot of variation. Note the
lack of length in *slip* for 'sleep', the reduced vowel in
minit 'minute', or the non-rhoticity in *bifo* 'before'. If one
understands these simplifications, it is possible to infer information on phonology. The vowel system has five vowels, i.e., /i, e, a, o, u/; there are rising diphthongs in *yai*
'eye' and *insai* 'inside'. Dental fricatives -*th*- are replaced
by the stop /t, d/ as in *da tin* 'that' and 'thing'. Syllable-fi-
nal consonants are deleted as in *insai*(de), *wan*(t) *kin*(d),
da 'that', etc. Simplification leads to a high level of homophony such as *we* /we/ 'when', 'why' and 'what'. *At*
means 'heart', but it could mean 'hat', 'hard', 'hurt' and
'earth'.

To turn to word-formation, *fain-fain* is called redupli-
cation technically and intensifies the meaning of a word.
Here it means 'very fine or good'. Irregular adverbs like
'well' for 'good' are not used. *Fo si* is a construction from
older varieties of English that still occurs in American
English in cases like "I want for you to win the race". If
the object is the speaker, it is omitted, which explains its
absence here. *Kot … at* replaces 'catch my eyes' or, as the
translation has it, 'stun'.

Louisiana's Cajun Creole

Louisiana spans the Mississippi. The eastern part was a French colony and was occupied by French settlers. It became British as a result of the Seven-Year War and was relinquished to the United States in 1783. The western part was purchased by the USA from Spain in 1803. Today's Cajun Creole was influenced from French as this well-known Christmas story shows:

10.4 "The night before Chrismas"
      'Twas the night before Chrismas
      An' all *t'ru de* house
      Dey don't a t'ing pass
      Not even a mouse …
      Den Mama in *de* fireplace
      Done roas' up de ham
      Stir up *de* gumbo [a soup or stew with okra pods]
      An' make bake de yam

Spelling is generally the same as in American English. There is evidence of departures from American English pronunciation and some common features with African American English. Dental fricatives are replaced by stops throughout. Consonant clusters at the end of a syllable can be reduced as in *roas* – but not in *don't*. *Done* in "done roas' up de ham" signals past tense, which is a significant grammatical departure.

Aboriginal Kriol and Aboriginal English

Australia was a settler colony so that the original population was forced into contact. The beginning was indeed difficult as Aborigines tended to refuse to interact with whites. The first Governor-General finally kidnapped several Aborigines so they would learn English.

The only successful case was Bennelong, who was used as an intermediary with Aboriginal tribes in the Sydney region in the 1790s. He is credited with the rise of a rudimentary pidgin, the Sydney Jargon that was then taken to other parts of Australia during the early 19th century. It localized somewhat in various locations but ensured a relative level of homogeneity across Australia. Some decades later the pidgin developed into an expanded one and turned into a creole. Its descendant, Kriol, is mainly used in the Centre and the Top End. Elsewhere it has disappeared and been replaced by the second result of contact, Aboriginal English.

Bennelong's role and that of a few other Aborigines is more complex. Their command of English must have developed further, as they lived in circumstances where more intensive contact was likely. The story of the second more developed contact language, i.e. Aboriginal English, is controversial. Leitner (2004b) argues that it may well go back to Bennelong and some other Aborigines who had more intensive contact with white people, while many Australian linguists maintain that it lost many of its pidgin features when it, to speak technically, decreolized decades later in the Sydney region.

For the purposes of understanding the following examples this controversy is unimportant. They illustrate some of the variation in Australia's Aboriginal contact varieties. The first one is a narrative (*quoted from* Leitner

2004b: 97) on a mass killing of Aborigines and is largely Kriol. The Aboriginal prisoners were lined up, shot, collected and burned:

10.5 "Well they *bin* putt*em* chain *longa* neck. Lin*em* up
  '*You altogether* run that way now. Line up,'
  Mak*em* ready …
  Kickem in the rib, one of them.
  All start. Right! Lin*em* up!
  Tu! Tu! Tu! Tu! Tu! Tu! Tu!
  Finish
  They bin gather*em* up all that now … Putt*em* *heap* there. Chuck*em* *big mob of* wood … And *chuckem* kerosene, strike some matches and *burnem*. Lot. All ashes. *Burnem finish*. Lot."

We see *bin* and *-em* in the first line. *Bin* refers to past time, while the suffix *-em* attached to 'put' has a very peculiar grammatical function. Reading the first line closely, one sees that an object (*chain*) follows so that *-em* cannot be the same as the shortened and non-standard English expression '*em*. It also occurs in *puttem heap* and *makem ready*. To cut a complicated explanation short, let me say that *-em* marks a transitive verb (as against an intransitive verb). As there is no such rule or function in native English, we understand, once again, that creoles do develop rules that do not exist in the input nor in the first languages of its speakers. Some other features will only be mentioned. *You altogether*, for instance, is a kind of plural pronoun for 'you'. In *finish* the past tense *-ed* is deleted and *lot* marks the end of the story. The story is mainly told in the active voice with events following chronologically. And yet, it shows a high level or oral narrative skill in creating pace and suspension.

The next example is a joke told in a collection of talks by the Aboriginal writer Mudrooroo which reveals the use of a broad form of Aboriginal English in the portrayal of the judge and the defendant. The passages of the defendant border those of Kriol.

10.6 [The judge asks:] "'What your address?' Tat woman tell im: 'Tis dress, I bin *ave* on.' ... And *ten tat* judge fulla, he say: 'How you been plead?' She tellim tat judge: 'I bin pleed from me 'ead, tat udder fulla, he bin *it* me tere.' Judge den tell*im* tat woman: 'I fine you five dollars.' And she 'appy, an she say: 'Oh tank you, I bin lose um tat five dollar last week.'" (*from* Mudrooroo, Narogin, 1995. *Us Mob. History, Culture, Struggle: An Introduction to Indigenous Australia*, Sydney: Angus & Robertson, 57)

The "phonetic" transcript has "t" that does signal a difference from other non-native varieties of English. We find *pleed* for 'bleed'. What we need to know is that Aboriginal languages do not have voiced consonants so that /θ, δ/ merge in /t/. The story is not entirely consistent as we find *udder* 'other'. The deletion of *h* in *ave*, *ead* and *it* is non-standard Australian English. There are grammatical peculiarities. *Bin* (*ave on*) marks the past tense; similarly in "How you *been* plead" 'did' and are the same as in many creoles worldwide. The *-im* suffix in, e.g., *tellim* (also *tell im* and *lose um*) mark transitive verbs.

That kind of variation has often been described in terms of a cline from a basic pidgin to Aboriginal English and on to non-standard Australian English. The Australian case is good example of that assumption.

Creoles and non-standard ethnolects in popular culture

Creoles and ethnolects can be used to express identities outside the mainstream – and yet be part of the mainstream in the end. Here is an excerpt from the lyrics of a Malaysian rap group that uses African American rap:

10.7 Too Phat, Malaysian Hip Hop duo
Hip hop *be connectin'* Kuala Lumpur with LB
(= Long Beach)
Hip hop *be rocking'* up towns laced *wit'* LV
(= Louis Vuitton)
Ain't necessary to roll in ice rimmed M3's
(= BMW) and be blingin'
Hip hop be bringin' together emcees (= rappers)

What is striking here is the imitation of African American English in a variety that does not use it. Recall that *be* followed by a present progressive *-ing* expresses habituality so that *be connectin'* or *be bringin'* means 'always connects' or 'always bring together'. Note in passing that the progressive form would not be possible in standard varieties of native English. The suffix *-ing* is spelt phonetically as *-in*, the dental fricative is replaced by "t", *ain't* is a nonstandard expression which is infrequent in Malaysian English. The name *Kuala Lumpur* is the only clear sign of Malaysian English. The acronyms show the in-group affinities.

The following passage is from an Aboriginal Australian rap group:

10.8 Ha ha I'm back all with South West Syndicate …
Slappin' high fives everywhere I go with
My lyrical flow that I know, so – Our

> *Nation of residence* is getting hesitant
> They *can't do shit* cos' they got no evidence
> *200 years* of this bullshit *us kooris* have had enough …

There is little evidence that signals the Aboriginality or the Australianness of the lyrics. The word *kooris* is an exception. "Our Nation of residence" is a cynical reference to Australia to express the feeling of disowning of Aborigines. The other italicized passages are non-standard in most varieties of English and are in Australian English.

Summing up, popular culture is an important part of English worldwide that can act as a counter-force to localization. We have seen that in the Malaysian example that mirrors a foreign creole. It can merge local and global patterns into a hybrid. The role of popular culture extends to soaps and serials, films, concerts. What should not be overlooked is that it can be seen in serious culture, museums, or culture marketing.

11 Pluricentric English Today

English appears in many guises. Viewers may be puzzled when they listen to interviews with people from West Africa, the Caribbean, Libya, China or Japan on CNN or the BBC. Their English may be hard to follow, when these speakers accommodate little to the English used internationally. Broadcast media cannot sub-title them as that could arouse animosity and may be seen as censorship and neo-colonialism. Broadcasting also shows the power that English exerts as any speaker with some command of it is more likely to be broadcast than those that speak Croatian, Arabic, Mandarin or Malay. Broadcasting reveals the pressure media are under that limits their choices. The 'natural' English of outside sources may reduce intelligibility and yet be unavoidable to avoid the loss of credibility. To the non-native user of English a good command of "English" need not be the gate-opener one thought it would be. The individual may need a very specific kind of competence to be successful. For nations or institutions it is a matter of choosing and implementing norms. This chapter will wind up what has been shown so far and move into the future of English and what the challenges are.

The socio-political path to pluricentricity

The spread of English is connected with a variety of factors such as power constellations, ideologies and beliefs, hopes, fears, demands, or default settings. These factors clustered in different ways during the various stages of colonialism and in the current perception of globalization. The following table gives a broad picture of the spread of English.

Timeline 8: The spread of English

5. to mid-11th c.	Anglo-Saxon dialects merged into Old English; major enrichments came from North Germanic (Vikings), Celtic, pre-Norman Latin and other languages; West Saxon became leading kingdom and developed early proto-standard; rise of Old Scots in Scotland.
late 11th to 15th c.	Norman invasion led to influences of Norman (later Central) French; created a triglossic situation; French and Latin took complementary domains, while English was demoted to folk language; substantial influence of French and Latin (carrying influences from Greek), Spanish, etc.; gradual bilingualism amongst French descendants; gradual expansion to Wales; north-east Scottish Lowlands, and south-eastern coastal Ireland (The Pale); blossoming Scots.
late 15th to mid-18th c.	With England coming under English control, beginning development of standard English and prestige accent; replacement of Latin and French domain by domain; hierarchical restructuring of dialect regions and standard English; fair amount of borrowing; growth of solid Standard English; decline of Scots; expansion to North America and Caribbean, India.
late 18th to mid-20th c.	Further codification of English; rise of Anglo-American bi-polarity; internal expansion to Ireland, Scottish Highlands; external expansion to Australia, South Africa, New Zealand; late 19th c. to Africa; USA acquire Philippines, Hawaii and Caribbean islands; Middle East protectorates post-World War I; rise of global English with League of Nations etc.; massive demand for English worldwide.

| mid-20th c. onward | Growth of national varieties; increasing distance from Anglo-American English locally; spread of English for conflicting reasons (Cold War, opening up, etc.); growth of global angle, resulting in a kind of diglossic situation with massive problems in education; growth of English as a *lingua franca*. |

English invaded the Celtic regions that had not been anglicized between the 17th and 18th centuries. That has been likened to colonialism but that concept has played a more convincing role outside Great Britain between the 17th and late 19th centuries. Colonies were and remained the object of European interests and conflicts. The problems of the East India Company around the middle of the 18th century were instrumental in the Declaration of Independence of the USA. The Seven Years' War, preventive actions of Britain during the French Revolution, the Napoleonic Wars and the Spanish-American War were clear examples of how European conflicts affected the colonial world. At times the acquisition of control was not achieved by power but in a more subtle way. Cases in point are the internal expansion of British control over Indian states or the installation of 'advisors' in Malay sultanates in the 19th century. The role of what has been called 'divide and rule' policy is so controversial that historians and politicians in Malaysia debate the question of whether the Malayan sultanates were really colonized at all. The 'advisors' had the consent of the sultans, one argument goes.

Colonial policies came to be accepted by the colonized and English acquired the role of a default option when competing sections of new states could not agree on a policy. India, Singapore, Cameroon, Nigeria and many other nations illustrate the fact that local languages were not always consensual and that English was felt to be an adequate, if not an ideal, solution. In Aboriginal Australia elders sometimes refused to pass on their ancestral languages and demanded that future generations shift to English. Accepting the 'death' of one's languages, rather than taking on the difficult battle for its survival!

The outcomes of World War I were a first step beyond colonialism. The League of Nations and the International Labour Office were founded in 1918 and represented the first global institutions. The fall of the Ottoman Empire and the British and French mandates that followed in the Middle East and East Africa were further signs of a new era. The British Empire reached its greatest extension by 1919. To get a full picture of the spread of English, one needs to add the USA and its possessions in East Asia and the Pacific, as well as in the Caribbean. What a map like this fails to show is the position of English as a foreign language such as in China, Japan or South-East Asia.

The geo-political position of English diminished during the period of decolonization that set in with the independence of India and Pakistan in 1947. But its socio-political role did not. Most former colonies retained English. That and the foundation of international alliances such as during the Cold War, the promotion of peace, the economic integration, the internationalization of education, etc., concurred to initiate a new phase in the growth of English. There was a deepening of its functions as it became an official language or a quasi-official language in many independent nations. The demand for a broader demographic base and an adequate command became important issues and both Britain and the USA responded with teacher-training and book publications. The creation of global institutions such as the UN, NATO, the

WTO, the IMF, etc., the foundation of non-English institutions like ASEAN, APEC, OPEC, or the African Union that opted for English made the need for good English even more pressing. Its traditional importance in postal, telegraphic and telephone communication, in air and maritime traffic, the role of the media and news agencies, of science and technology, military and peace operations increased its global presence. As globalization proceeded, English became the main foreign language worldwide. For the former colonies its retention was a mixed blessing. Many countries that did not have a colonial connection with English have adopted it as a first foreign language. Cases in point are the Arab nations that had an affinity to French and Thailand, Burma or Cambodia in South East Asia when they became members of ASEAN that require English.

Localization and globalization

The preceding chapters have looked at the development of English worldwide. It is natural now to ask what the four models of English introduced in Chapter Two tell us about the nature of English. The answers will be quite surprising. The models will be characterized briefly for ease of understanding:

1. Core-periphery (Quirk, British School)
2. Three Circles ("Englishes") (Kachru and his school)
3. International Standard English (McArthur)
4. English as *lingua franca* (Jenkins, Kirkpatrick)

These models capture two lines of developments. The first two highlight the dissociation of English from its historical core, England. The oldest model, the core-periphery one, started on the assumption that English was just a single language with some peripheries. There were registers such as in law that were difficult to integrate. Even the language of law in the USA remained close to that of Britain and that despite the different legal traditions. The peripheries of the core experienced a considerable widening at the end of the 19th century, when the influence of the languages worldwide on its vocabulary became a topic of research. Recall that English was used on all continents and that information could spread much faster than any time before as telegraph cables and regular shipping lines connected the major centres. There emerged a sense of globalism that was both an opportunity and a threat. Countless dictionaries and glossaries were being published and included in the compilation or revisions of major dictionaries like the *Oxford English Dictionary* and *Webster's* dictionaries. American English had been an undisputed target and Mencken's *The American Language* (1919) could be seen as the confirmation of linguistic independence. There was a flood of dictionaries and glossaries of localized varities of English in Austral-Asia, South and South-East Asia (*see* Leitner 2004a) that cannot be mentioned here for brevity. A few names like E.E. Morris (1898), Yule (1886), Hugo Schuchhardt and K. Lentzner (1891) must suffice. There were academic studies on the lexical impact of Malay and Chinese in Malaya (*see* Azirah/Leitner 2011). The lexical enrichment of English was well documented and many of the loan words made it into the core of the English vocabulary. Nevertheless, the varieties outside England as such continued to be seen as aberrations from the British Standard. The core-periphery model remained conservative.

Change came with Kachru's Three Circles in the 1970s.

He was inspired by the undeniable localization of English at all levels of linguistic organization at the end of the period of decolonization and nation-building. He rejected the core-periphery conservatism and insisted that these were natural developments, just like they had happened in American English before. "Englishes" would have to, and did, show regular departures from the original input and the growth of social norms. He called for an inclusive, realistic and socially responsible concept of English. Given the communicational realities of the time, his insistence on the three broad functions of English as native, second and foreign language was understandable. Local norms would be, so he believed, strongest in the Inner (or native) Circle, weaker in the Outer (or second language) Circle, and absent in the Expanding (or foreign language) Circle. We have seen evidence that his claim was and is well-founded. Having adapted to new environments, native varieties have a lot to do with non-standard varieties. They need to integrate new ethnic varieties that develop after first generation settlements. They need to create a new balance between speech and (public) writing which narrows the gap, so to speak, and makes writing open to expressions of speech. Second language English (in the traditional former colonies) is more concerned with the conflict between the heritage and the demands of globalization. It is marked by contact with local languages, the learning environment and patterns of informal speech. Some of the varieties concerned develop stable rules of their own, which show marked differences from any of the native varieties. Some of them develop away from another (recall the differences between Indian and South-East Asian English), and as they do that, they create powerful new epi-centres in pluricentric English. Depending on their regional size, they may present real challenges to English worldwide, according to David Crystal. They are also subject to pressures from Western cultures as the role of the politically correct language reform made itself felt or when media project American programme formats and cultural models.

Kachru's model has remained sterile and the social dimension has been ignored largely in research. An inflation of *Englishes* was the consequence. The expansion and development of English in China and adjacent countries has been seen as a serious threat to Kachru's distinction between the outer and expanding circle or, from a different angle, that between a second and foreign language English. It was abandoned and any sign of localization in the English in China is seen by many experts as evidence of a new instance of *Englishes*. While the implications of this change have not been discussed, a good case has been put forward by Kirkpatrick (2010) and others that Asian English develops common usage patterns, some of which can also be found in African varieties of English. I will return to that later. The dynamic models developed by Schneider (2007) and (in a specific case) by Leitner (2004a/b) laid out systematic and generally valid stages to the development of English. The path along these stages may, but need not lead to endo-normativity. Leitner foresees points of regression and restarts. We have seen cases of that in Malaysia's fluctuating policies and in the war-torn region of East Africa. Dynamic models are related to the *Englishes* perspective and are similar to the circles in that they highlight the use of English inside a nation or intra-national communication. They are sensitive to the role of global pressures and develop an interest in communication across nations, but this is peripheral.

The two other models target the second line of development, i.e., the communicative layers above localized varieties. Since the 1970s international communication in international relations, economy, tourism, academic exchanges, science and technology have been increasing significantly. One might point to the growth of such institutions as Wilton Park in Britain that gradually acquired a function in international relations and today counts as one of the centres of debate at a global level below ministerial levels. English has become the vehicle of access and participation, a *sine qua non* for future generations. The International Standard English model tries to salvage the core-view by redefining it as a standard in international contexts. The BBC follows its propaganda. Ignoring earlier developments, it is here that one finds the seedbed of International English and the continuing impact of Anglo-American English (*see* Leitner 2009).

English as a *lingua franca* models ignore national associations altogether and turn to the strategies of use in contexts where native speakers are absent or have no influence. That use of English is obvious in the interactions in institutions like the UN, the EU, ASEAN, the African Union and international tourism. Some experts are interested in the strategies used to secure comprehension (e.g., Seidlhofer 2003); others maintain that the use of English as a *lingua franca* has led to change in the texture of English (e.g., Jenkins 2007, Kirkpatrick 2010).

As the language with the greatest communicative footage inside a nation and across, English is no longer 'owned' by the British or Americans. Everybody has the right to use it creatively and to set norms locally. That development was seen as a danger in Australia in the 1940s (*see* Leitner 2004a). The BBC debated that issue in the 1930s, when its Pronunciation Advisor, Lloyd James, drew attention to the danger of American English moving away and to the impact of the Empire. It was recognized by the BBC in the early 1950s.

English today – and tomorrow?

These models reflect the historical stages from the dissociation from the English core, the rise of localization and the transition to international and global layers of communication. Some of the changes that accompany this development will now be illustrated again to provide background to the issue of the future of English and its impact on education. There are two points to discuss. The first is that the change in varieties worldwide may go to the heart of phonology, grammar and especially pragmatic rules of communication. Secondly, the path varieties take towards becoming epi-centres goes through a stage of *de facto* differences and more accepted differences (both called *localization*). These differences represent the realities of English worldwide and cannot be ignored in education though they have a very different role in discussing English Today from a sociolinguistic angle.

To begin with the impact of change in pronunciation, recall that words like *today* may sound like *to die* in Australian English. What sounds like *bed* in American English may sound like *bad* [a] in contemporary Received Pronunciation. The "t" in *letter* can be a glottal stop in British English, a flap in American English, or a retroflex "t" (the tongue curled back) in Indian English. There are considerable differences in the vowel systems. Many Asian and African varieties have a reduced system of seven or even five vowels only. Weak or unstressed vowels in *effect* and *affect* are reduced in Received Pronunciation and in Australia and New Zealand. But the targets are different, an [ɪ] here, a schwa [ə] there. In Asia and Africa they retain their original quality in a word like *address* or *comma*. Words that end in two or more consonants are reduced to one in Asia, Africa and in all contact varieties. The plural -*s* in, say, *kids* disappears. The accumulation of such characteristics makes accents difficult.

These differences do not occur by chance any more but are deeply rooted in local varieties. They are regular in Australian and Singaporean English. Similar developments are taking place in Indian and African English. Simplification and generalization are common tendencies whose outcomes need not be the same if one compares Indian with Malaysian English.

Turning to grammar, Crystal (2000) draws attention to the fact that the traditional tenet that "there is little macro-regional grammatical differentiation may not be applicable for much longer:

"older semi-modals (e.g. *have to, be going to*) are noted … to be 'considerable more common' in AmE, whereas recent semi-modals (e.g. *had better, have got to*) are 'more common by far' in BrE … .Variations are also noted with respect to aspect, modals, negation, concord, pronouns, complementation, and several other areas. Although each point is relatively small in scope, the potential cumulative effect of a large number of local differences, especially of a colligational type, can be considerable. It is this which probably accounts for the impression of Britishness or Americanness which a text frequently conveys, without it being possible to find any obviously distinctive grammatical or lexical feature in it." (www.davidcrystal.com/DC_articles/English19.pdf)

True, the accumulation of subtle differences may create misunderstandings. Even more serious ones may arise when we turn to varieties worldwide. Recall that the perfect and simple past in British and American English reveal opposing meanings. The extension of the progressive to verbs that describe emotional states like *to love* is more than just a generalization. It leads to the disappearance of semantic distinctions. McDonald's "I'm lovin' it" is a case in point. The violation of a rule is sanctioned by the picture that accompanies it. That is lost in Indian English where the extension is seen as a learner feature. Crystal makes a similar point when he discusses "*why + you*" constructions in Singaporean English. A sentence like "Why you eat so much?" calls for a justification and is a request, he says. There are two related constructions in British English. "Why do you eat so much?" is, he says, a genuine question and the speaker just wants to know – a somewhat doubtful explanation. "Why eat so much?" however, implies 'you should not eat so much' and requests a justification. Colloquial Singaporean and British English differ in the use of *you*. If *you* were there as in "*You* hold on, ok", it would sound aggressive. In Singaporean English it is polite. The reversal in politeness is not due to the context in which English is learnt but to the ability of Chinese speakers to impose rules and interpretations on English. Superficial structural differences thus find deeper explanations and signal the localization of English: "There is every likelihood of 'core' features of English grammar becoming a major feature in the description of New Englishes, as time goes by …," says Crystal. A core-periphery model is difficult to maintain.

The domain of lexis is undoubtedly the level where differences can be tied to cultural systems. A vast body of evidence shows that loan words have found their way into the core of English. *Hickory*, *amok* or *walkabout* are used worldwide but originate in America, Malaya and Australia, respectively. Nation-building has led to a young layer of loans that remains local. For instance, many Arabic words may turn up in, say, Malaysia and other Islamic nations, but not in Singapore. They are related to religion. A big Malaysian political party PAS has put the creation of an Islamic state on its agenda:

11.1 "Menteri Besar and party spiritual adviser Datuk Nik Abdul Aziz Nik Mat ... also said in response to a reporter's question that his state government had already laid out the foundation for *hudud* to be carried out." (*New Straits Times*, 23 Sep 2011)

Hudud, a word from Arabic Shyaria, refers to constraints on the freedom of action of Muslims and to the punishments foreseen; it is a central element in Islam. A cultural, but non-religious case is *kiasu*. Of Chinese origin, it expresses a Singaporean (Chinese) resistance to failure to avoid 'losing face'. In Malaysian English the word is used by all ethnicities. *H*-dropping, the omission of "h" in words like *'ouse* or *'onour*, is subject to social evaluations in native varieties. Features like these are closely tied to cultural, social or religious values and may carry sanctions or approvement. They are not neutral words or practices.

Despite the weight of change away from British English, the British seem confident that "Queen's English still rules the world". *The Independent* reported:

"The English-speaking world talks as we do in the UK, according to the biggest international study of English dialects ever undertaken. Researchers at the University of

Cambridge have shattered the myth that Americanese has taken an unshakeable hold on the Anglophone world. The findings, the result of a 10-year study of more than 70,000 people, also suggest that the legacy of the British Empire has played an important role in maintaining the pre-eminent position of British English. The researchers have been sifting through a vast internet database of responses from the world's English speakers, who were asked to choose which words they use to describe a range of everyday objects. Nearly 30 different words were given to describe a sandwich, including 'sub', 'hoagie' and 'nudger'. Contributors were also asked to enter the postcode, or zip code, of the town they believe most influenced their speech." (*The Independent*, 31 Oct 2010)

The paper reports on a study that has collected evidence from around the world. Malaysia is a case in point. The Education Minister described the target variety as "correct phonics" or pronunciation and said: "What is important is standard and the new curriculum will teach students according to the standard British English language phonics so that our students will know how to pronounce English words as spoken by native speakers." (*The New Straits Times*, 13 Feb 2010) For implementation 365 "master teachers" would be imported. It is unknown how many British teachers were brought in. The American Peace Corps sent 300 teachers and Australians were hired. There is a gap between policy pronouncements and implementation.

Both American and Australian English play a significant role in Asia. Japan has a longer association with American English that goes back to the 19th century. The same is true of China. And yet policy-makers go on proclaiming that British English is the guiding norm. In areas where policies cannot apply such as at university level and in popular culture American English clearly wins. In Singapore, which has been loyal to British English, a former Prime Minister argued the country should shift to American English, as it is the most dominant variety worldwide. European countries still favour British English in policy and practice but American English is gaining ground as a prestige variety in adult education and professional contexts.

The language preferences and practices worldwide call for change in European countries. With reference to Germany Anthea F. Gupta (1999) has said this:

"At least in Germany, the Anglo-American model of English is still seen as the point of reference, rather than a model of English which takes account of the range of Englishes in the world, and which sees English as a vessel of self-expression. As English does function in global terms … in due course those European countries where English has traditionally been a foreign language will have to adapt to a more open perspective which recognises the diversity of English in the world."

This is a clear call for change. But it will not do to say that education must open up to the "diversity of English in the world". Yes, teachers and students must be made aware of the richness of English today. But education must be founded on clear and achievable norms. One needs to retain varieties that promise greater communicational footage and are in line with a country's or a region's traditions. Choices must be akin to a nation's primary cultural or economic partners, while opening up avenues to widen the perspective.

What does that mean? We have seen important differences within and between varieties of English as a native and a second language. Native varieties are indeed closer to epi-centricity. They challenge the choices made in education as to which target varieties should be included. But even here and a lot more in second language varieties there's a lot of *de facto* usage. That usage is not part of the system of English, it occurs and maybe it is typical of and stable in the English of some country. As Kirkpatrick (2010) and others have shown, there is a great affinity across Asia and Africa, which makes it all the more important that we understand them. To give some examples, if vowel systems are reduced and consonant clusters are simplified, a lot of words sound the same (= homophony). If words come out of use, others fill the gap and associations may be unfamiliar. If the grammar changes, we need to misunderstand. And when all that is accompanied with code-switching – the alternation of languages – we will get lost. It is important to bring over the fact that there is no ground for prejudice just because that usage does not follow the conventions laid out in Germany or elsewhere. After all, one can observe that the participants who speak Singaporean or Nigerian English (or American English) have no problems communicating with one another.

How should one cope with the challenges? One could, for instance, consider the introduction of the reality of English by exposing learners to a selection of varieties. Some of that is common practice. The teaching curricula often contain literature from Australia, New Zealand, India, South Africa, and – not to forget, African American English. The titles selected for school use often contain loan words and local grammatical constructions. If they can be heard on a CD ROM or through a web link, one can hear the differences in pronunciation. What is lacking is the explanation of these usages. Little information is provided on the literary contribution that is made to describe a character. That path could be pursued more vigorously.

Another way to introduce change is to make distinctions between and within competence levels. One could emphasize the realities of English by binding them to the purposes for which English is learnt. Text books may avoid extreme local practices in speech and code-switching in multilingual habitats that will not be understood. There is no possible educational remedy there anyway. But awareness and skills in circumventing problems in intercultural communication can be practiced, as even a good command of English need not open up the doors to different worlds.

A note of thanks to Wolfgang Thiele (University Leipzig, Germany), Brian Taylor (University of Sydney, Australia), Azirah Hashim (University of Malaya, Kuala Lumpur), Tian Zhen Jian (Hulunbeier, China), Pramod Pandey (Jawaharlal Nehru University, New Delhi, India), Patricia McWilliams (London, Great Britian), Lim Beng Soon (Singapore Institute of Management), Hussaini Abdul Karim (Kuala Lumpur, Malaysia), Kirsten Middeke and Fenna Penning (Freie Universität Berlin, Germany) and many others for their advice and valuable help. I am grateful to my family for ideas, support and patience.

References

Aitken, John, 1979. Scottish Speech: A Historical View with special reference to the Standard English of Scotland, in: John Aitkin, Tom McArthur, eds., *Languages of Scotland*. Edinburgh: Chambers, 85–118.

Algeo, John, 2006. *British or American English? A Handbook of Word and Grammar Patterns*. Cambridge: Cambridge University Press.

Algeo, John, Thomas Pyles, 2005[5]. *The Origin and Development of the English Language*. Boston: Thomson.

Al-Issa, Ahmad, Laila S. Dohan, eds., 2011. *Global English and Arabic*. Frankfurt/M.: Peter Lang.

Azirah, Hashim, 2009. Not plain sailing: Malaysia's language choice for policy and education, *Association Internationale de Linguistique Appliquée / International Association of Applied Linguistics Review* 22, 36–51.

Azirah, Hashim, Rachel Tan, 2012. Features of Malaysian English, in: Ee-Ling Low and Azirah Hashim, eds., *English in Southeast Asia: Features, Policy and Language in Use*. Amsterdam: John Benjamins.

Azirah, Hashim, Gerhard Leitner, 2011. Contact Expressions in Today's Malaysian English, *World Englishes* 30(4), 551–568.

Baker, Sidney, 1945. *The Australian Language*. Sydney: Angus and Robertson.

Baskaran, Loga, 2008. Malaysian English: Phonology, in: Rajend Mesthrie, ed., *A Handbook of Varieties of English*, Vol. 4. Berlin: Mouton de Gruyter, 1034–1046.

Bragg, Melvin, 2003. *The Adventure of English. The Biography of a Language*. London: Hodder & Stoughton.

Britain, David, 2007. *Language in the British Isles*. Cambridge: Cambridge University Press.

Burridge, Kate, 2004. *Weeds in the Garden of Words*. Cambridge: Cambridge University Press.

Cheshire, Jenny, Sue Fox, Paul Kerswill, Eivind Torgersen, n.d., *Ethnicity, Friendship Network and Social Practices as the Motor of Dialect Change: Linguistic Innovation in London*. [http://www.lancs.ac.uk/fss/projects/linguistics/innovators/documents/sociolinguistica_Cheshire_etal_000.pdf]

Collins, Beverley S., Inger M. Mees, 2008. *Practical Phonetics and Phonology: A Resource Book for Students*. London: Taylor and Francis.

Crystal, David, 1995. *Cambridge Encyclopedia of the English Language*, Cambridge: Cambridge University Press.

Crystal, David, 2000. The future of Global English Grammatical Identity. www.davidcrystal.com/DC_articles/English19.pdf

Crystal, David, 2003². *English as a Global Language*. Cambridge: Cambridge University Press.

Crystal, David, 2004. *The Stories of English*. London: Penguin.

Darthorne, O.R., 1975. *African Literature in the Twentieth Century*. Minneapolis: University of Minnesota Press.

Dayag, Danilo T., 2012. Philippine English, in: Ee Ling Low, Azirah Hashim, eds., *English in Southeast Asia: Features, Policy and Language in Use*. Amsterdam: John Benjamins.

Deterding, David, 2005. Emergent Patterns in the Vowels of Singapore English, *English World-Wide* 26(2), 179–198.

Fasold, Ralph, 1990. Sociolinguistics of Language. Oxford: Blackwell.

Ferguson, Charles Albert, Shirley Brice Heath, David Hwang, 1981. *Language in the USA*. Cambridge: Cambridge University Press.

Fowler, Henry W., Francis G. Fowler, 1906. *The King's English*. Oxford: Clarendon Press. [Full text of the second (1918) edition available online at http://www.bartleby.com/116/, accessed 9/2011]

Fowler, Henry, 1926. *Modern English Usage*. Oxford: Clarendon Press [Second edition, edited by Ernest Gowers, 1965.]

Gibson, Mark, 2007. Mulilingualism, in: David Britain, ed., *Language in the British Isles*. Cambridge: Cambridge University Press, 257–275.

Graddol, David, 1997. *The Future of English? A Guide to Forecasting the Popularity of the English Language in the 21ˢᵗ Century*. [http://www.britishcouncil.org/learning-elt-future.pdf]

Graddol, David, Dick Leith, Joan Swann, Martin Rhys, Julia Gillen, eds., 2006. *Changing English*. Abingdon: Routledge.

Grataloup, Christian, 2007. *Géohistoire de la Mondialisation. Le temps long du monde*. Paris: Armand Colin.

Greenbaum, Sidney, 1988. *Good English and the Grammarian*. London: Longman.

Gupta, Anthea Fraser, 1999. Standard Englishes. Contact Varieties and Singapore Englishes, in: Claus Gnutzmann, ed., *Teaching and Learning English as a Global Language: Native and Non-native Perspectives*. Tübingen: Stauffenburg Verlag, 59–72.

Haugen, Einar, 1972. Dialect, Language, Nation, in: Einar Haugen, *The Ecology of Language. Essays by Einar Haugen*, selected and introduced by Anwar S. Dil. Stanford: Stanford University Press.

Hickey, Raymond, 2007. Southern Irish English, in: David Britain, ed., *Language in the British Isles*, Cambridge. Cambridge University press, 135–151.

Hung, Tony T.N., 2004. *Hong Kong English* [power point]. Hong Kong: Baptist University. [http://www.waseda.jp/ocw/Asian Studies/9A-77WorldEnglishSpring2005/LectureNotes/03_ HKE_TonyH/HKE_unit2.pdf]

Jenkins, Jennifer. 2007. *English as a Lingua Franca: Attitude and Identity*. Oxford: Oxford University Press.

Johnston, Paul A. Jr., 2007. Scottish English and Scots, in: David Britain, ed., *Language in the British Isles*. Cambridge: Cambridge University Press, 105–121.

Jones, Daniel, 1918. *An Outline of English Phonetics*. Leipzig: Teubner.

Kachru, Braj, 1983. *The Indianization of English*. Delhi: Oxford University Press.

Kerswill, Paul, 2007. Standard and Non-Standard English, in: David Britain, ed., *Language in the British Isles*. Cambridge: Cambridge University Press, 34–51.

Kirk, John, Jeffrey Kallen, 2006. Irish Standard English: How Celticised? How Standardised?, in: Hildegard L.C. Tristram, ed., *The Celtic Englishes IV: The Interface between English and the Celtic Languages*. Potsdam: Universitäts-Verlag.

Kirkpatrick, Andy, 2010. *English as a Lingua Franca in ASEAN. A Multilingual Model*. Hong Kong: Hong Kong University Press.

Leisi, Ernst, Christian Mair, 2008⁹. *Das heutige Englisch: Wesenszüge und Probleme*. Heidelberg: Winter.

Leitner, Gerhard, 1989. *BBC English und Englisch lernen mit der BBC*. München: Langenscheidt. [http://userpagers.fu-berlin.de/ ~leiger/papers/Leitner_1989_BBCEnglish.pdf]

Leitner, Gerhard, 1992. Pluricentric English, in: Michael Clyne, ed., *Pluricentric Languages*. Berlin: Mouton de Gruyter, 178–237.

Leitner, Gerhard, 2004a/b. *Australia's Many Voices*, 2 vols. Berlin: Mouton de Gruyter.

Leitner, Gerhard, 2009. *Weltsprache Englisch. Vom angelsächsischen Dialekt zur globalen "Lingua franca"*. München: C. H. Beck.

Leitner, Gerhard, 2010. *Die Aborigines Australiens*. München: C. H. Beck.

Mair, Christian, 2006. *Twentieth-Century English: History, Variation and Standardization*. Cambridge: Cambridge University Press.

McArthur, Tom, 1998a. *The English Languages*. Cambridge: Cambridge University Press.

McArthur, Tom, 1998b. Philippine English, in: *Concise Oxford Companion to the English Language*. Oxford: Oxford University Press.

McCafferty, Kevin, 2007. Northern Irish English, in: David Britain, ed., *Language in the British Isles*. Cambridge: Cambridge University Press, 122–134.

McCrum, Robert, William Cran, Robert MacNeil, 1986[1]. *The Story of English*. London: Faber and Faber.

McMahon, April, 2002. *An Introduction to English Phonology*. Oxford: Oxford University Press.

Melchers, Gunnel, Philip Shaw, 2003. *World Englishes*. London: Arnold.

Mencken, Henry Louis 2000[4] (1919/1921). *The American Language. An Inquiry into the Development of English in the United States*. New York: Alfred A. Knopf.

Meyerhoff, Miriam, 2006. *Introducing Sociolinguistics*. London: Routledge.

Platt, John T., Heidi Weber, Mian Lian Ho, 1983. *Singapore and Malaysia*. Amsterdam: John Benjamins.

Quirk, Randolph, Sidney Greenbaum, Geoffrey Leech, Jan Svartvik, 1985. *A Grammar of Contemporary English*. London: Longman.

Quirk, Randolph, Gabriele Stein, 1990. *English in Use*. London: Longman.

Schneider, Edgar W., 2007. *Postcolonial English*. Cambridge, New York: Cambridge University Press.

Schneider, Edgar W., 2011. *English around the World*. Cambridge: Cambridge University Press.

Sebba, Mark, 1997. *Contact Languages*. Basingstoke: Macmillan.

Seidlhofer, Barbara, 2003. *A Concept of International English and Related Issues: From "Real English" to "Realistic English"*. Strasbourg: Council of Europe.

Svartvik, Jan, Geoffrey Leech, 2006. *English. One Tongue, many Voices*. Basingstoke: Palgrave Macmillan.

Thomason, Sarah, 1997. *Contact Languages. A Wider Perspective*. Amsterdam: John Benjamins.

Thorat, Sandeep, 2009. Teaching English through Indian Writing in English in Rural India, in: *Language in India* 9. [http://www.languageinindia.com/oct2009/ruralenglishthorat.pdf]

Tian, Zhenjian, 2011. *Norm Orientation of Chinese English: A Sociohistorical Perspective*. Göttingen: Cuvillier Verlag.

Tottie, Gunnel, 2002. *An Introduction to American English*. Oxford Blackwell.

Trudgill, Peter, 2004. *New Dialect Formation. The Inevitability of Colonial Englishes*. Edinburgh: Edinburgh University Press.

Trudgill, Peter, Jean Hannah, 2008⁵. *International English. A Guide to the Varieties of Standard English*. London: Arnold.

Viereck, Wolfgang, Karin Viereck, Heinrich Ramisch, 2002. *DTV-Atlas. Englische Sprache*. München: Deutscher Taschenbuch Verlag.

Wee, Lionel, 2008. Singapore English: Phonology, in: Rajend Meshtrie, ed., *Varieties of English. Africa, South and Southeast Asia*, Berlin: Mouton de Gruyter, 259–277.

Wells, John, 1982. *Accents of English*, 3 vols. Cambridge: Cambridge University Press.

Wells, John, 1994. The Cockneyfication of R.P.?, in: Gunnel Melchers, Nils-Lennart Johannsson, eds., *Nonstandard Varieties of Language*, Stockholm: Almqvist & Wiksell.

Wolf, Hans-Georg, 2001. *English in Cameroon*. Berlin: Mouton de Gruyter.

Wolf, Hans-Georg, 2011. *A Dictionary of Hong Kong English*. Hong Kong: Hong Kong University Press.

Wyld, Henry, 1907. *The Historical Study of the Mother Tongue*. Charleston (South Carolina): Nabu Press. [Reprinted 2012].

Wyld, Henry, 1920. *History of Modern Colloquial English*. Oxford: Blackwell.

List of Illustrations

All illustrations have been redrawn based on the following sources.

31 Kachru's Three-Circle Model.
http://en.wikipedia.org/wiki/File:Kachru's_three_circles_of_
English.jpg
33 Family relations in English.
Peter Trudgill / Jean Hannah, *International English. A Guide
to Varieties of Standard English*, London: Arnold, [3]1994, [4]2002.
34 McArthur's circle of World English.
David Crystal, *Cambridge Encyclopedia of the English Language*, Cambridge: Cambridge University Press, 1995, p. 111.
39 One model for the depiction of internal variation.
Beverley Collins / Inger Mees, *Practical Phonetics and Phonology: A Resource Book for Students*, London: Taylor and
Francis, 2008, p. 3, Fig. A 1.1.
40 Internal variation in non-native Englishes.
Hashim Azirah / Rachel Tan, "Features of Malaysian English", in: Ee-Ling Low / Azirah Hashim, eds., *English in South-
east Asia: Features, Policy and Language in Use*, Amsterdam:
John Benjamins, 2012, p. 57.
42 The roots of English.
David Crystal, *The Stories of English*, London: Penguin, 2005,
p. 19.
47 Viking settlement areas.
David Crystal, *The Stories of English*, London: Penguin, 2005,
p. 51.
60 The shift to English.
Manfred Görlach, "Sprachliche Standardisierungsprozesse im
englischsprachigen Bereich", in: *Sociolinguistica* 2 (1988).
61 The varieties of English in terms of accent and dialect.
Gerhard Leitner, *Australia's Many Voices*, Berlin: Mouton de
Gruyter, 2004, p. 239.
83 Stages towards non-rhoticity.
John Wells, *Accents of English*, vol. 1, Cambridge: Cambridge
University Press, 1982, p. 215.

Glossary

acrolect: a term used to refer to the upper (social) end of a scale that describes the extent of variation in a variety of English or other languages (→ **basilect, mesolect**). The entire scale derives from the study of contact languages (→ **creole, pidgin**) and has been introduced into the study of English as a second language; it does not apply to native varieties of English.

acronym: is a short form of a complex word that uses the initial letters or syllables of a complex word or phrase, see NATO, EU, UK or Interpol.

agent noun: a term used to refer to complex nouns like *runner* or *actor* that denote an agent or someone who performs an action related to the base verb. Simplifying somewhat, 'a runner runs' and 'an actor acts'.

allophone, allophonic: The noun and the adjective denote a variant of a phoneme that is typically used under specifiable conditions. The /l/ phoneme occurs in a 'dark' form after vowels or as a syllable of its own in the south-eastern English of England (*fall* and *continental*), but in a 'light' variant elsewhere (*leaf*). (→ **phoneme, phonology**)

alveolar (stop or fricative): describes a place of articulation between the back of the incisors (= dental) and the palate (= palatal)]. It is the typical place of articulation of /t, d, s/ but not of /θ, ʃ/.

archaism: a term that refers to words or grammatical forms that have become obsolete.

aspect: a grammatical system of the verb that is used to express, for instance, an on-going activity (→ **progressive form**) or something done regularly or habitually (as in African American English "You be my friend a long time"). It differs from tense which is used to locate an event in time.

aspirated, aspiration: a term used to describe the audible release or opening phase of a stop consonant with a puff of air (passing the vocal cords). Aspiration in English occurs after voiceless stops in stressed position as in *time* or *keep*, but not in *liquor* or *lack*. Aspiration occurs in the south-eastern English accents, but not in Scottish English.

basilect: a term used to refer to the (socially) inferior end of a scale that describes the variation in a language or variety (→ **acrolect, mesolect**). The scale comes from the study of contact languages (→ **creole, pidgin**) and has been introduced into the study of English as a second language; it does not apply to native varieties of English.

brogue: refers to the playful style of speech of Irish English that is used to create effect such as in good narration. In a broader sense it refers to general cultural properties of the Irish, esp. in the USA or Australia.

calque: loan translation.

citation style: a term used to refer to the style of speech or pronunciation used when words are articulated in isolation. In this form the sounds are, so it is believed, with the greatest amount of care and it is this form that is used in dictionaries. (→ **connected speech**)

cline: a term used like *scale* that describes patterns of linguistic variation. Acro-, basi- and mesolect are located on a scale or a cline.

clitic: is a short form of a word attached to the end of a preceding word, esp. in speech but also in writing. The negative *not* or the (modal) verbs *will* or *shall* typically occur as "n't" or "'ll" in *won't* or *she'll*. Clitics are common in colloquial speech and writing.

code-switching: a term used to describe the shift between different languages or varieties of a language. In Middle English it was not uncommon to switch between English and French, in today's Malaysia or Nigeria one can observe shifts between English and Malay or English and Yoruba.

codification: a term used to describe the process (or development) whereby certain features of a language become a part of a standard variety. A case in point is the development of the present perfect with *have* and the past participle (e.g. 'have done') to express the current relevance of some event that is not located at a given point in time such as "I've been to England a long time ago" in contrast to "I was in England last year". The avoidance of the loss of /h/ in words like *hut* or *history* is another example.

collective noun: a term to refer to nouns that refer to a body of members or items such as *police* or *audience* or *tools*. They raise problems of whether they should combine with a plural verb as in "the audience are applauding vehemently" or permit the singular as in "the audience is applauding vehemently".

colligational, colligation: refers to words that appear in proximity with one another or in a text to produce the effect of, say, 'Americanness' or ''Britishness''. A cluster of Americanisms in one text would exemplify the term.

collocation: a term to describe the typical company of a word. Thus, *may* has a tendency with *well*, while *can* goes with *hardly*.

colloquialism: an expression, such as a word, a grammatical construction or a pronunciation common in colloquial, informal conversation or writing. Examples are the words *cop* or *pal*.

complement, complementation: a grammatical or syntactic constituent in a sentence. There are several uses. In "John's <u>the winner</u>" the underlined constituent is a subject-complement, in "The declared John <u>the winner</u>", it is an object complement. In a different sense the term is used to include objects, and in a third one embedded clauses (or sentences) as in "John wanted <u>to be the winner</u>" one speaks of complementation (triggered by the verb *to want*) and the clause is the complement.

connected speech: refers to the 'normal' style of speaking where words are linked with one another into utterances (unlike in isolation). The particular manifestations of connected speech can be quite slow or very fast, it may show signs of individual speakers.

connotation: a feature of the meaning of a word or a longer expression. Thus a word like *cop* 'means' the same as 'policeman' but implies (→ **connotation**) something derogatory or very informal or slang.

constituent: refers to one or several words that belong together as a grammatical phrase such as "John" or "the long train journey from Delhi to Mumbai" or "very good".

contraction, contracted form: a process or result of merging two words into one such as *can't*; *I'll* would be a contracted form.

corpus, corpora: a small or very large collection of authentic speech or writing of a language. In the past such collections were assembled manually, today they are assembled by computer. Corpus linguistics is a dynamic and influential branch of linguistics.

creole: is one outcome of intensive and long-term language contact such as in large farms during colonialism. Unlike a pidgin, which marks a beginning stage and has very reduced forms of pronunciation, a small lexicon and a peripheral grammar, a creole is increasing in complexity over time, as it has native speakers and is used as a main language by its users.

declarative (sentence): describes a sentence type where, in English, the subject occurs before the predicate. This is not so in interrogative and imperative sentences.

dental (fricative or stop): describes a place of articulation behind the upper front incisors. Dental fricatives are the underlined consonants in *fath*er or in *th*in; a dental stop occurs in *width* as the /d/ is articulated in the same place as /th/.

deontic meaning: a type of meaning of mainly modal verbs like *may*, *must* or *should* that express some kind of obligation (*must*, *should*) or permission (*may*).

derivation, derivative: that part of morphology that looks at complex words derived by adding a prefix like *untruth* or a suffix like *derivation*. *Derivative* refers to the outcome of derivation or a complex word.

diachronic linguistics: Unlike → **synchronic linguistics** this branch looks at the development or history of a language or variety. Thus, the study of the loss of inflexion from Old English to Middle English illustrates this area.

diglossia, diglossic: describes a bilingual or multilingual situation where one language or one variety of a language is used in the public or prestigious domains, while the other is used for ordinary purposes. In Middle English Latin was the so-called 'high' language in religion and writing, French in the national and administrative domain and English was the 'low' language used amongst the common folk.

diphthong: a vowel whose sound quality is not stable but shifts. The vowels in *like* or *boy* are diphthongs. (→ **monophthong**)

donor language: In a language contact situation where languages influence each other, the donor language is the one that provides loan words etc. for the other or others.

endo-normative, endo-normativity: a term to refer to a situation where the norms of a language (or standard variety) come from inside the community or nation where it is used. The norms of standard (British or American) English originate from Britain or America. But it is still uncertain if the norms of Nigerian English come from within Nigeria or are modeled on Standard British English. The opposite is exo-normative. On one reading endo-normative varieties are instances of 'Englishes'.

epistemic meaning: a type of meaning associated with mainly modal verbs like *may*, *might* or *should* that expresses some kind of inference (*may*). Thus, "He might be might be at home, the lights are on" expresses the speaker's conclusion from seeing some evidence.

ethnolect: a variety of a language such as Afro-American English in the USA or British Black English (in Britain) used by descendants or migrants from some region outside the country. Ethnolects are typically minority forms of a variety or language.

etymology: deals with the history of words, esp. of words from very old periods of the language or from outside. One can thus explore the etymology or origin or words like *street* (from continental Latin influence) or of *ketchup* (from Chinese or Malay).

exo-normative: a term to refer to norms of a language (or standard variety) come from outside the community or nation where it is used. The norms of today's Nigerian English may still come from without Nigeria and a modeled on Standard British English. The opposite is → endo-normative.

flap: refers to the manner of articulation of a stop consonant where the tongue makes a very brief closure of the oral cavity. Flaps are common replacements of /t, d/ in words like *letter*, *ladder* or *continental*. In English Received Pronunciation, the /r/ between vowels as in *very* can be articulated as a flap.

folk etymology: a term to refer to the popular but false etymological explanation of a word *Amok*, for instance, used to be also written as "a muck" which was to suggest that it is like 'afar' or 'afire', where the "a" derives from a former preposition "on" so that such adjectives mean something like 'on fire', '(on) being far', etc.

fricative: refers to the manner of articulation of a consonant where the tongue makes no closure of the oral cavity but comes close to some part to produce a noise or friction. Examples are /f, s, v, z/.

genderlect: a variety of a language used by or typically associated with women or men.

glottal stop: a type of sound produced by the closure and abrupt opening of the vocal cords. It can be heard in German in words beginning with a vowel like *aber*. In English it may be used as a replacement of /t/, but also /p/ in words like (see underlined) *le**tt**er* or *u**pp**er*.

glottalization: describes the articulation of a glottal stop before or after another stop consonant. Thus the /t/ in a word like *letter* may be accompanied by a glottal stop.

homogenization: a term that is used in linguistics to describe the fact that different dialects of a language may become very similar. Thus, the Germanic dialects that were transported to Britain in the 5th century became ultimately so similar to be called English.

homophony: a term used to describe two (or more) different words that sound the same but are spelt differently. Examples are *to lead* and the chemical element *lead*.

hybrid: a term for a complex verb that combines elements from two languages. *Koala bear* consists of an Aboriginal and an English word.

idiolect: a term used for a way (or variety) of a language that draws heavily on individual speakers. The former American state secretary Henry Kissinger had, for instance, a strong accent in both English and German that made him immediately recognizable.

idiosyncracy: describes the grammatical or semantic property of some lexical item that cannot be explained by a general rule. One *talks about* something but *discusses something*. It is hardly possible when 'about' is used.

inference: is a term used in semantics and pragmatics to describe the situation when the meaning of an utterance is 'inferred', but is not explicitly contained, from what is said.

inflectional, inflectional morphology: is that part of morphology that deals with inflectional endings like the plural -*s* or the past tense -*ed*.

informalization: describes the process whereby formal language as it was used, for instance, in newspaper commentaries as replaced by expressions that are 'colloquial' or 'informal'. Contractions like *it's* or the use of *cop* for 'policeman' are cases in point.

interrogative: a term used for a sentence type that is used to ask questions. In questions that are answered by "yes" or "no" the subject and the verb (auxiliary) are inverted. Thus, one says "Did you see that film?".

intonation: a term used to describe the pitch movement (or speech melody) in connected speech. If you say "Singapore is a `fascinating island state" (→ **declarative sentence**), the pitch is falling in the English of England. Adding a facet of doubt to qualify the "fascinating" is done by having a falling intonation, followed by a rising one, such as in "´fascinating island state". In an interrogative construction it would be rising. All languages use intonation to express shades of meaning.

inversion: a term used to refer to, e. g., the movement of the (auxiliary) verb before the subject, as in "May I come in?".

jargon: a term with several meanings. In a loose sense it describes the typical technical language in, say, the press or in sports. In another sense it describes the rudimentary but unstable styles used in intensive contact situations. The 'jargon stage' may lead to, some experts belief, into a → **pidgin**.

labio-dental: describes a place of articulation where the lower lip comes close to the upper incisors and produces a friction typical of /f, v/.

lateral: describes a manner of articulation where the air can escape along the sides of the tongue rather than through the centre passage. That is the case in the articulation of /l/ in English.

lexeme: another, more technical, linguistic word for 'word'.

lexicalization: describes the process whereby a loan word or a complex, derived word, to take two examples, becomes fully integrated into a language. The word *kangaroo*, for instance, is an Australian Aboriginal word but has acquired a wider meaning and produced numerous derived words like *to kangaroo*, *the Kangaroos*. (Australia's national rugby league team).

lexico-grammar: that part of grammar that is closely related to lexical items or words and is not associated with general rules. Thus, the verb *to deem* is typically used in the passive form ("something is deemed [to be] worth referring to"), while *consider* is not limited to the passive. In contrast, the simple present and past are possibilities of sentences in general.

lexis: a term used to refer to the words of a language.

lingua franca: refers to a language that is used in multilingual contexts such as Nigeria, South Africa or India whose linguistic diversity is so large that English is often used as a *lingua franca*. English is said to be used as a lingua franca in Europe and Asia.

loan (word): refers to a word that comes from another language. English has provided many Anglicisms in German and many languages around the world.

loan blend: → **hybrid.**

mesolect: a term used to refer to the middle (social) space of a scale that describes the extent of variation in a variety of English or other languages (→ **acrolect, basilect**).

modal: a term used to refer to modal verbs like *can, could, shall, should, may, might*, but also *need* and *ought to*. These verbs express modal meanings such as epistemic or deontic meaning.

modality: describes the area of study of modal meanings. Apart from modal verbs the term refers to nouns like *possibility* or the adjective *possible* that refer to inferences or belief.

monophthong: a vowel whose sound quality is stable and does not shift. The vowels in *lid* or *bug* are monophthongs. (→ **diphthong**)

morpheme: refers to the smallest meaningful unit of a language (→ **morphology**). Thus, words like *table* are (free) morphemes (or words), the prefix *un-* in *untruthful* is a (bound) morpheme that cannot occur on its own; *-ful* is a suffix that cannot be used on its own.

morphology: that branch of linguistics that deals with morphemes in inflection and word-formation. The area is quite complicated as many bound morphemes trigger changes in pronunciation (= morpho-phonology). Thus, -*ee* in *awardee* ('a person that is awarded something') or *employee* causes the (word) stress to be on itself.

non-rhotic, non-rhoticity: describes an accent like English Received Pronunciation and many other south-eastern English accents as well as, for instance, New England where the /r/ is not pronounced after a vowel. Thus, the "r" in *bird* or in *far* is not pronounced. However, it is pronounced between vowels as in *mirror*.

patois: a French word used to refer to colloquial dialects of little standing. It is rarely used for English but it is used in the context of English as a Second Language such as in Malaysia in the same sense as basilect.

phoneme: the smallest unit of pronunciation that causes a shift in meaning. Thus, the first consonant in this list of words is a phoneme as it produces different words: *till, will, sill, kill, bill,* etc. In contrast, /t/ is aspirated in stressed positions as in *till*, while it lacks that in words like *still*. Aspiration is not phonemic in English.

phonology: that branch of linguistics that deals with the sound system (e. g., phonemes and intonation) of a language.

phonotactics: a term that describes the possible combinations of phonemes. Thus, words that begin with three consonants like *street* or *spread* must have /s/ at the beginning and /r/ or /l/ as the third one. The middle one is always a stop consonant.

pidgin: the outcome of intensive language contact in situations where speakers do not share a language but still need to communicate. That was the case during colonialism and slavery. (→ **creole**)

pitch (movement): same as intonation.

plosive: describes the manner of articulation of sounds like /p, t, k/, where the oral cavity is closed for a brief moment and opened abruptly, producing a kind of 'plosion'.

post-vocalic: refers to a sound or phoneme after a vowel. Thus, rhoticity applies to the "r" after a vowel as in *rear*, /l/ has a 'dark', velar quality after a vowel in English English.

pragmatics: refers to the study of language (or of utterances, as against sentences) in context or in 'real' situations. When words refer to something concrete they have reference, while in isolation they have meaning. Sentences typically express a speech act as they are intended to influence the addressee; they may inform, request something or express one's feeling (= speech acts). Speakers must monitor a situation by using polite (or sometimes impolite) expressions.

pre-vocalic: refers to a sound or phoneme before a vowel. Thus, rhoticity does not apply to the "r" before a vowel as in *rear*, /l/ has a 'light', palatal quality before a vowel in English English.

progressive (form or aspect): refers to the *-ing* form of verbs such as in "John's going down the road, as you see from the window" to refer to an action in progress (or related meanings).

prosodic (phonology): refers to intonation, stress etc. (→ **phonology**)

putative (should): *should* is used typically in native varieties of English instead of the subjunctive to refer to utterances related from others or to express a meaning that is inferential and not necessarily a fact.

Received Pronunciation (RP): RP is the most prestigious accent in England that goes back to the accent at the Court (from Early Modern English), became a fashionable accent of the Upper and Upper Middle Classes by the 19th century and turned into the dominant social accent by the mid-19th century. Its social prestige assured it status in all colonies where it was the 'yardstick' for the elite until the late 20th century.

reflexive (pronoun): refers to (personal or possessive) pronouns like *myself* or *themselves* that refer 'back' to a noun before.

regionalism: refers to words or pronunciations, etc., that are closely associated with regional dialects or accents. In general American English this term was used to express the idea that, while it is highly variable, it excludes regional forms like the *Southern drawl*, the slowed down speech rhythm, or nasalization.

register: a term used to refer to the typical variety of a language used in some profession like academic writing, chemistry, or car repairs or in (some) sport. Registers have typically a number of specific words, grammatical constructions or forms of pronunciation.

retroflex: refers to a manner of pronunciation whereby the tip of the tongue is curled back somewhat. American English has a retroflex /r/ and Indian languages have a set of alveolar plosives that are articulated with the retroflexion of the tongue.

rhotic, rhoticity: refers to accents like general American English or Scottish English that articulate "r" after a vowel (= post-vocalic). The noun refers to the property of an accent using postvocalic "r"s. (→ **non-rhoticity**)

schwa: refers to vowel (sound and phoneme) articulated in the central oral cavity (or area). In many varieties of English it is used in unstressed syllables like *comma*, *behavior* (Australian and New Zealand English), or *entertain*.

sibilant: refers to a manner of articulating some sounds behind the alveolar ridge (*Zahndamm*) or the pre-palatal area (*vorderer Gaumen*) such as the consonants in *silent*, *sugar* *zoo*, etc.

sociolect: a term used to refer to some variety of a language that is tied to a particular social class or group. English Received Pronunciation, for instance, is an upper middle class accent. Standard varieties such as Standard Indian English are typically also sociolects.

stratification: a technical term to describe the patterns of variation in any variety of a language or a language. Malaysian English, for instance, stratifies in terms of ethnicity, educational background and professional status.

subjunctive: a grammatical mode that is required or possible in certain syntactic contexts such as in reported speech *indirekte Rede*). It does not imply that the speaker is committed to what he is saying – he is reporting. In English the subjunctive (*Konjunktiv*) only exists in phrases like "if I were him", otherwise it tends to be replaced by the putative *should* or is paraphrased like "..., he said".

suffix: a bound morpheme like *-dom*, *-ful*, or plural *-s* attached to another word at the end; witness *kingdom*, *truthful* or *tables*. The opposite is → prefix. (→ **morphology**)

syllabicity (loss): a term used to refer to consonants that act as the centre of a syllable such as /l/ in *continental* or /r/ in *centre*. The loss of post-vocalic "r", for instance, went through a stage where the vowel before "r" was followed by → schwa as a syllable. When it was attached to the preceding vowel as in *rear* to produce what is called *centring diphthongs*, which end in a schwa, one speaks of 'syllabicity loss'.

synchronic (linguistics): is concerned with studying a language at some period of time. Typically, this is the current period but it could refer to, say, Old English, the 14ᵗʰ or 17ᵗʰ century. (→ **diachronic linguistics**)

tense: a grammatical system of the verb that locates an event in time. If tense is defined as a system that must have a formal expression inside a verb, English only has the simple present (not marked) and the simple past (marked with *-ed*); there would be no future tense. This limitation is often not used so that one can speak of the English future tense (with *will*).

triglossic, triglossia: refers to a situation where three languages are used in a country, which are used for different purposes. In Middle English, Latin was the language of writing, sciences, etc., French the language of government, and English the language of the informal interaction amongst the English. (→ **diglossia, diglossic**)

velar: refers to a place of articulation in the soft palate (*weicher Gaumen*) used for, e.g., /g, k/.

vocalization: a term used to refer to a process whereby a consonant becomes a vowel. The post-vocalic /l/ in words like *school* can become a velar or 'dark' vowel, similar to /o/.

vowel shift: a term mainly used in historical linguistics to refer to a process where vowels move in similar direction. The Great Vowel Shift, for instance, accounts for the pronunciation of *meat* with /iː/ but also of *fire* with /ai/ or *pub* with /ʌ/. In modern English one tends to speak of vowel shifts in Australian English and in northern American cities.